D1191200

Agricultural
Options

Other Books by George Angell

Computer-Proven Commodity Spreads (Windsor Books, 1981)
Sure-Thing Options Trading (Doubleday & Company, 1983)
How to Triple Your Money Every Year with Stock-Index Futures (Windsor Books, 1984)
Real-Time-Proven Commodity Spreads (Windsor Books, rev. ed., 1986)
Winning in the Commodities Market (Doubleday & Company, rev. ed., 1986)

Agricultural
Options

*Trading Puts and Calls in the New
Grain and Livestock Futures Markets*

George Angell

American Management Association

This book is available at a special
discount when ordered in bulk quantities.
For information, contact Special Sales Department,
AMACOM, a division of American Management Association,
135 West 50th Street, New York, NY 10020.

Library of Congress Cataloging-in-Publication Data

Angell, George.
  Agricultural options.

  Includes index.
    1. Grain trade — United States.   2. Cattle trade —
United States.   3. Put and call transactions — United
States.   4. Options (Contract) — United States.
I. Title.
HG6047.G8A54   1986   332.64'25   85-48215
ISBN 0-8144-5822-X

Printing number

10 9 8 7 6 5 4 3 2 1

Acknowledgments

Special thanks are due to Jay Sorkin, an options trader at the Chicago Board of Trade, who was kind enough to send me the "delta printout" from the Board's floor computer. I would also like to thank the Options Group in New York for permission to reprint its sheet listing the delta information. John Hopson, who trades options at the Chicago Mercantile Exchange, also offered a number of suggestions and carefully explained some of the subtleties of options trading to me. He deserves a note of thanks.

I would also like to thank my agent, Evan Marshall, for his encouragement on this project, as well as Ron Mallis, my editor, who saw the promise of a book on agricultural options.

Among those who contributed in an indirect, but nevertheless helpful fashion are Lesley Dormen and Laurie Sutton, who didn't hesitate when I called upon them for special assistance; David Carren, who provided a West Coast office during one of my many journeys; Duane Davis, who worked overtime on our competing software project when time was at a premium; and Marci Hertz, who minded the mail.

Contents

Contents

Introduction

Options!

Puts and calls, spreads and straddles, conversions and reverse conversions. It may sound like the pre-game locker room strategy of the Dallas Cowboys, but, in fact, this is the jargon of a whole new world of financial trading. This increasingly sophisticated language of Wall Street was once confined to the few blocks around Chicago's Jackson and LaSalle and the canyons of lower Manhattan. With the introduction of the new agricultural options, however, options strategy is now being discussed amid the cornstalks of Iowa and the cattle ranches of Texas. Word is spreading. Options limit risk. Options can make raising crops and livestock safer. What's more, options can earn you a hefty profit — fast.

But aren't options limited to stocks?

Hardly. Although an established market for listed stock options exists in four U.S. cities today, in recent years the concept of options trading has spread to foreign currencies, precious metals, interest-bearing financial instruments, and even stock-index averages. Now there's a new wrinkle in options trading: agricultural options. For a little money down, they can buy you admission into the fast-track game of commodities. Moreover, this new market for your money can have you dealing in thousands of bushels of grain or carloads of livestock. What would you do with a railway car of live cattle? Doesn't matter.

The point is, you can make a ton of money speculating in cattle futures with strictly limited risk by buying and selling agricultural puts and calls. And to do it, you don't have to know a steer from a hog, a soybean from a jellybean. Of course, if you are already in agriculture, you don't have to be told the value of being able to hedge against the vagaries of the marketplace. To those in agriculture, risk is a way of life. Droughts, floods, and high interest rates can all wreak havoc with a grain farmer's marketing plans. Options can help take some of the risk out of this high-risk business.

Options were not always popular with the agricultural community, however. First introduced in the 19th century, when regulatory authorities were virtually nonexistent, they were subject to insider abuses that resulted in them being outlawed in the 1930s. Those were the days when markets were cornered and manipulation by a few well-financed speculators could hurt a lot of people. A number of farmers went broke speculating in grain options. Today, in an era when regulation exists, the fluctuations can still be wild. But thanks to regulation and wide participation no one can successfully manipulate the market.

Agricultural options, which, as we shall see, are actually options on agricultural futures, are the first new products to be introduced in the grain markets since the Chicago Board of Trade first opened its doors in 1848. Then, as now, the primary purpose of the grain markets was to transfer risk from the farmers and processors, who grew and used the raw crops, to the speculators, who were out to make a quick profit. Over the years, through floods and droughts, good times and bad, the futures market provided for the transfer of risk from hedger to speculator — as it still does today. The only difference between yesterday and today is the scope of the market. As recently as 15 or 20 years ago, grain trading was the province of a few, notably farmers and professional floor traders. But no longer. Today's speculator might be a housewife in California or a sheik in Saudi Arabia, so diverse and widespread have the markets become.

Despite the popularity of futures trading — the markets have grown enormously in recent years to include financial futures and contracts on such exotic commodities as leaded gasoline and heating oil — the one stigma the markets have been unable to throw off has been the high, and often intolerable, risk. Now, thanks to this newest wrinkle, the agricultural option, you can participate, for the very first time, in the highly volatile grain and livestock futures market with strictly *limited risk*. This is a meaningful development that promises to make agricultural options one of the most popular new trading vehicles.

Put yourself in the place of a futures trader. When he buys, say, soybeans, he does so with just 5 percent to 10 percent down in the form of margin money. Given the fluctuations in the market, however, the trader soon finds that he has a tiger by the tail. He might double his money in the first hour's time; but, then again, he might lose his margin and receive a margin call. Due to the high leverage involved, the chance of having his margin impaired at some time when he holds the contract is rather high. In short, he *must* be right almost from the outset of the trade if he isn't going to be forced to sell out at a loss or commit more margin to the trade.

The margin, or "earnest money," in futures trading assures that you are good for the potential losses — at least at the start. But it doesn't limit your liability. Thus, as a buyer of soybeans, you stand to lose $50 every time the price moves 1¢ against you *regardless of how much margin money you initially deposited with your broker*. One cent, by the way, is nothing in soybeans; the soybean market can move 30¢ up or 30¢ down from the previous day's close. When it does, you have what is known as a *limit move*. Indeed, in a panic situation (which happens more often than commodity brokers would care to admit), the price of soybeans might move limit down today, tomorrow, and the day after that. When the market is said to "lock limit," you can be in real trouble. It won't happen to you, you say? You would simply sell out your soybeans and take the loss? Well, occasionally, the market opens limit down and is "offered at limit." This means there are no buyers, only sellers. Try telling your broker to sell out your soybeans when the market is locked at limit down, and he'll probably laugh — or cry! (Actually, you'll probably be the one crying, since it is your money.) Remember, for you to get out of your obligation as a buyer, you have to sell — or, of course, keep the position fully margined and come up with the cash for the beans. In the meantime, you can lose many, many times the initial margin. In fact, you can lose your house, your car, your bank account — everything you own, and then some. Is it any wonder you hear futures trading is risky?

Enter the new agricultural options. Options give you the right — but, significantly, not the obligation — to buy or sell a fixed amount of a commodity before a specific date at a specific price. In return for a premium fee, you maintain the right to exercise the option. But in the case of adversity, such as a series of limit moves, you simply forget the whole thing and absorb the loss on the option. Instead of exposing yourself to a limitless risk, you know the entire risk at the outset. Whatever you pay for the option is your risk. Period. Happily, the upside potential is not limited. If you buy calls just before a runaway bull market, you can parlay a few thousand dollars into a small fortune!

For hedgers, who rely on futures markets to make the money they are losing in the field, options offer a new and sophisticated way to fine-tune their marketing decisions. In theory, a pure hedger is not supposed to worry about money lost in the futures market, because he's making it elsewhere, namely in the cash market. But try to tell that to a farmer faced with a series of margin calls when his cash crop is yet to be harvested. His broker wants cash, and all he's got is a potential for cash that could be wiped out overnight by a freak weather pattern. With options, a cattle rancher in Oklahoma can sell his steers without the possibility of margin calls. Likewise, a meat packing plant in Illinois can guarantee its purchasing price with options. And if the cash market improves still further in the hedger's behalf, well, he can just absorb the loss of the option premiums and sell higher or buy lower as his needs dictate. Options provide the versatility to enable speculator and hedger alike to interact in the best interest of everyone. Our task will be to outline the various strategies both can use to maximize their profits.

You can often spot the winners in the futures and options markets by their ability to change their trading habits. Anyone who has been around for a while knows that nothing works all the time. At the least, you have to be willing to change with the market. Yet, so many first-time futures traders, operating in a game that is notoriously unforgiving, refuse to examine their trading strategies when they lose.

Chances are you may have already taken a flier in corn or cattle, wheat or soybeans. You've tried your hand at the fast-paced game of futures trading. You've listened to brokers, you've played by the rules —and you've lost!

You may even have redoubled your efforts. Met margin calls. Poured good money after bad. All to no avail. How can something that looked so promising at the outset develop into such a disastrous investment? Where did you go wrong? Perhaps you didn't. Perhaps you were playing the wrong game from the outset.

Now's the time to get a fresh start. Options, as I will stress over and over again, are incredibly versatile and permit you to limit your risk while participating in the profit potential of the highly leveraged futures markets. In the pages ahead, you will learn a host of strategies for playing a highly sophisticated financial game. You'll learn how to size up an options trade. You'll learn how to resist manipulation by floor traders. Most important, you will learn how to match your strategy to market conditions, so you aren't employing the wrong strategy at the wrong time. You'll learn how to write options. How to spread and strad-dle options. In short, how to win!

Some of the strategies we'll discuss are more difficult to understand than others. Not every strategy is appropriate for every trader. In fact, one of the messages of the book is that you must know how to select the right trading strategy for a particular circumstance. But stay with it. The principles are valid, and the rewards are worth the effort. In few endeavors can you start with virtually nothing and make a substantial amount. Options trading is one of them. Now let's get started.

1

Agricultural Options: The Newest Wrinkle in the Futures Market

Glance at the financial pages of *The Wall Street Journal*, and there, amid the endless columns of numbers, you will find hidden fortunes waiting to be gleaned by the astute investor. Even a cursory glance will reveal daily opportunity. Nowhere is this hidden profit potential more apparent than in the high-stakes futures markets, where fortunes often change hands in minutes, even seconds — where getting on the right or wrong side of the market represents prosperity or ruin. Consider this: the nearby contract of soybeans, over its short lifetime of perhaps 18 months, has fluctuated in value by almost $18,000. The same contract could have been margined for about one-tenth as much, or less. Even if you could have captured just a third of the move (no one, after all, can sell at the top and buy at the bottom), you would have walked off with several hundred percent in profit!

But there's more. What if you could participate in a potential $18,000 move by putting down, win or lose, just $1,000 or less? Now we are talking about investing $1 to make $18. (More realistically, we're talking about investing $1 to make $5 or $6 — but what kind of investment offers you those odds over a few months' time?) What's more, we're talking about limited risk; and even then, if things look like they aren't working out, you can generally recoup 20¢ or 30¢ on the dollar.

Just the day before I wrote this, soybeans had a daily range of $14\frac{1}{2}$¢. Translated into English, this means the value of a single contract fluctuated a total of $725 in a single day! Now compare this with the stock market, where a $7\frac{1}{4}$-point move in a low-cost stock is extremely unlikely. Moreover, consider the amount of cash you would have to invest in a stock to participate in a $7\frac{1}{4}$-point move. Even 100 shares in IBM will cost you more than ten grand. And when was the last time IBM had a $7\frac{1}{4}$-point range in a single day? By comparison, a put or call option on the soybean contract might have cost you peanuts. Depending on the option you select, your cost might range from $175 to $4,000. At recent price levels, an option on a futures contract with six months left prior to expiration traded as low as $\frac{1}{2}$ percent to 12 percent of the value of the contract. With low premium costs as these, you have a chance to make enormous percentage profits on invested capital.

The Importance of Agriculture

It is not just a cliché. Our agriculture markets feed the world. Think about this: the value of the commodities traded each year exceeds the total value of all the stocks traded on the New York Stock Exchange — more than a trillion dollars! Yet how many people think about actually speculating in the commodities futures markets? Relatively few. And for good reason. Until now, the risks outweighed even the high profits to be had. Moreover, relatively few, brokers among them, really understood how these highly leveraged and often volatile markets worked.

Agriculture has never been an easy field in which to succeed. For the farmers, who grow the crops, and the ranchers, who raise, feed, and market the livestock, agriculture has been an increasingly difficult profession. High interest rates, changing growing conditions, low prices — all have put the poor farmers on the ropes in recent years. Yet one-fifth of our population depends either directly or indirectly on agriculture for its livelihood. And despite the trend toward fewer and fewer farmers, agriculture remains of vital importance to our national economy.

What is certain in the uncertain world of agriculture is that risks will remain. Risks related to weather. Risks related to soaring interest rates. Risks related to the marketplace. And even risks related to risks. The market is highly dependent on a boom-and-bust psychology. During good times (high prices), farmers will grow more crops. This, in turn, will result in abundant supplies in following years and lower prices. Likewise, low corn prices will translate into low hog prices, since hog raisers feed corn to their animals. What is worse, a temporary lessening in interest rates will send farmers to the bank to obtain additional financing. Thus leveraged to the hilt, these same farmers find themselves unable to meet their payments when interest rates rise. Indeed, there are so many things that can go wrong in agriculture, you wonder what makes farmers continue to farm.

Why Trade Ag Options?

Managing risk, then, has become a life-or-death situation for many farmers. Farming is hard enough without being at the mercies of the marketplace. But surprisingly few farmers hedge their risks in the commodity futures markets. According to the Chicago Board of Trade, the largest commodity exchange in the world, only 10 percent to 15 percent of all farmers hedge their risks in the futures market. Now, with the introduction of agricultural options, this percentage can be expected to rise as more and more commercial growers and users, drawn by the limited risks of futures trading, will turn toward this new tool for managing risk.

For the speculator, there are also problems. While the hedgers, or farmers, use the futures markets to *avoid* the natural risks associated with growing or processing commodities, the speculator embraces the risk in pursuit of profit. But his task hasn't exactly been an easy one either.

Because of the high leverage of commodity futures trading coupled with the sudden price moves, the speculator frequently finds himself on the losing end. Futures trading is, after all, a zero-sum game. This means the pie doesn't get any bigger; for you to make money, someone else has to lose money. And in the high-stakes world of futures trading, the well-financed speculators and hedgers, who can frequently ride out huge paper losses, often grab the lion's share of the profits. There simply isn't enough money to go around for all the participants. It's been estimated that as many as 90 percent of all speculators end up with trading losses. Again, the culprit is the high leverage (a double-edged sword) together with the price volatility. Traders tend to get whipsawed, so that even once-promising positions can turn sour on short notice.

For hedger and speculator alike, the new agricultural options have been a godsend. Because the options enable the purchaser to limit his risk to a one-time premium fee, he is free to sit back and await favorable prices, oblivious to the often highly erratic short-term price moves.

Options are the answer to the age-old lament "If only I'd stayed with my position!"

Futures versus Options

We've talked about leverage. We've talked about limiting risk. Now let's talk about choice. The main feature of an option is choice: the choice to exercise or not exercise the option, the choice to buy or sell. A grain or livestock option gives you the right, but not the obligation, to buy or sell the underlying futures contract. In turn, the futures contract, if held to maturity, provides you with the opportunity to take or give delivery of the underlying grain or livestock.

Let's take an example. A June 65 call on live cattle futures gives you the right to *buy* June cattle futures at the guaranteed *strike price* of 65 (read $65 per hundredweight, or 65¢ per lb) at any time prior to expiration of the option. For this privilege, you will have to pay a premium fee, which is nonrefundable. As long as June cattle futures prices are *below* 65, the call will remain *out of the money*, which means you would not exercise it, since you could purchase cattle futures more cheaply in the futures market. Significantly, the fact that the option remains out of the money does not mean the option will not retain value. In fact, as long as time remains before the expiration, the option will maintain what is known as *time value*.

Above 65, of course, the option will have added value, known as *cash value* or *intrinsic value*. At any time June cattle futures trade above 65, the option is said to be *in the money* by the amount the market price exceeds the strike price. Thus, at 73, the June 65 call is $8 per hundredweight in the money. The option holder, or buyer, alone retains the choice either to exercise the option and receive a long June cattle futures contract at the price of $65 or to sell the option. If he decides to sell the option, he will receive at least the intrinsic value of $8 plus whatever time value the option retains.

The futures contract, in contrast, is characterized by the absence of choice. The holder of a long futures contract, for example, must maintain margin on his contract regardless of its price movement. Thus, a speculator who purchases June cattle futures at $65 stands to sustain a loss if futures fall below that price. At a price of $62, for instance, the trader of long futures will have a loss of $3 — or $1,200 in total, since each $1-per-hundredweight movement in price on a standardized cattle contract of 40,000 lb translates into $400.

Now let's compare the two. One speculator buys a June 65 call for a premium of, say, $2, or $800. Another speculator buys a long June futures contract at the price of 65 and deposits, say, $1,000 in margin. As prices move higher, the long futures trader stands to benefit because he purchased on margin and does not have to pay anyone for the privilege (aside from commission costs). His margin payment will be returned to him should he sell the June cattle futures contract at a price higher than 65. Let's say prices rise to $69. The June cattle trader simply sells his futures and realizes a $4 profit, or $1,600 minus commissions. The purchaser of the June 65 call, however, having paid $800 to the *writer* of the call, must recoup this money in the market if he is to profit. As a result, the option buyer's first $2 per hundredweight in profit will go to offset the cost of the option. At a price of $69, therefore, the buyer of the June 65 call will have only an $800 profit, again minus the transaction costs. He will earn the difference between the strike at 65 and the market price of 69, or $4; $2 of this profit, however, will go to offset the cost of the call.

As I mentioned, the option buyer has a choice. He can take his profit by simply selling the option, or he can exercise the option and receive a *long*, or buying, position at the strike price of 65. In the latter case, the option buyer, once he receives the long position (which will appear as a bookkeeping entry in his brokerage statement), will be treated as a futures trader. That means he must maintain margin and will be subject to margin calls. For this reason, and because an additional commission is involved if the option buyer exercises his call, many option traders simply sell their options for what they will bring in the market.

Now, you might be thinking, why buy an option—and pay a premium—if you can start making money right from the outset by going long in the futures market? Good question. The answer rests with safety. For the premium payment of $800, you receive the right to buy cattle at the strike price at any time prior to expiration of the option, *regardless of the subsequent movement of cattle prices*. So, if cattle prices fall to 50, you can hold onto your call option and, assuming a rally, still make money if prices are above the strike at expiration. But the futures trader has no such luxury. The buyer of June cattle futures, remember, must margin his account at all times. Thus, if he buys at $65, he is out $400 at $64, $800 at $63, $1,200 at $62, and so on. Indeed, if prices drop to $50 per hundredweight, the hapless long cattle futures buyer at 65 is out $15 per hundredweight, or $6,000! All with no guarantee that he won't lose even more money. At the same time, the call buyer has risked only his initial $800 call premium. The point is, option buying can be a lot safer than simply outright speculation in the futures market.

There are all sorts of variations on this scenario that can turn disastrous for the futures trader. Let's say, for instance, that the buyer of June cattle futures at 65 realizes his poor timing when cattle futures fall to 64. So he sells out his position at 64, sustaining a mere $400 loss. At that stage the buyer of the June 65 call has also probably lost a portion of his premium, and if prices stay below 65 at expiration, the call buyer will indeed lose his entire $800 premium. So the futures trader might indeed still feel at an advantage. But what happens if the once bullish cattle trader turns bearish as prices fall and he *sells short* June cattle futures at, say, 64 — and, as so often happens, prices rally? Now the futures trader will have a loss on the short futures position, since prices have risen above where he had sold. Indeed, he is in the process of being whipsawed, a common enough event in the futures market, whereas the option holder can sit clamly, knowing his call will guarantee him the right to purchase June cattle futures at any time prior to expiration of the option.

As you can see, options offer a certain peace of mind in a notoriously stressful business.

Why an Option on a Futures Contract?

There are all sorts of options in the financial world — stock options, cash options, even options on real estate. Why have an option on a futures contract?

Futures, which are standardized, widely traded contracts in widely used commodities and financial instruments, have several advantages for both option buyer and writer (seller). For one, the futures price for an agricultural commodity such as soybeans, corn, or wheat is determined in the fairest way possible by having a great many buyers and sellers in a single centralized arena. This centralization also provides liquidity: because there are many buyers and sellers in a single arena, hedgers and speculators can be assured that they can move both in and out of the market without costly price dislocations.

Then there is standardization. Imagine what a chore it would be to write a specialized contract with every option. One option would cover 5,000 bushels, another, say, 23,000 bushels. Each buyer would be dependent on a single seller, and vice versa. This could be particularly difficult for writers seeking to buy back their options in order to escape a deteriorating situation. By basing an option on a futures contract, which is standardized and widely traded, each buyer assures himself of a seller, and vice versa.

Lastly, by basing the option on the futures contract, one is assured of being able to take delivery (in the case of long futures) or give delivery (in the case of short futures) if one so wishes. Thus, the economic justification of the contract is met and the vehicle becomes a genuine hedging tool.

The Role of Futures Trading

For years, the U.S. futures markets have played a vital role in the national and world economies. By providing a risk-transfer mechanism, the agricultural futures markets have enabled growers and processors of agricultural products to hedge against risk in the producing and processing of agricultural commodities. The markets have made agricultural production both efficient and abundant—indeed, some would say, too efficient. Centralized and serving as a price-discovery medium, the futures markets have often come under attack as the *cause* of low prices. But no speculator in the world can cause prices to decline, except momentarily, unless an abundance of the underlying commodity exists—and in recent years, this has been precisely the problem. If anything, a speculator would prefer raising prices; bull markets, after all, provide the necessary fuel to draw new players—and profits— into the markets. It is the bear-market psychology that results in a lack of liquidity and the accompanying doldrums that farmers and speculators alike seek to avoid.

Far from being the culprit, the futures markets merely reflect, often months in advance, the underlying economic conditions. During times of high interest rates and low inflation, money will naturally be drawn away from real commodities and inflationary hedges in favor of the far safer and surer debt markets. After all, if an investor can readily gain a fixed high yield, often guaranteed by the government, why speculate in high-risk commodity futures? This has recently been the situation, but market uncertainty is sure to persist and the agricultural futures markets will continue to provide an important risk-transfer role.

There are several ways to participate in the futures markets, depending on your objectives.

First, the markets are, as they have been since 1848, a centralized arena in which so-called "hedgers" shift the risks of growing and processing agricultural commodities to willing speculators. For the hedger, therefore, the role of the marketplace is to make owning and processing commodities safer, not riskier. For the hedger, the futures market serves as an insurance exchange. In return for the potential for earning a profit, the speculator takes on the risk of the hedger, guaranteeing the hedger a fixed price for his grain or livestock at some time in the future.

Consider the case of the farmer who grows corn. By using the futures market, the corn farmer can establish a price for his product while it is still in the ground. Let's say corn for delivery nine months later, in December, is selling for $2.95 per bushel. By selling corn futures, the farmer can establish this as his selling price. Time passes. Suppose corn prices decline to $2.20 per bushel when the farmer is ready to deliver his crop. He is still guaranteed his price of $2.95 per bushel. How? Simply by buying back his short (selling) positions in the futures and capturing the difference between his initial selling price and the now lower purchase price. In fact, he has two alternatives. He can sell his corn in the cash market for the going price after picking up his profit in the futures market. Or, as an alternative, he can hold his short futures position until maturity and give delivery against the corn futures contracts and receive the $2.95 a bushel for his corn. In either instance, commission costs aside, his net price is $2.95 per bushel.

For the user of corn — say, a hog raiser — the hedge works in reverse fashion. Knowing he will require corn to feed his animals, the hog farmer can contract to purchase futures that will enable him to pay a fixed, predetermined amount. In the event of rising corn prices (higher feed costs), the hedged hog raiser will know his costs are fixed. Obviously, this can be a great help to the farmer's bottom line. This latter hedge strategy is known as the *buying hedge*.

From the standpoint of the grower or user of farm commodities, therefore, the futures market serves as a risk-reduction mechanism. The only drawback is that the hedger, seeking to limit risk, might ''lock out'' a windfall gain by contracting to sell or purchase at a fixed price. For example, in the event of a bull market, the farmer who contracts to sell corn at $2.95 per bushel might sorely regret his decision if, nine months from now, the cash market is willing to pay him $3.40 per bushel. Likewise, for the user of corn who contracts to purchase futures at $2.95 per bushel, the decline of the market below that price would mean the loss of a windfall profit, since he will be obligated to pay the higher futures price. For many growers and users, reducing risk is worth forgoing some windfall profits; but for others, more willing to assume the risks associated with growing and processing commodities, the futures-market hedge is best left alone.

Options Offer a New Wrinkle

Now let's look at a totally new hedging tool: the farm option. Unlike the futures contract, which obligated both buyer and seller to perform, the agricultural option allows the call buyer to exercise *only if it is in his financial interest.* In the case of the buying hedge, the farmer will purchase corn futures (exercise his call option) only if the call will enable him to purchase more cheaply than he can in the cash market. And the same is true for the selling hedge. The potential seller of grain would purchase put options. If, in time, the puts prove profitable — that is, enable the seller to achieve a more favorable selling price — the farmer will exercise his options and assume short futures positions at the now higher selling price. The hedger who uses puts and calls has the flexibility that his fellow farmers who just use futures do not have. The holder of the call or put is never obligated to perform; the holder of a long or short futures contract, in contrast, must always perform, regardless of the economic benefits or costs. Of course, there is a cost associated with this strategy. And that is the premium price one pays to purchase a put or a call.

For the speculators who willingly take on the risks the hedgers would prefer to do without, the futures markets are anything but a means of reducing risk. On the contrary, the speculator embraces risk in pursuit of profit. Unlike the hedger, the speculator doesn't have the underlying commodity growing in the fields outside his home. The fact is, the speculator can't deliver thousands of bushels of grain or thousands of pounds of livestock. For that matter, given his limited resources, he probably couldn't take delivery of grain or livestock either — even if he wanted to. His only "out" in the futures market is to "pay up" when he's wrong. When, for instance, in the midst of a bull market, a speculator buys wheat contracts, he does so with the understanding that he will be able to sell it at a higher price — high enough, certainly, to justify his risk. But when his judgment proves faulty or the market turns into an unrelenting bear, the hapless speculator has no choice but to sell out his position at a lower price and sustain the loss.

Faced with a declining market for grain, the speculator who holds long wheat futures has alternatives, but none of them are any good. He can continue to margin his position by posting additional margin funds — indeed, he'll have to post additional money if he wants to maintain his position — but this only puts off the day of reckoning if prices decline further. He can hope for a rally, of course. He can, in fact, even take delivery on the wheat at the maturity of the contract, but even this extreme action will not gain him a profit if prices fall. The bottom line is: he'd better be right about the direction of prices, or it will cost him money.

Let's compare this futures strategy to one in which the speculator purchases put or call options. With options, the speculator can participate in the highly leveraged futures market without the risk attendant to buying and selling futures. He can use his options if they prove profitable. That is, he can sell an option or exercise an option if it goes into the money. If the option shows little sign of proving profitable, he can walk away from it — or even resell it for what it will bring in the market. As the holder of an option, he is never obligated to perform. The choice is his.

For the buyer, the advantage that options have over futures is staying power. Even in the most volatile markets, an option won't ever cost a buyer a penny more than the initial premium. And this, compared to the futures market, where both buyers and sellers are threatened with margin calls, is a genuine advantage. But this is not to suggest that options are somehow superior to futures — only different. In fact, some of the most successful strategies involve trading options and futures together, such as in several so-called "buy-and-write" strategies, where the options provide a sort of safety cushion for the futures position. Certainly, futures serve as the foundation for the new agricultural options; the futures are the dog, to borrow a well-worn analogy, and the options the tail. Hence, the options will reflect the performance of the futures, and the seasoned ag options trader will track the futures closely.

Options are clearly versatile trading tools. On the one hand, they enable you to profit from a move in the market with strictly limited risk; on the other, they complement futures trading by protecting against risk and providing a cushion of profit, as when options are written against futures positions. While the risk associated with purchasing options is strictly limited, they still enable an investor to participate in the high leverage of futures trading. Leverage, which is nothing more than using a small amount of money to control an asset worth many times as much, is one of the most attractive features of the futures market — except that it can turn against you. Well, options, by virtue of their limited risk, blunt the double-edged sword considerably, while allowing an investor unlimited potential profit. By any measurement, the new agricultural options are an exceptionally flexible and versatile investment tool. And for futures traders, they provide the perfect complementary hedge, resulting in a sophisticated trading tool that is unparalleled in its adaptibility to specific market situations.

Are the New Agricultural Options Safe?

You may have questions concerning the safety of ag options. Given the commodity-option scandals that have plagued investors over the years, your fears are understandable. But if the question is, "Will you be paid?" the answer is an unqualified yes. Despite the numerous scams that have received wide publicity over the years, the new ag options are an animal of a totally different stripe. Let's consider the safeguards and features of the new options on futures.

Exchange-traded options, which are comparatively new, are heavily regulated by the Commodity Futures Trading Commission (CFTC), the federal regulatory agency that monitors the futures market. In addition, the exchanges themselves monitor trading activity and discipline members who do not conform to exchange regulations. In options, as in futures, a third party, the clearinghouse, stands between every buyer and seller. The clearinghouse, an independent nonprofit corporation, exists to ensure the financial integrity of each contract. Thus, if you purchase a call option on, say, soybean futures on the Chicago Board of Trade, the Board of Trade's clearinghouse will stand between you and the seller of the option. If the market moves in a favorable direction and you exercise your call, the clearinghouse will see that you are credited with a long futures contract at the stipulated strike price and that all terms of the contractual agreement between buyer and seller are met. In short, the clearinghouse ensures the performance of every contract.

The key to the performance of the contract is the *margin* that is required of every option seller. Futures contracts are margined by both buyer and seller. Options contracts are similarly margined and *marked to the market* every day — but only for the sellers. This means the sellers are obligated to post funds to ensure that the contract can be fulfilled anytime. Moreover, the seller's obligation persists as long as he holds the short side of the option. The buyer, however, who pays cash for his option, is free to exercise or walk away — the choice is his. Since credits and debits are calculated daily after the close of trading, any undermargined position would receive a margin call. This is a call for additional funds, which must be deposited immediately. If they are not deposited with the clearing member in a forthright fashion, the position is liquidated at the best possible price on the next day's opening. At that time, the option seller is obligated by law to repay any debit in his account.

What if he doesn't pay? Well, first of all, he must have funds on deposit in his account in order to trade; should his resources be depleted, the clearing member firm, who stands between the individual floor trader and the clearinghouse, will be responsible for the loss. The bottom line is, everyone gets paid. The exchanges and the futures industry have far too much at stake to default on any trade, no matter how small. In fact, with the exception of a default of the potato contract at the New York Mercantile Exchange about ten years ago, no one in recent memory has lost a dime in the futures industry through the failure of a contract on a U.S.-regulated exchange.

But don't exchange members go broke? Sure, all the time. But this doesn't mean the safeguards of the exchange prevent winning traders from receiving their profits. The safeguards include a daily accounting of profits and losses on all open positions. Thus, an option writer who sells a July 675 soybean call and holds the position overnight will be scrutinized by the clearinghouse's computer to see that he has sufficient funds in his account. Moreover, his clearing firm, which in turn is responsible to the clearinghouse, will be monitored daily for sufficient margin funds. The exchanges and the CFTC have the right to perform audits on the books of any firms they suspect are not meeting exchange regulations concerning financial safeguards. As far as the exchanges are concerned, the would-be investor in agricultural options can therefore be assured that the terms of the options agreements will be met.

Regulated versus Unregulated Options

The integrity of the new agricultural option contracts is best illustrated by considering some of the abuses of the past. In the past, regulation didn't exist, resulting in losses to many hapless investors.

The concept of an option contract on agricultural futures is not new. The Chicago Board of Trade has been trading futures contracts for more than 137 years. During the late 19th century, grain traders engaged in trading what were then known as "privileges" — essentially, options on grain contracts. In the freewheeling days of early grain trading, regulation was unheard of, and abuses resulted. At first, exchange officials simply looked the other way where options trading was concerned. Then, in 1874, when Illinois law made privilege trading illegal, privileges were banned.

Privilege trading persisted, however, moving to the hallways of the Board of Trade and to another Chicago exchange, the Open Board of Trade, which is today known as the MidAmerica Commodity Exchange. Just as prohibition didn't put a stop to drinking, a ban on privileges didn't put a stop to options trading of farm commodities. Instead, privilege trading flourished in one form or another. Banned from Illinois, Chicago-based traders turned to Milwaukee, where they telegraphed their orders. Finally, the Board of Trade forbade members from trading privileges in any form in outside markets.

Despite the prohibitions, traders were attracted to the concept of grain options trading. And this is where the first real option based on a futures contract was born. Known as "indemnity of sale or purchase," the new privileges that were introduced in the first years of the 20th century worked essentially as options on futures do today. For example, if the contract was exercised, the buyer agreed to make a futures contract with the seller and pay the difference between the indemnity, or option, and the futures contract.

The concept of options received a boost when the 1874 Illinois statute prohibiting all options trading was amended to allow trading in which the settlement would result in an actual transfer of a cash grain or futures contract leading to actual delivery or sale of a commodity. Under the new rules, in which options served a legitimate hedging function, the trading of privileges flourished until 1921, often accounting for as much as 10 percent of the Board of Trade's volume.

The Futures Trading Act of 1921 imposed a 20¢-per-bushel tax on all privilege trading. At a time when corn was trading at between 60¢ and 70¢, the tax put an end to options trading for the next five years. In 1926, the tax was declared unconstitutional, and the on-again, off-again love affair with options trading was definitely on once more. Yet a few years later, in 1933, attempts to corner the wheat market resulted in a huge run-up and a subsequent crash in wheat prices. Options trading in agricultural products was finished for the next 50 years. The Commodity Exchange Act of 1936 made the prohibition on options trading formal.

Scandal in the Seventies

Some 40 years later, in the early 1970s, options trading surfaced once more. Because the prohibition on agricultural commodities remained, some seasoned con operators saw an opportunity to profit by offering the unsuspecting public options on the so-called "world commodities" — sugar, cocoa, silver, and plywood. These were unregulated commodities, not covered by the original Commodity Exchange Act. Then, as now, the concept to offer an option to purchase or sell a futures contract was a good one. For a fixed premium price, the buyer of an option could hope to profit from the volatility of a number of popular commodities.

The timing was ripe, since a number of commodities had begun to soar in value. Buyers of such options were literally doubling their money overnight. Word spread. And the Los Angeles firm that had started the new options business, Goldstein, Samuelson, Inc., soon found a host of competitors clamoring for business as the demand for these seemingly high-profit instruments mushroomed. Alas, as most investors soon learned, the options were too good to be true. The firms selling the options were operating nothing more than Ponzi-type schemes — taking money from Peter to pay Paul. The options were ''naked''in the truest sense. Nothing stood behind them. The sellers maintained that they hedged in the futures market to protect the client. Perhaps some did; others simply pocketed the money. With the markets soaring, the paper profits on the options were enormous. Most investors were pressured to buy more options. As a result, the firms ended up owing huge sums of money with no way to make good on their contractual agreements. It was as if a bookie had taken bets on only one team in a sports event, and that team had won. There was no way to pay the winners. Goldstein, Samuelson, the principal firm engaged in the options scandal, was reputed to be responsible for customer losses amounting to $70 million. Finally, the authorities stepped in, and the business folded like a house of cards overnight. Another speculative bubble had burst.

The Birth of Exchange-Traded Options

In the more than ten years since the California debacle, the concept of options trading has been scrutinized carefully. First, there was the birth of listed options on stocks, led by the Chicago Board Options Exchange, which commenced business in the early 1970s. Today, trading in listed stock options is an enormous business. As a response to the excesses in the 1970s, the Commodity Futures Trading Commission was formed and put in charge of regulating the commodities industry. Starting in 1977, the CFTC debated a pilot program for options on futures contracts. At first, all domestic agricultural commodities were excluded from this program. Then, in 1981, the CFTC approved the limited trading of options in a few specific futures, including Treasury bonds, gold, and sugar. The contracts fluorished. Today, Treasury-bond options have a daily volume of approximately 50,000 contracts. Because much study was devoted to the proper margining of these contracts, with numerous built-in safeguards such as daily marked-to-the-market variable margins, the contracts have been scandal-free. Indeed, they've proved as solid as any futures contract.

Next, the time had come for farm options. In January 1983, a bill lifting the ban on agricultural options was passed. A committee was formed to solicit comments on the new proposed options from commer-

cial users and interested participants. Would ag options serve a legitimate hedging function? The answer was a resounding yes. So far, the
regulators have little reason to doubt that they made the right choice in
allowing the resumption of farm options trading after more than 50
years. In fact, given the range of new strategies available to both commercial hedger and speculator, options on ag futures are likely to become one of the most welcome new financial products in a long time.

2

Getting Started in the New Agricultural Options Market

To many readers familiar with equity options, a book on agricultural options might seem redundant. Aren't puts and calls essentially the same, regardless of their underlying instruments? Well, yes and no. While it is true that many of the strategies are similar — you buy a call in anticipation of rising prices and buy a put in anticipation of declining prices — there are fundamental differences.

Most of the nonequity options introduced in recent years, including the successful options on U.S. Treasury bond futures, have been on financial instruments that don't present problems of delivery or perishability. The options on stock indexes, for example, have a cash settlement provision that allows the buyer or seller of the underlying instrument to settle for cash on expiration of the futures contract. Thus, if you purchase a put on, say, a New York Stock Exchange Composite Index future and exercise it, you will receive a short futures position. If the market closes below the strike price, you will get cash credited to your account. The index contract, being nothing more than a legal fiction, entails a bookkeeping entry — nothing more. In contrast, a traditional stock option calls for the delivery of the underlying stock. Even an option on a popular commodity such as gold involves contracts to give or receive a nonperishable, universally recognized store of value. This is something investors worldwide can understand. But agricultural futures? For most, agricultural futures are an entirely new breed of financial animal.

Futures on farm products are quite different from shares of stock or legal fictions such as stock indexes. Live hogs and cattle literally live and breathe. And the supply of grains and cotton is highly dependent on weather patterns and "acts of God," which are outside the control of man. Certainly, farmers and futures traders have lived with these imponderables for years. But to the new trader of agricultural options, the nature of the underlying vehicle has to be taken into account.

What affects farm futures prices? Weather, for one; seasonal patterns in supply and demand for another. A host of government reports that are issued regularly. Interest rates and the cost of money, as reflected in the carrying charge market. And isolated events such as the success or failure of the Peruvian anchovy harvest, the weather for Brazil, and Soviet growing conditions. All can generate substantial changes in farm commodity prices on the U.S. futures exchanges. For someone who has limited himself to trading options on IBM and Xerox, the number of new variables that have to be taken into account when you trade ag options can prove a rude awakening.

In addition, there is the difference between stocks and futures. Futures are highly leveraged, and as a result, even a modest move in prices of a commodity can generate panic by those speculators who are suddenly losing substantial amounts of money. Then, too, stocks have a lasting quality. They can be passed down from generation to generation. But futures contracts are short-lived. As they approach expiration, the contracts will be liquidated *regardless of price.* Most speculators simply haven't the means to take or give delivery of the underlying commodity. This difference in the nature of the underlying instrument will change the option buyer's or seller's attitude toward his investment.

Another difference between stocks and futures is the size of investor participation. A company that issues stock has only so many shares outstanding, but a futures contract, whose particpation is measured by "open interest," or the number of contracts which have yet to be offset prior to expiration, can be created at will.

Lastly, stocks differ from commodities in terms of volatility. Because of different crop years and expiration months, volatility can't be measured easily in the futures market. Moreover, the volatility in an agricultural commodity is apt to be greater than stock volatility. For instance, in a recent 12-month study of stock prices, the volatility of IBM shares ranged from 15 percent to 25 percent. Over the same period, soybeans had a volatility ranging from 15 percent to 45 percent.

As a result of these differences, the traditional methods of recognizing "fair value" in an option are apt to prove inadequate for agricultural commodities under actual market conditions.

Understanding the Nomenclature

Every field — whether it's law, medicine, or finance — has its own specialized nomenclature, and options trading is no exception. Rule number one is not to be put off by seemingly nonsensical terms, especially the ones that brokers are apt to use. Options trading is relatively straightforward once you understand the terms. The fact is, options present another financial opportunity for investors and hedgers alike, and the potential rewards are well worth the effort involved in learning the basics.

First and foremost, you have *puts* and *calls*, the two main types of options. Second, you must remember that there are two sides to every options transaction: the buying side and the selling, or writing, side. The buyer pays a *premium* to the seller, who in turn guarantees to uphold his part of the bargain in the contract — namely, to allow the buyer to buy or sell (depending on whether he purchased a call or a put) the underlying futures contract at the agreed-upon price, known as the *strike price*.

The call option, as you may remember, permits the buyer to purchase the underlying futures — that is, "call" it away — at the strike price; the put allows the buyer to sell — or "put" — the underlying futures at the strike price. The option buyer may or may not *exercise* his option; the option writer, on the other hand, has no such luxury: he *must* perform once he writes an option. His only alternative is to offset his short position by liquidating (or covering) in the market. And when the option proves profitable to the buyer, this covering is accomplished only at a loss.

Finally, options are said to be "wasting" instruments. This is because they're priced partly according to their *time value*, which must inevitably "waste" away as they approach *expiration* or *maturity*. At maturity, all time value ceases to exist; at that point, an option will be valued at its *cash* or *intrinsic value*.

Options are designated according to the delivery month of the underlying futures. Thus, a call option for November soybeans will be designated as, say, the November 775 call; but — and here's the tricky part — the November 775 call will actually expire in October, in time for the buyer of the call to receive the underlying futures contract. If he so wishes, he can then hold the futures contract until maturity, a month later, and take delivery of the actual soybeans. He can also sell the futures contract if he wishes.

Actually, not all options on futures expire the month before the expiration date of the futures contract. The exception is options on cash settlement instruments, such as the S&P 500 options on the underlying stock-index futures. Because these cash-settlement instruments do not involve delivery of an actual commodity or financial instrument, the options expire at the same time as the futures.

If thoughts of thousands of bushels of soybeans piling up at your front door have you worried, don't concern yourself. Of the million of contracts traded each year, only a small minority are held to maturity; the rest are *offset*, or liquidated, before that date. The same, by the way, is true of options contracts. Most are offset prior to expiration, and the profits and losses are calculated according to the prices at which the buyers and sellers bought and sold.

As a would-be options trader, you'll want to acquaint yourself with the terms *in the money*, *at the money*, and *out of the money*. To keep the illustration simple, let's first deal with calls. A call gives you the right to purchase the underlying futures at the strike price. Thus, if you owned a call to purchase live cattle futures for December delivery with a strike price of $68 per hundredweight, and the underlying December futures contract were trading at, say, $76 per hundredweight, you'd have a built-in cash profit of at least $8, or the difference between the strike price and the current market price of $76. (In actuality, such an in-the-money call would be trading for more than its $8 cash value, depending on the time left to expiration.) To summarize, a call is *in the money* when the strike price is *below* the underlying futures price.

An *at-the-money* call is one in which the strike price is *identical* with the current market price of the underlying futures.

Out-of-the-money calls have a strike price *above* the current market price of the futures. Thus, the December 76 cattle call would be out of the money if December futures were trading below $76 per hundredweight. Why pay more than the prevailing market price of the underlying futures? Obviously, you wouldn't want to exercise such a call. But this doesn't mean that an out-of-the-money call will not have value. On the contrary, it could prove quite valuable should cattle prices rise. Hence, even out-of-the-money options will retain what is known as *time value*, or value attributable to the remaining time left to expiration. Because of this time value, options with identical strikes but different expiration dates will have different values. If this is March, which of two options with identical strikes will have the greater value: one expiring in July or December? Obviously, the one with the greatest amount of time, the December option, will retain the greatest value.*

Let's now turn the situation on its head. Let's consider puts. The put gives you the right to *sell* the underlying futures at the strike price. Thus, an in-the-money put will have a strike which is *above* the market price. If the price of January soybeans is $7.10 per bushel, a put providing you with the right to *sell* those January soybeans at, say, $7.50 has an intrinsic value of 40¢ per bushel. Conversely, an out-of-the-money put would have a strike price *below* the current market. Who would want to sell January soybeans at $7.00 per bushel if the very same soybeans were trading at $7.50 per bushel in the futures market? No one. For this reason, out-of-the-money options trade for considerably lower prices than in-the-money options.

What about the cost of an option? Option prices, which are known as *premiums*, are determined by competing buyers and sellers gathered together in a trading pit on the floor of a futures exchange. Typically, an options pit will be situated adjacent to the trading pit for the underlying futures. This facilitates the trading of both instruments for those engaged in sophisticated buy-and-write strategies.

Option premiums are tied closely to the price of the underlying futures. As futures prices rise, call-option premiums will typically rise too — but not necessarily in a one-to-one fashion. Conversely, puts will decline in rising markets and rise in value in falling markets. Failure for one to keep pace with the other would present such an unmistakable profit opportunity that traders would quickly buy the undervalued option or futures and sell the overvalued one until they came into line. This simultaneous buying and selling of two similar, though not necessarily identical, trading vehicles is known as *arbitrage*. It is a popular trading strategy among a few well-financed traders. But because of the small profits to be had on each trade, a commission-paying non-member would have difficulty in capitalizing on arbitrage opportunities.

The premium price is determined by open outcry in the pit. The reason for the open-outcry method is that it provides for the fairest and quickest way to make current prices known to all traders in the pit. Thus, an option buyer *bids* and an option seller *offers* or *asks*. The difference between the bid and the asked is known as the *spread*, or the

---

* The exception to this rule occurs with different crop years when the nearer month, or old crop month, has an option of greater value because of heightened volatility or uncertain supply-and-demand factors.

difference between what the buyer is willing to pay and what the seller is willing to offer.*

For a trade to take place, both buyer and seller must agree on a *single price*. That is, the buyer must agree to trade at the seller's asked price; or, conversely, the seller must be willing to trade at the buyer's bid price. Through the open outcry method, all traders in the pit are able to hear the bids and offers, so the opportunity exists to achieve the best possible price in such a competitive market. That kind of options trading in a centralized arena during normal business hours makes for an efficient and liquid market that offers both buyers and sellers the best possible deal.

Such so-called "listed" options are in sharp contrast to unlisted options, which involve a buyer and seller who do not come together in such a competitive environment. In such cases, the seller is holding the important cards, since the buyer is totally dependent on him for both buying and, later, selling or exercising the option. In such cases, the premiums are apt to reflect the lack of liquidity, and the buyer will be at a clear disadvantage.

Option premiums are quoted in terms of the underlying futures contracts. Grains are quoted in cents, or dollars and cents, per bushel; for instance, corn might be quoted at 361 (meaning 361¢ per bushel) or $3.61. Grain futures and options are also quoted in $\frac{1}{8}$¢ increments, although the smallest price tick in a grain futures contract is $\frac{1}{4}$¢. Thus, 361-6 means 361$\frac{6}{8}$¢, or 361$\frac{3}{4}$¢, per bushel. Since all futures and options on futures in grain contracts call for delivery or sale of the standardized 5,000-bushel contract (the MidAm 1,000-bushel soybean option is the sole exception), the value of 1¢ is $50, or multiplied by the 5,000-bushel size. A half-cent would be worth $25; a quarter-cent would be worth $12.50 on a single futures or options contract. Now, if your broker quotes you a premium of 105$\frac{1}{2}$ on a March 750 call, you know you will be paying 105$\frac{1}{2}$¢ per bushel, or $5,275 (105$\frac{1}{2}$¢ per bushel × 5,000 bushels per contract = $5,275). Obviously, this is a pretty high premium. But if March futures are trading at $8.29, you can see that 79¢, or about $3,950 of this premium, are intrinsic value, the balance being time value.

In the livestock complex, the quotes similarly reflect the size of the underlying futures. Cattle, which trades in standardized contracts of 40,000 lb, is quoted in dollars and cents per hundredweight, or cents per pound. The smallest increment in cattle is .025, meaning that prices

---

* Do not confuse this usage of "spread" with "spread position," in which one buys one option or futures and sells another.

will move in increments of that amount. For example, the price might move from 64.35 to 64.37 (meaning 64.375), to 64.40, to 64.42 (meaning 64.425), to 64.45, and so on. In live hogs, you have a similar situation. The key difference between cattle and hogs is the size of the contract. While cattle are traded in a 40,000 lb contract, hogs are traded in a 30,000 lb contract. As a result, a 1¢ move in cattle is equal to $400 per contract ($.01 × 40,000 = $400), whereas a 1¢ move in hogs is equal to $300 per contract. A February 64 cattle call quoted at, say, $5.90, would therefore cost 400 times as much, or $2,360. And a February 60 hog call quoted at $6.00 would cost 300 times as much, or $1,800.

How an Option Is Traded

The scene of a commodity trading pit can be either bedlam or boredom. Depending on the time of day—the open and the close are the busiest—and the market action, an options pit will either be a mob of traders waving hands and arms and gesticulating over yells and shouts or a relatively placid group of traders standing around waiting for some "paper," as the public orders are known, to come into the pit. On a slow day, the "locals," or traders who make a living trading for their own accounts, will temporarily come alive as the scalpers and other floor traders fight for the elusive "edge," or spread between the bid and the asked price, to make a hard-won living by "clipping" a half-cent or less off an order.

To the uninitiated in the ways of the floor, the scene appears entirely uncontrolled and undisciplined. Yet to the professionals on the floor, who use a sort of financial shorthand in yelling out their bids and offers—"four on forty, forty at a half"—the terminology is clear and unambiguous, with everyone in the pit knowing precisely what is taking place.

Traders use hand signals—palms out for selling, palms inward for buying—to further clarify their intentions in the pit. This is accompanied by a lot of body language, including the wavings of hands, shouts, and jumping up and down to attract the attention of an order filler or another local. Amid the seeming bedlam that occurs in a trading pit, one wonders how the traders can make sense out of such confusion. Yet the trading proceeds with precision. With the flick of a wrist or the nod of a head accompanied by the single word "Sold!" thousands of such transactions occur daily, involving contracts valued at millions of dollars.

"I sold you sixty 675s at the orders," a soybean option trader might yell out in confirming an order just consummated, although no such confirmation is necessary. The opposing trader will know precisely what he said: simply that he, the buyer, *purchased* sixty calls at a premium of whatever the prevailing price was at the time plus "the orders," which is shorthand for three-quarters of a cent. Let's say the seller was offering the calls at 5¾¢. The buyer might have yelled out "sold" and the transaction was completed. Thus, for each of the sixty 675 calls, the buyer would have paid 5¾¢, or $287.50, to the seller, who received a like amount. The "orders," as it is known to grain traders, refers to "three-quarters" — it's just easier to yell out.

Despite the seeming complexity of the transaction, the standardization and relatively few variables involved make the completion of a trade rather straightfoward. For example, each commodity is traded in only one pit, with each contract month limited to a specific area of the pit. The most active month occupies the bulk of the trading area. But with the introduction of agricultural options, the task immediately became somewhat more complex. With options, not only do you have contract months — January soybeans, March soybeans, and so on — but you have puts and calls for each month *and* different strike prices for each. As a result, the options trader has to be precise in his intentions. He can't just buy and sell at will without paying attention to the specific option he is offering or bidding on.

For example, looking to trade the January 700 calls, a soybean options trader might yell out into the pit, "What's the market for the Jan.* 700 calls?"

"Two at three-eights," might come back the reply, meaning they are bid at 2¢ and offered at 2⅜¢.

He then has to make a decision. If he decides to buy, he knows he'll be bidding against the previous bid of 2¢. Thus, his bid must be identical or higher (in the same time frame) but never lower. To bid lower would be considered "off the market" — a violation of the rules. The same is true for selling. With the offer at "three-eights," the would-be seller must match the previous offer or offer it lower — "at a quarter," for example — but never higher.

Let's say the trader wants to buy the January 700 calls for 2¢, or $100 per option. "Two bid!" he'll shout. "Two bid on sixty!" Chances are he'll be met with a chorus of sellers offering to him at a slightly higher price — say "two-and-a-quarter." Either the buyer or one of the

---

* Note the use of the abbreviated form of the month here. To save time the trader would say "Jan." rather than "January."

sellers must then relent for a trade to take place. That is, either the buyer must increase his bid or the seller must lower his offer — or, more likely, simply "hit" the bid by yelling out "Sold!"

Now that we've seen the theory involved in a trade being consummated on the floor, we can look more closely at the practical situation facing the public investor. Simply put, *everyone* wants the best possible price. If they had their way, buyers would always buy at the bid and sellers would always sell at the offer. In reality, however, buyers frequently buy at the offer and sellers frequently sell at the bid; if it were otherwise, no trading would take place.

When either buyer or seller relents, it is known as "giving up the edge." Almost all so-called "market" orders involve giving the edge to the floor. In highly liquid markets, the edge is apt to be small — typically $\frac{1}{8}$¢ or $\frac{1}{4}$¢ in the grains. But in less liquid markets, the spread between the bid and the asked is apt to widen, and you'll have to pay more to enter or exit the market.

For example, let's say you decide to trade an option that doesn't enjoy a wide degree of participation. In the grains, the spread between the bid and the asked in a thinly traded option might be 2¢ or more. Let's say a July 675 soybean call recently changed hands at 40¢ or $2,000 for the option. Knowing the last trade occurred at 40¢, however, may not be that helpful to you. After all, the last trade may have occurred a half-hour or even an hour ago. Just because the futures are actively traded is no guarantee that the options, especially the deep in- and out-of-the-money options, will enjoy a similar degree of wide participation. Moreover, perhaps the futures have moved up since the last trade in the options market. When your order hits the pit, the market for the July 675 call may be "43 bid, 47 asked," representing a 4¢ spread. If you are a buyer, therefore, your market order will probably be filled at 47; if you decide to sell a moment later, however, you will receive only 43. Such are the hazards of trading thin markets.

The Current Options

Currently, there are seven agricultural commodities for which options on futures are traded on seven exchanges. Under a pilot program approved by the CFTC, the federal regulatory body of the futures industry, the exchanges have been allowed to introduce ag options, commencing with just one commodity each. A number of exchanges are now trading two or more options. Here are the options currently traded:

1. *Sugar.* Considered a "world" commodity rather than a domestic agricultural commodity, sugar was the first commodity to have listed options trading. Sugar options were introduced during the initial options program, which preceded the ag options by about two years. Traded at the Coffee, Sugar & Cocoa Exchange in New York, sugar options have not won the widespread acceptance among traders once expected. Whether the problem rests with the lackluster sugar market no one knows, but this is certainly one factor militating against the widespread acceptance of sugar options. Sugar options have an open interest of less than 4,000 contracts. By comparison, the widely traded U.S. Treasury bond futures options have an open interest of 250,000 contracts. Like the world sugar futures contract, the sugar option is quoted in 1/100ths of a point, with the minimum tick equal to $11.20.

2. *Wheat.* Wheat options are traded on three exchanges, but the type of wheat is slightly different on each exchange. On the Minneapolis Grain Exchange, options are traded on futures contracts of hard red spring wheat; at the Kansas City Board of Trade, options are traded on that exchange's hard red winter wheat contract; and in Chicago, the MidAmerica Commodity Exchange offers options on soft red winter wheat, which is traded both at the MidAmerica Commodity Exchange and the Chicago Board of Trade. The MidAmerica wheat option is for 5,000 bushels of wheat, despite the fact that the MidAm's mini-futures contract in wheat is limited to just 1,000 bushels.

3. *Cotton.* Options on cotton futures are available at the New York Cotton Exchange. The underlying cotton contract consists of 50,000 lb of cotton, with a minimum price tick of $5, or $500 for a 1¢ point.

4. *Live Cattle.* Options on live cattle are traded at the Chicago Merchantile Exchange, the nation's leading futures markets for livestock products. The standard futures contract is 40,000 lb of live cattle, and the premium quotes are for dollars per hundredweight, or cents per lb, with the minimum .025 tick equal to $10, or $4 for 1/100¢.

5. *Live Hogs.* Options on live hog futures were introduced at the Chicago Mercantile Exchange in early 1985, on the heels of the successful live cattle options introduced the previous fall. The standard contract is for 30,000 lb of live hogs, with the premium prices quoted in dollars per hundredweight, or cents per lb. The options, like the underlying futures, are quoted in increments of .025 points, with each point valued at $3.

6. *Soybeans.* The most successful farm options contract to date, soybean options are traded at the Chicago Board of Trade. The options, like the futures, are for the standard 5,000-bushel contract, with each option quoted in minimum ticks of $\frac{1}{8}$¢, or $6.25.

7. *Corn.* Options on corn futures were introduced at the Chicago Board of Trade in early 1985, following the success of the soybean options. Like the underlying futures, the corn options are quoted in cents per bushel, with strike prices placed at 10¢ intervals.

The Four Basic Strategies

There are two parties to every options contract, just as there are two parties to every futures contract. But in the case of options, the buyer and seller have different rights and responsibilities. Since there are just two types of options — puts and calls — let's deal with one and then the other.

The Call-Option Buying Strategy

The call-option buyer purchases, for a fixed premium price, the right to buy the underlying futures contract at the strike price at any time prior to expiration. The buyer, however, is not obligated to exercise the option or to sell the option; if he wishes, he can simply abandon the option. Should he wish to sell the option at any time prior to expiration, he may do so. The option premium at the time he sells the option will be determined by the relationship of the underlying futures price to the strike price; the amount of time left to expiration; the volatility of the market; and other factors, such as interest rates, that might affect the chances for the option's ultimate profitability. Should the option buyer decide to exercise his call, he will receive a long futures position at the strike price.

For example, let's say it is May and you purchase a July 390 wheat call for a premium of 30¢, or $1,500. (The standardized wheat contract is for 5,000 bushels; thus, a 30¢ per bushel premium will work out to $1,500.) At the time, July wheat futures might be trading at, say, $4.10 ($4.10 per bushel), suggesting that the 30¢ premium reflects 20¢ in cash value and 10¢ in time value. That is, the option might be exercised for 20¢ on the day it is purchased. But, expecting still higher wheat prices, you are willing to pay an additional 10¢ in time premium for the privilege of being able to "call in" July wheat futures at a price of $3.90 a bushel.

Let's assume you're correct in your market judgment. In mid-June, when the call option is about to expire (in general, options on futures expire a month before the expiration of the futures contract), July wheat is trading at, say, 465. You can either exercise the July 390 wheat call at that point or sell it at a profit. If you exercise the call, you'll be given a long July wheat futures at the strike price of $3.90 per bushel. Since the market price for July wheat is now $4.65, the position will have a built-in profit of 75¢. As an alternative, you can simply sell the July 390 wheat call. At expiration, the option will be worth its cash value (the difference between the strike price and the July futures), or 75¢ per bushel. Prior to expiration, the call will be worth even more, since it will retain some of its time value. Assuming a 75¢ cash value, you can sell the call for $3,750. Since it originally cost $1,500, the profit will amount to $2,250 before commissions. An example of call buying is shown in Figure 1.

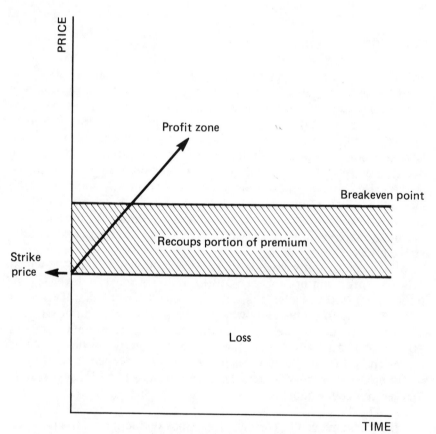

Figure 1.   Example of call buying.

The Call-Option Writing Strategy

The seller, or *writer*, of the call is on the other side of the transaction. The seller guarantees the buyer the right to purchase the underlying futures at the strike price. Because the price of the underlying futures may rise, at least theoretically, to infinity, the writer has an unlimited risk. In fact, the writer has the very same risk as a short seller of futures contracts. He is liable for the strike price of the call and more. To guarantee the performance of the call contract, the writer must post margin, which is marked to the market on a daily basis.

Let's examine how this might work in practice. You decide to purchase a July wheat call with a strike of 390 for a premium of 30¢ per bushel, or $1,500. As a writer, I might decide to take the other side of the trade. You pay me a 30¢-per-bushel premium ($1,500), and I provide you with the opportunity to "call away" the underlying futures at the strike. To guarantee my end of the bargain, I must post margin. My margin may increase or decrease, but I must post something as long as I hold the "short" side of the call.

Why would I write a call and assume an unlimited risk in pursuit of a fixed profit? There are several reasons. For one, I might think the buyer's judgment is simply wrong. In that case, I anticipate lower wheat prices. Remember, if the price of July wheat futures settles below the strike at expiration, the call is totally worthless to the buyer. His loss, my gain. As the writer, I would keep the entire 30¢ premium. Or I might write a call if I think call premiums are overpriced. The 10¢ time premium for only 30 days may seem a bit excessive. For the call to have value at expiration, the futures prices must rise by 10¢. Even if July futures trade at $4.20 per bushel (390 strike + 30¢ premium = 420 breakeven) at expiration, I will still break even, because I will then be paying out 30¢ on the call for which I received an identical amount. Thus, even if wheat prices rise, the writer stands to make money *if* the rise does not exceed the premium received.

In the case of a July 390 call, the buyer is paying 20¢ in cash value when the market price is $4.10. The balance, or 10¢, is the time value. The call writer also operates on the notion that he has time value working on his behalf. As a call option approaches maturity, it loses time value — at first slowly, then, as it nears the end of its life, rapidly. That's why an option is known as a "wasting asset" — to the buyer. To the seller, however, an option is an "appreciating asset"; those "wasting" dollars, in the form of eroding time value, are going right into his pocket.

The writer, therefore, has quite a different situation from the buyer. In return for an unlimited risk, the writer can receive only a fixed, predetermined premium, for which he must post margin. No matter how far below the strike the futures price falls, the writer will receive no more than the original premium income. Conversely, if his judgment proves wrong, the writer can lose an infinite amount in the form of margin calls—if he doesn't take defensive action. What sort of defensive action? Well, just as the futures trader can buy back his position and offset his position, the option writer can do the same. Thus, if the writer of a call decides to limit his losses—or profits—he may *buy back* (cover) the call at the prevailing market price. He is then absolved of his responsibility to continue margining his call.

Let's say that, having written a July 390 wheat call for 30¢, the writer finds himself in a losing position as wheat prices move higher and the call is worth 40¢. Not wishing to sustain greater losses, the writer can buy back his July 390 call for 40¢, sustaining a 10¢ loss in the process.

In the same manner, the writer may decide to take profits if prices decline. Let's say time passes and the July 390 call is now worth 25¢. The writer can earn a 5¢ profit by buying back the call. Having received 30¢ for selling the call, he will profit by 5¢ when he buys it back at 25¢. Moreover, he may have earned the 5¢ while the market stayed stationary, the price decline reflecting time premium alone.

Why not just hold onto the short call? Again, there are many reasons. Perhaps he wanted only a small, short-term profit. Perhaps he anticipated higher prices, and a corresponding disappearance of his paper profit. Perhaps he had better uses for the money that was tied up in margin. Lastly, no matter how far out of the money an option trades, it will always retain some time value until expiration. Why hold onto an option and tie up margin in pursuit of the last few cents in writing calls?

Figure 2 shows an example of writing a call.

The Put-Option Buying Strategy

The put-option buyer tends to expect lower prices, since the put option provides him with the right, but not the obligation, to sell the underlying futures at the agreed-upon strike price. Let's say you are bearish on hog futures. You might buy a put on October hogs with a strike of $60 a hundredweight for a premium of $3, or $900 on the 30,000 lb contract. In the case of the put, the option will have cash value when the price of the underlying futures falls *below* the strike price. Thus, $58 live hog futures would mean an in-the-money July 60 put, but

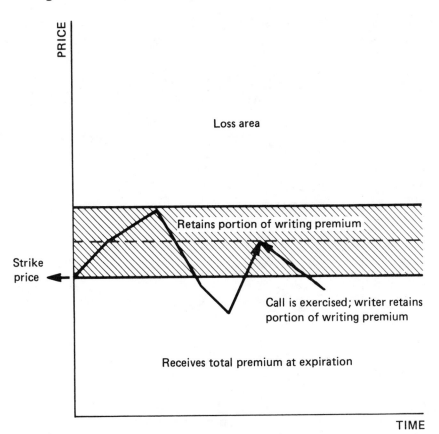

Figure 2.   Example of call writing.

an out-of-the-money July 54 put. Why sell hogs at $54 if you can sell them at $58?

The put is the mirror image of the call. The put is a separate option from the call. Thus, you do not exit a put position by selling a call. Each has to be treated separately. If you buy a put for, say, $3, you will profit if you can sell it for $4 or $5. But the value of the put moves inversely to the value of the underlying futures. Thus, if futures *rise*, put prices will fall; if futures *fall*, puts will rise in value.

The put buyer's risk, like the call buyer's risk, is strictly limited. The initial premium is the maximum risk. If the price of the underlying futures contract is *above* the strike at expiration, the put will expire worthless and the put buyer will sustain a 100-percent net loss.

The put buying strategy is illustrated in Figure 3.

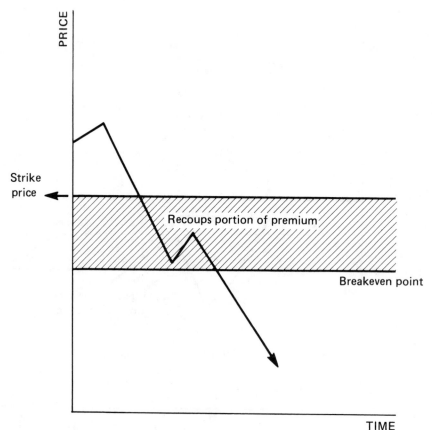

Figure 3.   Example of put buying.

The Put-Option Writing Strategy

The writer of a put, like the writer of a call, guarantees the other side of the trade. By agreeing to have the underlying futures "put" to him, the writer is willing to *buy* futures at the strike. The writer of a put receives a "long" futures position when the option is exercised. The call writer, on the other hand, receives a "short" futures position. There are always a buyer and a seller in every transaction.

Why write puts? For the very same reasons one would write a call —income. Like the call writer, the put writer knows the market must move (albeit in a different direction) for the buyer to make money. He knows the market must move down for the put to prove profitable to the buyer. And he doesn't believe it will.

As a put writer, you might anticipate steady to higher prices. Or you might write the put knowing that the premium income will offset, in part, any downward move in prices — a sort of profit cushion below the strike. Thus, if you write a put for $3, you know you can lose that much in a declining market and still break even. Put writers, like call writers, take an income approach to the market. Occasionally, they reason, a position will move against them, but over time, the likelihood is that decreasing time value will work in their favor.

What are the drawbacks to put writing? The same, essentially, as call writing. The position must be fully margined at all times and is marked to the market daily. What's more, the put writer can lose many times what he stands to gain.

Figure 4 illustrates put writing.

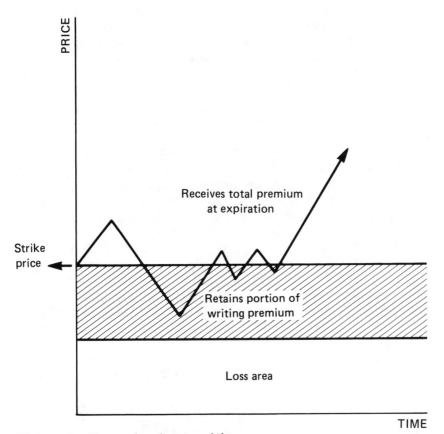

Figure 4. Example of put writing.

What Influences Premium Prices?

Now that we know the meaning of option quotes and understand how prices are established in the pit, we need to know what influences premium levels. Why can you buy one option for $600 and another for $1,600?

There are a number of factors that influence premium prices. The most important, no doubt, has to do with the relationship between the option's strike price and the level of the underlying futures. An option, after all, is merely the right — not the guarantee — to buy or sell futures at the strike. It may very well be that the option you purchase today will never have a cash vaue, only a time value that represents potential.

We have seen that an in-the-money option commands a greater premium than an out-of-the-money option. The in-the-money put or call has intrinsic value. That is, its value is composed of real cash value (meaning it could be exercised at a profit today) plus time value, or the value accruing from the remaining time left to expiration. For the same reason, an option that is said to be *deep in the money* will have a greater value than an option which is *slightly in the money*. Out-of-the-money or at-the-money options, of course, are priced according to what the market feels the remaining time warrants.

Next, in considering an option premium, you have to consider the volatility of the underlying futures. Since the value of the typical soybean contract moved approximately $17,000 over the past year, compared with a fluctuation of about $5,000 for a contract of corn, an option to buy or sell soybeans at some time in the future is understandably more costly than an option to buy or sell corn — assuming a comparable relationship between the options strike price and the price of the futures. In addition, you have to consider the influence of economic factors such as interest rates, which affect almost every financial decision today. If rates are likely to rise, people can earn virtually risk-free profits simply by purchasing T-bills. Investors are therefore going to be reluctant to put money into the very risky options market, which might lower option premiums. Finally, there is the influence of the remaining time on option premiums. As I've mentioned, a longer-term option has more value than a comparable shorter-term option.

The options specifications, as we've seen, are pretty straightforward. You decide whether to purchase or sell (write) a put or a call. Again, the call gives the buyer the right to purchase the underlying futures at the exercise or strike price. In fact, if exercised, the call will result in a long, or buying, futures position being credited to the call holder's account. The put is the reverse. The put gives the holder, or buyer, the right—but, again, not the obligation—to sell the underlying futures at the strike price. When exercised, the put results in a short, or selling, position being credited to the account of the put holder. On the writing side (remember, there are always two parties to an options or futures contract), the *writer of a call* receives a *short* position at the strike price when the option is exercised. Conversely, the *writer of a put* receives a *long* position at the strike price when the option is exercised.

The exercise prices are standardized and straddle the market price at the time the options commence trading, usually with at least seven options trading for each cash commodity. In time, as the market prices change, new options are added to accommodate the change in prices. For instance, with June live hogs trading at $50, puts and calls with strikes at 44, 46, 48, 50, 52, 54, and 56 might be introduced. Should hog prices move to the $60 level, higher strikes that are closer to the market price will be added.

Now let's see if we can work with these new terms to identify an option precisely. Remember, we must identify *all* the terms of the option in order to make sure we are talking about a specific put or call and not just all calls or all puts on, say, live-cattle contracts. Let's say it is May and you are bullish on grains, particularly soybeans. You might call a futures broker and get a quote on August soybeans and the accompanying August call options. "The August beans are at 781½," the broker might reply. "The August 775 calls are at 12 bid, 13 asked." Will you understand his quote? The underlying futures are trading at $7.81½ per bushel, whereas the *right* to purchase the August soybeans at a price of $7.75 per bushel (or 6½¢ per bushel under the market) is bid at 12, or $600 per contract, and asked at 13, or $650 per contract.

Once you receive this information, you'll want to know what to do with it. Will you buy soybean futures? Will you buy the calls? Or perhaps write soybean puts? Or engage in a slightly more exotic strategy such as buying a bull spread in calls? Because you are concerned about risk, you might want to limit your trading activities to purchasing soybean calls. You can instruct your broker to purchase an August 775 soybean call *at the market*, in which case you'll probably pay the asked (or seller's price of 13¢ per bushel, or you can place a *limit order* to purchase the August 775 call at, say, 12½¢. In the latter case, your order may or may not be filled. It all depends on whether a seller who had previously been offering 13 is willing to sell at 12½. By the way, a limit order of 12½¢ means "12½¢ or better." That is, the order may be filled at 12½¢ or even 12¢, but never 12¾¢ or any price higher than your specified limit of 12½¢.

Let's assume you buy one August 775 soybean call at the market and receive the fill price of 13¢. What have you purchased? The right to buy August soybean futures at a price of $7.75 per bushel at any time prior to the call's expiration in late July. Remember, agricultural options expire the *month before* the futures. As you might suspect, the value of the call will be determined by the rise or decline of the underlying August soybean futures. If soybean prices decline, the likelihood is that the value of the call will also decline; rising prices, of course, will probably enhance the value of the call.

For the sake of our illustration, let's say time passes and bean prices decline. Because the August 775 soybean call will be out of the money below the strike of 775, the call might trade at only 7¢ a month later. The entire premium now reflects so-called *time value.* (If the option remained out of the money at expiration, this value would cease to exist and the option would expire worthless.) As the call holder, you are now faced with a decision. Should you continue to hold the call? Or should you sell it at a loss? On the one hand, the price of soybeans may rise and you may recoup your paper losses; on the other, bean prices may be headed lower, and you may stand to lose your entire investment.

Let's say you decide to sell. Having paid 13¢ per bushel for the option, or $650, you now receive just 7¢ per bushel, or $350. Your loss is limited to the difference between what you received and what you paid, or $300 plus your commission cost. Should soybean prices subsequently rise, you may wish you had held on a little longer.

When you sell, you simply reverse your order to your broker. Having purchased one August 775 bean call, you now sell one August 775 call, and the transaction is complete. As the buyer of the option, you are not obligated, however, to ever sell the option. Had you held onto the call and prices stayed below the strike price, you would have simply abandoned the call at expiration. Your loss, however, would have amounted to the full premium in that case.

There are other possibilities, of course. Let's say soybean prices rise after you purchased the call. Now you are in the enviable position of having a profit. Again, there are decisions to make. Should you sell the call or exercise the option? Again, it depends. By selling the call, you will receive whatever it will bring in the market. Let's say by the first week in July, the price of August soybeans rises to $8.50 a bushel. Now you have at least 75¢ of intrinsic value in the August 775 call plus whatever time value remains — say, another couple of cents. The same call you purchased for just 13¢ per bushel is now valued at 77¢. You can simply sell the call for 77¢ per bushel ($3,850). Your profit will then be the difference between what you received for the call and what you paid for it.

An alternative is to exercise the call. By exercising, you will be given a long August soybean futures with a net purchase price of $7.75 per bushel. Since August beans are now trading at $8.50 per bushel, you will have a paper profit of 75¢, or $3,750, in your account. With August futures at 850, your paper profits will be more than adequate to margin one position. But should soybean prices drop precipitously, you will be requested to post additional margin, just like a futures trader, to maintain the position. To realize your profit, you must then sell the long August futures. Your profit will be determined by the difference between selling and buying price, minus the initial cost of the call.

For example, let's say prior to the last trading day in August, you sell your beans for $8.63 per bushel. Your profit is 88¢ in the futures (863 − 775 = 88) minus the 13¢ you paid for the call, or 75¢ per bushel. That's $3,750 exclusive of commissions. The point is, as a holder of a long soybean futures position, you will be treated like any other futures speculator, and the same rules governing profits and losses will apply. The only difference will be that you initiated your position by exercising a call option rather than by simply purchasing a futures position. The end result, of course, will reflect the added cost of purchasing the call.

How to Write Ag Options

So far, our emphasis has been on purchasing options. But put and call contracts, like the underlying futures contracts, consist of two parties: a buyer and a seller, or writer. The writer, in the parlance of the option market, *grants* the option to the buyer. That is, in return for the premium income, the writer agrees to have the call or put option exercised against him. In the case of the call, the writer will receive a *short futures position at the strike price* in the event of exercise. The put writer will receive a *long futures position at the strike price* in the event of exercise.

This is an important concept to grasp, so you should think about it for a moment. Remember, there are both a buyer and a seller for every transaction. In the options market, the writer grants the option to the buyer. The buyer or holder of the option alone determines whether or not he will exercise his option. Once the buyer exercises, the writer must fulfill his contractual agreement. What is that agreement? In the case of the call, the buyer is entitled to a long futures position in the underlying commodity futures at the strike price. In order for the call holder to have a long position (or buying position), there must be a seller on the other side of the transaction. The writer is that seller.

Let's take an example. An option writer offers to sell a March 270 corn call for a premium of 17¢, or $850 on the 5,000-bushel contract. In return for writing the call, the writer *receives* the premium in his trading account. This money is now his to keep, but he cannot remove it from his account unless he maintains margin. Thus, the writer, unlike the buyer, must margin the option just like a futures contract. And the option is marked to the market daily just like a futures position. The reason? The option writer faced an unlimited liability. In return for writing the option, the writer has agreed to provide the option buyer with a long futures contract at the strike price of the option at any time during the life of the call. In return for the fixed premium, therefore, the writer can lose an infinite amount.

Writing options sounds like a risky business; but once understood, it is not as risky as it might seem at first. For one, most options expire worthless. That's right, the odds favor the sellers, not the buyers. After all, for an option to prove profitable at expiration, it must rise above the strike in the case of a call or fall below the strike in the case of the put.

But let's return to our example. Let's assume the March 270 call is trading *at the money*. That means the price of March corn futures is right at 270¢ per bushel. If the price of March corn futures were below 270, the call would be said to be *out of the money*, and if prices were above the strike price, the call would be termed *in the money*. Option traders also make finer distinctions by saying an option is *slightly* in the money or *deeply* out of the money. At any rate, the writer grants or sells the call to the buyer for, say, 17¢ per bushel. He receives the premium money and is obligated to perform on his side of the contract — namely, providing the buyer with a long futures position at any time he wishes, at the strike price of 270¢ per bushel.

Let's say that, as time passes, corn prices rise and the at-the-money call becomes an in-the-money call. The call buyer decides to exercise. What happens? The buyer receives his March corn futures at the strike price of 270, and the call writer receives a short position at the strike of 270. Unfortunately for the writer, however, the market is now above 270 — say, 300 — and the difference represents a loss to the writer, who, you must remember, has sold futures short at 270.

For the writer, the full 30¢ difference, however, is not a loss. Remember, the writer received the initial premium of 17¢ per bushel. The writer's real loss, therefore, is the difference between the premium received and the amount paid out on the losing futures position. In this instance (assuming he liquidates the losing short position he receives by virtue of exercise), the writer has sustained a net loss of just 13¢, or the difference between the 30¢ he lost and the 17¢ he received for writing the option. The buyer, of course, profits by the 13¢. He paid 17¢ per bushel for the call and receives a futures position with 30¢ in paper profits—again assuming he liquidates the futures position immediately. He may increase his profit by continuing to hold the futures position. But then again, the market may reverse, and he may lose on the futures position.

Why would you write options? To achieve writing income. In our example, the writer sustained a loss—but only because the market rallied after he sold the call. What would have happened if the market had remained stationary over the life of the call, or rallied only slightly, or even declined? For the writer, all these possibilities would have proven profitable. If the option expired when the price of March corn futures remained at 270 or fell below, the entire 17¢ premium would have been his to keep. That's $850 in writing income. Had the call expired when the March corn futures was slightly above 270—say, 272—the call would have had just 2¢ in profit to the buyer, and he would receive back only 2¢ on an option that originally cost him 17¢. The difference, of course, is the writer's profit—in this case, 15¢ per bushel.

Protecting the Short Position

As you can see from the example in the preceding section, option writing entails considerable risk. But there are measures you can take to minimize the risk. There are defensive actions you can take before an adverse move gets out of hand.

The simplest and most straightforward strategy is simply to buy back (cover) your short option position when the market goes against you. Although this will most probably result in a trading loss, it is often the best course of action. Paradoxically, learning to take losses is often the key to market success. Losses are a part of futures and options trading, and one must learn to keep them small by getting out of losing positions without hesitation. While it is true that prices might reassert themselves in a more positive direction, more often than not hesitation only results in a small initial loss growing into a larger one. The reluctance to accept small losses has been the undoing of countless traders over the years.

In addition, one must take into account the risk/reward ratio when writing options. The potential gain is limited to the cost of the option premium to the buyer; hence, at best, the writer can receive 100 percent of that premium, not a cent more. More likely, if he offsets his position before expiration, his gain will be only a portion of the premium — maybe only 10 percent or 20 percent. Thus, if you write a call for, say, 17¢ ($850) and you buy it back for 16¢ because you anticipate higher prices, your gain will be only a penny per bushel — that's $50, hardly enough to pay commissions. What is it worth to you to gain 1¢ profit (or, for that matter, 17¢)? Four cents in risk? Five cents? Or even 10¢? The point is, as a writer, you must concern yourself with the risk — and you must be willing to take losses when the market moves against you. In later chapters, we will deal with setting stop-loss points and other ways to hedge risks associated with writing options.

For hedgers, such as a wheat farmer who owns the underlying commodity, the writing of a call might be a riskless strategy if he is willing to sell his grain at the strike price. For instance, let's say a farmer writes a December 370 call that's out of the money for a premium of 12¢, or $600. At the time he writes the call, December wheat futures are trading at $3.60. By writing the call, the farmer is, in effect, agreeing to sell wheat at the strike price of 370 *plus* the premium of 12¢ — or $3.82 per bushel, a full 22¢ over the current market. At that price, he might reason, he has received a fair price for his wheat. By writing the option, however, he locks out a more favorable price above 382¢ per bushel. In addition, by writing the call, he sets up a profit cushion of 12¢ per bushel. Should prices drop precipitously, however, this profit cushion may not be sufficient to offset unhedged losses in the market.

To fully understand the strategy involved here, let's assume prices remain stationary at $3.60 through the expiration of the December call in late November. At a price of $3.60 for December wheat, the 370 call will expire worthless. Hence, the buyer will lose his premium. But the writer of the call will realize the 12¢ premium as his gain. Below a price of 348¢ per bushel (360 − 12 = 348), however, the writer will realize a real loss on his unhedged wheat, since the 12¢ writing income will be insufficient to offset the decline in the market.

What happens if prices rise? Say prices rise to 370 at expiration. The call will remain unexercised and expire worthless, resulting in a 12¢ gain to the call writer. (Actually, he nets an additional 10¢ gain on the futures price rise, since his cash wheat is now more valuable). Above $3.70, however, the call will be exercised. Even at $3.71 at expiration, the call will be worth 1¢, and the call writer will receive a December wheat short futures at the strike price of $3.70. The wheat farmer can then either hold the short wheat futures to expiration in December and deliver against the contract (receiving $3.70 per bushel) or buy the futures in the market and offset his short position. If he offsets the short futures above the 370 selling price, of course, he will realize a loss equal to the difference between where he sold ($3.70) and where he bought. However, the initial 12¢ premium income should more than offset any loss in the futures as long as December wheat futures stay below 382 — or the strike price plus the writing income.

The hedger who writes calls against his cash commodity must be willing to live with the strike price plus the writing income as his ultimate selling price. As a hedger attempting to use this strategy, therefore, ask yourself: Am I willing to sell my grain at the price represented by the strike plus the premium? If not, you must monitor the position closely and be prepared to buy back short options *before* they go into the money. American options (as opposed to European options, which are exercisable only at expiration) can be exercised at any time prior to expiration. Another alternative for the would-be option writer, of course, is to write only those calls which are far enough out of the money to justify the risk involved. For example, if you are unwilling to sell wheat at $3.70 but willing to let your wheat go for $4.00, then write the higher-strike call. The only drawback will be a substantially lower premium for a call that is far out of the money, but that's one of the trade-offs one must contend with in the market.

You can write options ''naked'' — in which case you do not own the underlying futures — or ''covered.'' The latter strategy is more conservative, since the risk is limited. (If you write a call and already own the futures from a lower price, you probably won't mind having it ''called away'' at a higher price. Your only regret will be that you hadn't written a higher-strike call, since you will sustain an opportunity loss.) Precisely how, when, and why to write options of varying strike prices and durations will be the subject of Chapter 4. For now, it is sufficient to understand that writing options on a consistent, income-generating basis is a viable market strategy for hedgers and speculators alike.

For the noncommercial trader, agricultural options represent an excellent way to take advantage of a particular market situation. By combining buying and writing options, often in conjunction with buying and selling futures contracts, one can set up a profit zone for virtually any type of market. The innovative options trader can use a given options strategy to capitalize on rising, declining, and even stationary markets. Indeed, these new agricultural options are so versatile that one is hard pressed to keep abreast of the possible strategies. Fitting the appropriate strategy to the appropriate market condition will be the task of much of the material in subsequent chapters.

Which Contract Should You Trade?

Options, like futures, trade in different contract months. The contract months will differ for each commodity. In soybeans, options may be exercised for futures that expire in January, March, May, July, August, September, or November. In cotton, the expiration months are March, May, July, October, and December. Since there are no June soybean futures, there will also be no June soybean options.

Although all options are standardized, you must be careful to offset an option position by selling (if you originally bought) an option with the same strike and delivery month. Hence, if you initially buy a November 625 soybean call, you must then sell the same November 625 call when taking profits. Not to do so will result in your having two positions. For example, if you then sell a January 625 call, you will have a spread position—long on the November 625 call and short on the January 625 call. Also, when you buy a call, you don't offset the position by selling a put. If you buy calls and you wish to offset your position, you must sell calls; and the same is true for puts.

Now, what contract month should you trade? This will depend on the strategy you are employing. If you are using a strategy that calls for using adjacent months or front and back months, such as a horizontal spread, the strategy will dictate the months. However, if you just want to buy or sell puts or calls, a very simple but important rule applies: *always trade the most active month.* And a corollary to this rule: *always trade the most active option.**

Generally, the activity will be measured by the size of the *open interest*, or the number of outstanding contracts still to be liquidated. Open interest tends to measure a contract's liquidity. A large open interest suggests ample liquidity; small open interest suggests an illiquid or thin market. The most active — and most liquid — option contracts will tend to be in the nearby month, and as expiration approaches, activity will pick up in the adjacent month and traders will *roll over* their positions into those months. It is important to remember that agricultural options expire the *month prior* to the expiration month of the underlying futures. Hence, options on April live hogs will expire in March, options on December live cattle will expire in November, options on May wheat will expire in April, and so on. Once an option expires, the underlying futures tend to trade about another month.

Let's say it is July and you are looking to trade wheat options.

* With few exceptions, the nearby month will be the most active month, and the most active options will be those with strikes closest to the market.

Which contract month would you select? Since the July futures contract is about to "go off the boards" and the July options have already expired in June, the nearby futures and options are the September contract. But even the September options will have only one month to trade, since they expire in August. You may therefore want to consider the December options.

The option you select will also influence the quality of your fills. If you trade an illiquid contract month, you will find the bid and asked prices farther apart. With fewer buyers and sellers, the incentive to buy and sell must be greater to offset the greater risks involved. Hence a market that might have a $\frac{1}{4}$¢ spread in the nearby option might have a much larger spread in the back-month option. As a public trader, you will often, if not always, be given the less favorable end of the deal—that is, you'll be buying at the asked price and selling at the bid price—and you'll find this lack of liquidity will really hurt you on the fills.

Which Strike Price Should You Trade?

As a rule, the best strike prices, like the best contract months, are those enjoying the greatest activity—again for the same reason, liquidity. When it comes time to offset your position, you want to be sure there will be a buyer for your option. The at-the-money calls and puts tend to enjoy the greatest participation, for reasons that will be covered in depth in later chapters. For now, look to the most active options with the greatest open interest as the best trading vehicles for your initial entry into the agricultural options markets.

Calculating the Breakeven Point

We know that every option buyer's risk is limited to the cost of the premium, or 100 percent of his investment. And we know that every option writer's risk is virtually unlimited.* But what about calculating profit? What's the breakeven point on an option? Simple: the call buyer will reach breakeven on his investment when the futures are valued at the strike price *plus* the premium and commission cost at expiration. In

---

* The put writer's risk, in theory, is limited in the sense that the value of the underlying futures contract cannot fall below zero. But in fact, the put writer's risk is much lower, since the underlying futures are certain to maintain *some* value.

the following example, we'll leave out commission costs.

Let's say you purchase a call on December cotton with a strike of 70 when the premium is equal to 3¢, or $1,500 on the 50,000 lb cotton contract. In order to break even at expiration, you must recoup the $1,500 premium fee in the market. Hence, for the call to retain the $1,500 value at expiration, December cotton futures must trade at 73¢ per lb, or 3¢ *above* the strike price. In that case, the intrinsic value of the call will offset the initial premium cost of the call and you will break even.

What about still higher prices? Above the price of 73¢, you will earn a profit. Since the 70-strike call provides you with the opportunity to purchase one long position at the strike, any rise in December cotton will be reflected in the value of the call.

What about the cotton call writer? Where is his breakeven point? At the same price as the call buyer's. At 73¢ per lb (strike plus premium), the writer will have the call exercised against him. The exercise will result in a *short futures position* at the strike of 70 entered into his account. Assuming he immediately liquidates at the market price of 73¢, his loss will be just 3¢, or $1,500 — the exact amount of money he received for writing the call. The result will be a wash, neither profit nor loss, commission costs aside. Neither buyer nor seller will profit with December cotton futures at 73¢ at expiration of the December calls. Between the prices of 73 and 70, the writer will gain some profit (although not the entire premium) on his short call. And at 70 or below at expiration, the call writer will make a 100-percent profit on the call.

Puts, being the mirror image of calls, work in reverse. The buyer's breakeven is the strike *minus* the premium. The writer's breakeven occurs at the same price.

Naturally, the buyer of the put wants prices to decline, whereas the writer is counting on a steady or rising market to keep prices *above* the strike so he can capture the full premium. Figures 5 and 6 illustrate the concept of breakeven for calls and puts.

Understanding the Newspaper Reports

Quotations for agricultural options are listed in the financial press according to the final settlement prices for each put and call. In Table 1, I've listed the results for options on soybean futures as they appeared in the following day's *Wall Street Journal*. Note that the lower-strike calls and higher-strike puts, reflecting options that are deeper in the money, command higher premium prices.

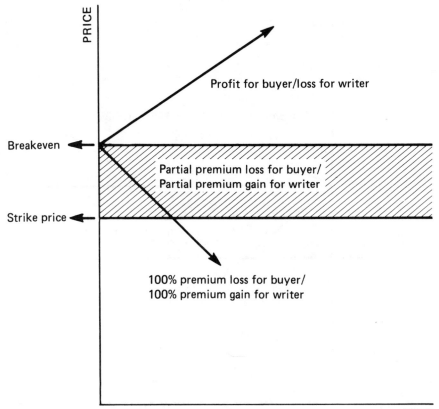

Figure 5.   Breakeven point for calls: breakeven occurs at the strike price plus the premium.

The settlement prices of the three nearest futures are also listed. It's important to understand precisely what each price signifies.

Under "strike price," four digits are shown — 6750, 7000, 7250, and so on. Placed at 25¢ intervals, the strike prices have a zero following the number to indicate "no eighths." Thus, 6750 means "six dollars, seventy-five cents, and no eighths." For the call buyers, the January 675 call that settled at 5¼¢ gives the buyer the right to purchase one January 1985 soybean futures contract at a price of $6.75 at any time prior to expiration (mid-December). The cost of 5¼¢ per bushel translates into a $262.50 premium plus commission on the 5,000-bushel contract. Since January soybeans, however, are trading at only $6.30½ per bushel, the January 675 call is far out of the money. In fact,

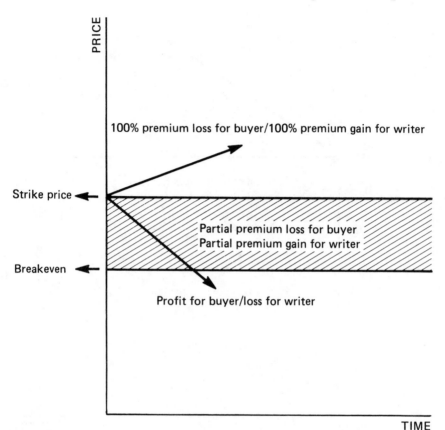

PRICE

100% premium loss for buyer/100% premium gain for writer

Strike price

Partial premium loss for buyer
Partial premium gain for writer

Breakeven

Profit for buyer/loss for writer

TIME

Figure 6.   Breakeven point for puts: breakeven occurs at the strike minus the premium.

at today's settlement, the January 675 call is exactly $44\frac{1}{2}$¢ out of the money—the distance between the strike price and today's settlement price.

Is the opportunity to purchase January soybeans at $6.75 per bushel worth $5\frac{1}{4}$¢? Perhaps, but probably not. Unless soybeans stage a substantial rally in the seven or eight weeks before expiration of the call, the option will expire worthless. For the writer of the 675 call, of course, the small premium, given the long odds, perhaps warrants the risk involved.

Why are there no 550 or 575 calls? Probably because they are too deep in the money. The premium would almost certainly reflect the $80\frac{1}{2}$¢ cash value in the January soybeans and the $95\frac{1}{2}$¢ cash value in the

Table 1. Quotations for options on soybean futures, Monday, November 5, 1984, Chicago Board of Trade (CBT). Contract size 5,000 bushels; quotations in cents per bushel.

Strike Price	Calls — Last					Puts — Last				
	Jan	Mar	May	July	Nov	Jan	Mar	May	July	Nov
5500	...	...	...	...	...	1	...	...	...	...
5750	...	...	...	...	...	2½	...	...	...	...
6000	36½	...	67	...	...	7	12	...	...	...
6250	21¼	40½	51	...	...	15¾	20½	22	...	26
6500	11½	28½	42	...	40½	31	33	31½	...	35
6750	5¼	18	30	38	31	51½	47½	...	...	...
7000	2⅝	12	22	29	22	...	...	...	...	65
7250	...	...	...	17½	16	...	...	...	...	...

Est. vol. 1,500: Fri vol. 739 calls, 450 puts
Open interest Fri: 1,986 calls, 854 puts
Soybean Futures—5,000 bu; cents per bu

Nov	Jan	Mar
616½	630½	645¼

Source: *The Wall Street Journal*, November 6, 1984.

March soybeans on the 550-strike calls. In addition, each call would command a few more cents in value for the time left to expiration. For the buyers, the $4,000 to $5,000 premiums would just tie up premium money needlessly and seriously impair the advantage of high leverage that so many option buyers seek. And for the writers, the high premiums would not offset the considerable amount of funds involved in margining such deep-in-the-money calls. As a rule, those strike prices which are closest to the market price of the underlying futures enjoy the greatest participation. And although the volume is not broken down here by individual call, one would suspect that the 625 and 650 calls would enjoy the greatest participation.

The prices also illustrate how the value of call options will increase as one considers a more distant option. Consider the out-of-the-money 650 calls for January and March expiration. Both calls have a strike that is *above* the current market value of the underlying futures, hence both have only time value. The January 650 call settled at $11\frac{1}{2}$¢ and the March 650 call at $28\frac{1}{2}$¢, or $575 and $1,425, respectively. Unlike in stock options, the underlying futures trade at *different* prices, reflecting their different carrying costs, and therefore each option has a different price. For instance, when the January soybeans futures are trading at $630\frac{1}{2}$, the January 650 call is $19\frac{1}{2}$¢ out of the money, but when the March soybean futures are trading at $645\frac{1}{4}$, the March 650 call is only $4\frac{3}{4}$¢ out of the money. Thus, the higher premium for the March call reflects not only the greater time to expiration but also the higher likelihood that the option will go into the money and ultimately prove profitable to the call buyer.

One exception to this rule seems to be the $7.00-strike calls. You will notice that the May 700 call is 22¢ and the July 700 call 29¢. But the November call is only 22¢, the same amount as the May call. Why would anyone pay the same price for a call that has six months less than another? If the underlying security were stock, this would truly be nonsensical. But since the underlying security is a commodity, the reason for the comparable value becomes more apparent.

The main reason for the different valuations of the two options is that they are for two different crop years. In perishable commodities, futures for different crop years can trade almost like two entirely different commodities — one going up while the other declines in price. More likely, supply and demand are quite different for the two crop years, and the premium values of the respective calls reflect this.

In puts, as you can see, the lower strikes are less expensive and the higher strikes more costly. This is the opposite of calls, and for good reason. Put options, remember, give the holder the right to *sell* the underlying future. In Table 1, you can see that the January 575 put settled at 2½¢. This translates into a $125 premium to control a futures contract worth $31,525. This would seem a bargain if it weren't for the high likelihood of the put expiring worthless. After all, the 575 put would have value at expiration only if the January soybean futures declined by 55½¢ — all in seven or eight weeks!

An unlikely event, you say? Precisely. And that's why buyers are unwilling to pay a lot for puts that are so far out of the money. As you move to a higher strike, the risk to the writer understandably rises, and the puts become more valuable. With January soybean futures at 630½, the out-of-the-money 625-strike put commands a 15¾¢ premium to compensate the put writer for the higher risk of the option proving profitable.

A number of options with various strikes didn't trade on the day shown. This is not to say that outstanding options didn't exist. They may have. But on the day shown, no trading took place. The volume for the previous Friday shows the number of contracts traded, both in puts and calls. The open interest is the number of contracts that remain unliquidated or offset on the day shown.

Options as an Insurance Policy

For the commercial user or producer of agricultural products, the new farm options offer an array of opportunities to hedge risk. In fact, because of the variety of strategies, a commercial can fine-tune his option hedging program to satisfy his own attitude toward risk as well as his market expectations.

For instance, let's say a cotton grower is about to harvest his crop but is uncertain about prices. A part of him is eager to "lock in" current prices by selling cotton futures. But another part is a bit more adventurous and wants to remain unhedged. Indeed, if cotton prices rise, the unhedged position would yield greater profits; then again, he could live with today's prices. The risk? That prices decline while he is unhedged. In that case, he could find himself in financial difficulty.

A third possibility is for the commercial cotton grower to buy cotton put options. The puts will prove valuable if prices decline. At the same time, they will permit him to participate in any rise in the cotton market. The only risk: the premium cost. And even this risk can be heightened or lowered by selecting different put option strike prices. The commercial cotton grower might select out-of-the-money puts that will protect him only down from, say, 50¢ per lb. By paying more for a higher-strike put,

Figure 7. Using options as an insurance policy: a cotton grower purchases out-of-the-money puts to establish price floor at strike price regardless of later price movements.

the cotton farmer lowers his "deductible," in the parlance of the insurance profession.

This notion of farm options as an insurance policy with varying degrees of protection and deductibles is important for the commercial trade. Too often, the world "option" is associated with the notion of high risk. But, as you can see, to the commercial engaged in growing or processing farm products, options make the task of growing, raising, and processing commodities safer and more stable. Figure 7 shows how a cotton grower might purchase an out-of-the-money put option on cotton futures to ensure a floor price for his commodity regardless of subsequent price movements.

Higher-Strike versus Lower-Strike Prices

By selecting a higher-strike put and paying a higher premium, the commercial hedger lowers his "deductible" and thereby establishes a higher minimum price for his cotton. By doing so, the hedger is able to sell his cotton at a higher price. The only drawback to this approach is that a continued rise in cotton prices will result in a somewhat lower net price, since the hedger bought a relatively expensive put—which, due to the rise in cotton prices, will now be allowed to expire worthless.

By selecting a lower-strike put, the commercial hedger achieves downside protection but at a somewhat higher risk. His "deductible" rises in the sense that he will have to pay the difference in losses between today's market price and the put's strike price. In a rising market, however, he benefits by not purchasing the higher-strike puts. Should prices rise and the puts expire unexercised, the premium costs will be lower than for the more expensive puts and, as a result, the commercial hedger's profit will be greater.

An Abundance of Option Strategies

For both commercial and noncommercial traders, the new markets in agricultural options offer a wealth of innovative and challenging trading strategies. In the following chapters, we'll examine many of these new strategies in depth. You'll learn how to create synthetic puts and calls, synthetic long and short futures positions, and many other exotic combinations of the new options and futures. You'll learn how to place conversions and reverse conversions, strangles and straddles, combinations and spreads.

3

Secrets of the Professionals: Twenty Time-Tested Rules

If you spent your daily life in the trading pits — and learned well the lessons to be gathered from such an experience — you could become rich, as many have, without ever sitting down to dwell on the many pitfalls of trading. But if you are new to trading futures and options on futures, you can save yourself a fortune by simply following the "golden rules" of the professionals, who survive by a mixture of wit and discipline that guides them in their day-to-day trading activities.

So take the time to master the rules set forth here on buying and selling options the way professional floor traders do. You'll want to add some rules of your own, but the ones included in this chapter should help you get started on the path to trading success.

What Can You Learn Down on the Exchange Floor?

Every would-be trader of agricultural options owes it to himself at least to visit one of the commodities exchanges offering the new puts and calls. Virtually all the exchanges today have a visitors' gallery where members of the public can watch the trading in process. Some even offer conducted tours and recorded tapes to explain the many gyrations, perplexing cries, and hand signals used by the members. Better yet, have an exchange member get you a pass to the floor where you can get a close-up view of the trading. You may even wish to consider becoming a member yourself and joining in the fray firsthand. It will be an experience you'll never forget.

To a first-time observer, the floor action will appear to be no more than gibberish. Grouped together in trading pits, options and futures traders appear to be taking part in some mysterious ritual, yelling and screaming, waving their hands and arms, jumping up and down. Yet every hand signal, every yell, has a meaning. The financial shorthand the traders use is designed to convey their wishes as succinctly as possible. Despite the seeming mayhem — and, yes, despite the occasional fights and violent words — this universe is tightly controlled and understandable. Indeed, considering the amount of money at stake, one wonders why emotions aren't *more* volatile.

If you aren't trading on the floor, you may wonder what relevance the mechanics of the floor have to you. The point is, however, every buyer must find a seller, and vice versa – and, significantly, every trade must be consummated on the floor.

With each floor trader operating as his own auctioneer, the open-outcry method of trading requires buyers and sellers to call out their bids and offers to the entire pit. The reason for the open-outcry method is that it ensures the best possible price, since it provides everyone an opportunity to take a trade — or, of course, decline the opportunity and leave it alone. Presumably, in such a competitive atmosphere, with buyers seeking the lowest possible price and sellers the highest, price discovery will work best. At least, that's the theory. In practice, unless you have some experience in reading the market from a floor trader's perspective, you may get confused by some of the price action.

On or off the floor, trading options and futures is a tough business. A seasoned floor trader has the mind of a computer with the nerves of an air traffic controller. An active local might be long 60 or 70 calls at one strike and short 60 or 70 at another; he might have an equal number of put positions. And somehow, through it all, he must have an idea if he is net long or short, and what the contingencies should be in the event of a sharp market rise or fall. At the same time, he may be laying off risk in the adjacent futures pit. The number of dilemmas he may find himself in in a single trading session is enormous. What if the market goes limit bid? Should he run or stay? What if a big order hits the pit? Should he fade (take the other side of) the paper, the public orders? Should he scalp (trade in and out of) the market? Or should he look for a trend and try to ride it? Will the stops be run? And so on.

There is virtually no single correct answer to these questions. Surprisingly, some of the most accepted rules are often the most unprofitable strategies to follow. For instance, take the well-worn expression

"Cut your losses and let your profits ride." The rule is fine — as far as it goes. But how do you put it into practice? Generally, this rule translates into placing stop-loss orders. Yet, to the floor, the stops are red flags — easy money for those with the ability to second-guess the stop-placers. Does this suggest you shouldn't place stops? Not exactly. After all, a refusal to place stops can result in disastrous losses. So what is an intelligent options trader to do? In a word, learn — learn the options game from the professionals.

Twenty Rules of the Professional Trader

In the next sections, we'll look at some of the basic principles that guide the professional floor trader. As you should realize by now, there isn't one way to earn profits in the ag options market. There are many. Not all of them, however, will be right for you. But you can profit by following the general rules of successful ag options traders.

Rule 1: Be Flexible

Markets change. You don't have to look far to understand this simple fact. The high-flying markets of the 1970s gave way to the more sedate markets of the 1980s. If history is any guide, chances are the markets will change again. In order to profit in a changing market, you must be flexible and tailor your trading strategies to different economic climates.

Stories abound of traders who made hundreds of thousands of dollars only to lose all their money when the markets changed. The reason? They kept doing the same thing. Granted, it isn't always easy to know when the market is about to change in character. So let your trading success be your guide. If you have been, say, successful writing calls, and then you recognize one day that your call writing program is only resulting in losses, give yourself a break and get out of the market. Chances are, the reason the calls are being exercised against you is that the market has entered a bull phase. This notion of being flexible cannot be emphasized enough. The best traders know when to be bold and when to be cautious.

Rule 2: Be a Specialist

The more specialized you are, the greater your chances of understanding the pulse of the market and knowing when the inevitable changes occur. Professional floor traders are almost always specialists concentrating on one commodity and, often, one particular strategy in one pit. If soybeans are your specialty, why fool around with cattle calls? Sure, you may from time to time spot an opportunity in cattle calls. But you are probably better off looking at one thing. For the floor trader, of course, there is the problem of being physically in one pit or another. For instance, the soybean options trader at the Chicago Board of Trade would have to run over to the Chicago Mercantile Exchange, several blocks away, to trade cattle options — assuming, of course, that he held a membership there.

Because the forces that propel different markets are often too divergent for one individual to keep on top of both, the old bromide about not putting all your eggs in one basket doesn't make sense in the options market. Rather, the idea is to put all your eggs (within reason) in one basket and then watch that basket very, very carefully. That's what the professionals do, and that's how you can win. Down on the floor, members are often identified informally according to the commodity they trade. Hence, you'll hear someone say, "He's a bean trader" or "He's a corn trader," or whatever. Rarely do you find a professional who trades everything. Yet nonprofessional traders are often burning up the phone lines to trade everything in sight. Better to increase the size of your position in a single commodity than to jump all over the place looking for opportunity.

The same rule, of course, pertains to your individual strategy within the commodity of your choice. If you develop a profitable strategy writing calls, why get involved in another strategy that might not work as well? Stick to what you know best.

Rule 3: Learn to Love Your Losses

One's attitude toward trading losses is what separates the professionals from the amateurs. Professional traders recognize that losses are an occupational hazard that one must quickly deal with. They take their losses and forget about them by getting on to the next trade. The nonprofessionals, in contrast, will hold onto a losing position because, in their opinion, they "can't get out." This is a sure sign of impending disaster. By trying to avoid a small loss, these traders almost guarantee a large one — often when their margin is depleted.

This rule is especially important for option writers. The buyers know their risk at the outset. But even then, the buyers can improve their results by selling losing options and looking for a better buying opportunity. Isn't it better to lose a small portion of your investment than the whole thing? It should be obvious. Yet, time and again, the nonprofessional will hope, pray, and talk himself into holding a deteriorating position. At this stage, one can almost be certain that the best course of action would have been to get out. If you can learn to accept the idea that you were indeed wrong, and *act* on that idea, you will improve your trading immeasurably. Everyone has losses. Why should you be any different?

Rule 4: Nail Down Those Profits

Knowing when to take profits and losses is the key to trading success. Too often, we grow to love a position and become reckless right at the point when we should be most cautious. An almost surefire rule is to do the *opposite* of what your emotions tell you: plunge when you are scared to death; run like hell when you become confident you have the market beat. Knowing this rule and following it, of course, are two different things. The best professional traders take profits as a matter of course. Overstaying the market is a real problem of novice traders who don't recognize how fast things can change. Despite the runaway bull and bear markets we've had over the years, the statistics would probably tell you that "everything tends to move back toward the middle." Rallies precipitate profit-taking and decline bargain-hunting; the result is a change in the short-term trend. Capitalize on this tendency and take those profits.

Rule 5: Know the Trading Characteristics of Your Commodity

This rule is a corollary of Rule #2 about specialization. Commodities have different trading characteristics. If your commodity is corn, you will want to acquaint yourself with all the crop reports and fundamentals that will affect corn prices. Sometimes this might include monitoring the prices of other commodities. Since corn is a feed grain, the number of cattle and livestock on feed might be an important factor in corn futures prices. You'll also want to know how corn trades. What is the daily volatility? How far does corn tend to move in the first hour of trading? Once the open is known, what is the "morning bulge," when prices move up or down in response to an overnight demand or weakness? All this information can help you make intelligent decisions.

Every commodity tends to have its own characteristics. The professionals, who trade the same commodity every day, will know these characteristics. Since you will be competing with them for trading profits, doesn't it make sense that you know the market as well as they do?

Rule 6: Know When They Are Running the Stops

One of the favorite, and most profitable, games of the floor is to run the stops. There is nothing illegal about this practice. After all, no one holds a revolver to your head and forces you to place a stop just above the day's high. But given the conventional wisdom of trading, practically every broker in the country will advise his client to place such a stop-loss order. The problem is, most of the stops are at the same price. As a result, when one order is triggered, several hundred more may follow. Too much buying — or selling — can only cause the market to move in the direction of the buying or selling. What then happens, of course, is that the buying or selling suddenly dries up once all the stops are run. With no one left to push the market higher or lower, guess what happens? That's right. Prices generally retreat back to where they were *prior* to the running of the stops.

How do you spot a market in which you are having a short-covering rally or brief break due to a run on the stops? One sign is a market that moves quickly and then goes dead. When this happens, it means there is no follow-through buying or selling. And prices will move back to where they were. One problem: occasionally, what looks like a brief short-covering rally turns into the real thing — a genuine bull market. When this occurs, you better be prepared to get in on the right side, because prices may never return to present levels.

For the options trader, stop-running is particularly worrisome. The futures, remember, are the dog that wags the tail, the option. Because of thinness in the options market, a move in futures may result in the floor not wanting to let you out at a reasonable price. If you panic and send in a market order at a time when the stops are being run, chances are you will be absolutely killed on the fill. It often pays to allow reason to re-emerge in the market before you do anything. That way, you will ensure yourself a more favorable price.

Rule 7: Try to Trade Only the Most Active Contracts

Professional traders have one recurrent nightmare. What if I can't get out? If you trade an inactive month — say, December corn, when most of the open interest is in the July corn — you'll be trading against a handful of professionals who will count on your making mistakes. Because there are fewer traders to "take the other side of the trade," they can pretty well set up the situation to take advantage of the public's tendency to make mistakes. A tight bid/asked spread in the nearby month might be complemented by a wide spread in the distant months.

It only makes sense. The traders want to be paid to take on the added risk associated with a thinner market. Remember, the time will come when they, too, will have to exit the market. The better the deal they can get from the "paper," or public order, the better their chance of making money on the trade.

The same considerations apply to strike prices. Deep-in-the-money options will have less participation, because the buyers won't want to tie up their money buying cash value in the options. Similarly, deep-out-of-the-money options typically suffer from lack of participation, because the buyers realize that their chances of being profitable at expiration are very slim. This leaves the at-the-moneys. In general, the at-the-moneys will be the most active. Trade where the bulk of all traders are willing to buy and sell, and you will receive the best possible prices.

Rule 8: Beware Expiring Options

As Chicago Board Option Exchange S&P 100 traders have found out in recent years, funny things happen to options just prior to expiration. As a matter of course, floor traders write out-of-the-money options that are soon to expire. The reason? The chances of the options expiring with any cash value is slim. Very slim. By writing the soon-to-expire options, the floor often counts on a sure thing. The problem is that sometimes large traders decide to move the futures in such a fashion that the increased volatility alone often results in *higher premiums* even if the time value is down to the last fraction of a point, with just a day or two to expiration. And when this occurs, the option writers can lose a fortune.

To bring the problem into focus, consider this: let's say you write soon-to-expire options for a fraction of a cent, hoping to capture the remaining time value. Remember, one may write hundreds, even thousands, of options at a time. If the option is out of the money and only a day or so remains to expiration, the chances are very good that the writer will earn the premium income. But occasionally, due to market manipulation or whatever, options, even out-of-the-money options, will *gain* in value on the last trading day. Hence, if you have written a soon-to-expire out-of-the-money soybean call for $\frac{1}{2}$¢ and it rises to 1¢, you have lost 100 percent of your potential maximum gain. This could result in real problems. A genuine rally that takes the option into the money could result in huge losses for the call writer.

Rule 9: Pare Commission Costs to a Minimum

Professional floor traders don't pay commissions, only modest transaction and exchange fees that can lower their costs to 50¢ to $1 a trade. Nonmembers, in contrast, can pay $20 to a discount firm and even $60 to $70 to a nondiscounter. Even a modest commission cost eliminates many of the more popular strategies, such as writing soon-to-expire out-of-the-moneys. If the entire profit on a trade is only $25 or $50, you can't afford to pay a commission.

There are two things you can do about commission costs. The first is to negotiate with your brokerage house for the lowest possible commissions. To begin with, start with a discounter who is used to dealing with reasonable commissions. Twenty dollars is reasonable; $60 isn't. Then make a deal. Ask him what he will charge if you do so many trades a month and deposit so much money in margin. As a bargaining chip, offer to leave a certain portion of the money in cash; the rest will go into Treasury bills. This may help you get the best possible commission. What the discounter can't make on the lowered commission expense, he may be able to make off the added interest he picks up on the additional cash you keep in the account. Remember, he has floor expenses as well as the expenses related to running his business. With any luck, you may be able to get $15 or $16 on a round-turn basis.

The second approach is to consider purchasing an options membership yourself. Contrary to popular belief, you don't have to be physically on the trading floor to use your membership. You can live in California and trade over the phone and pay the off-the-floor fees that members pay. Depending on your clearing firm, your fee could be as low as $3 or $4 a trade. Remember, if you aren't in the trading pit, someone still has to fill the order. That order-filler must be paid. But certainly, $3 or $4 a trade is more reasonable than even the best discounter can offer. This is for active traders only. Because a well-financed active floor population is a key to the success of a contract, the exchanges prefer members who are going to use the seats in person.

Another excellent argument for purchasing a seat is the likelihood of making a genuine capital gain. With inflation declining, membership prices have fallen in recent years. So a buying opportunity may indeed now exist. With the deficit unlikely to decline significantly in the near future, however, chances are excellent for higher inflation and higher seat prices, not to mention higher grain and livestock prices. In general, membership prices reflect overall interest in the commodities market. A bull market in the next few years will almost certainly cause exchange seat prices to rise.

Memberships, like futures and options prices, are determined by a bid/asked market. So a given membership might be quoted at, say, $40,000 bid and $45,000 asked. The price you will ultimately pay will be based on where you place your bid and what you are willing to pay at the time you qualify for membership.

An exchange may offer more than one type of membership, so you'll have to inquire about the rights that each seat provides. In general, an options seat—such as the Chicago Merc's Index and Options Market (IOM) seat—will enable you to trade all the options on a given exchange or division of an exchange. To join an exchange, you must file certain papers, including a financial-suitability form and an application listing past employment and schooling. If you have no history of financial irresponsibility and have sufficient funds to purchase the seat and deposit trading capital, you have a good chance of being accepted for membership.

Most exchanges have a $300 to $500 filing fee for membership and allow you 60 to 90 days after you are approved to purchase the seat, although the precise procedure will differ from exchange to exchange. Membership prices will vary from exchange to exchange. Annual fees are about $1,000 to $1,200 a year.

Rule 10: Learn to Be a Knowledgeable Risk-Taker

The best traders are comfortable with risk. The novice trader, on the other hand, is apt to be either too reckless in his trading activities or, at the other extreme, too desirous of a sure thing and hence too conservative. Either attitude spells trouble. The person who is afraid of risk will wait until he is absolutely "certain" of the market's direction. The problem is that this leads to mistakes. The most dangerous time to invest is once the trend is known. At that stage, the knowledgeable traders, who took their chances when the outlook was unknown, are nailing down their profits. The result is a market that is ripe for reversal.

Don't be afraid of risk. Rather, learn to embrace it and accept the fact that no one really knows the future. This point was adequately shown to be true several years ago when studies were done on investor attitudes. The study revealed that the more risk-adverse an investor, the more likely he was to wait for a "sure thing." As a result, the risk-adverse traders were always late in their timing, whereas those who weren't risk-adverse had a greater chance of buying weakness or selling strength—in other words, betting against the crowd. In the uncertain world of options trading, you really must be a risk-taker. If you don't include yourself among their ranks, you are probably better off doing something else.

Rule 11: Buy Strength and Sell Weakness

This rule flies in the face of just about every prudent thing every investor has been taught. But it's the way to bet — that is, if you want to win. Most investors are afraid to buy strength and sell weakness. How can I buy it now? reasons the novice trader, when the market has risen 10¢ on the day. The same is true of declining markets, especially when new life-of-contract lows are being made. *The market is never too strong to buy and never too weak to sell.* Remember, by definition, for a market to rise, it *must* take out prior highs; and the reverse is true on the down side.

A good example of this rule occurred in the currency markets in the winter of 1984/1985 when the dollar made its meteoric rise. Because the dollar had never risen to such heights, the conventional wisdom was that it was certain to move down. It eventually *did* move lower — but not before many, many investors who had purchased currencies had been wiped out. Just prior to the break in the value of the dollar, it zoomed upward, bankrupting the hapless currency speculators who bet against the dollar. They met their fate because they refused to sell weakness, preferring instead to outguess the market.

Rule 12: Stick to Your Game Plan

While it is important to be flexible, you want to have an idea that you are making intelligent decisions in the market, not haphazard ones. For this reason, you want a game plan, a set of golden rules that you won't violate, no matter what. The rules have to be ones you can live with and implement without hesitation.

For example, let's say you are strictly an in-and-out trader. One rule is: *no losses overnight.* You might be looking for a writing opportunity in the market, but you want to get in when the trend is with you. If you are wrong, you want to take the losses quickly and get out. By refusing to hold a loss overnight, you ensure yourself of small losses. By refusing to do this, by changing your game plan in the middle of the trade, you are only inviting trouble. Losses not taken have a definite tendency to grow larger. In fact, this should be a corollary to Murphy's Law.

Let's consider another example. Let's say you never want to give back a profit. Once having achieved a profit, therefore, you must be willing to take the profit. Having once gained the profit, you only invite trouble by increasing your position. Don't do it. Stay with your original game plan.

Rule 13: Always Have a Contingency Plan

The best-laid plans tend to go awry. So be prepared for the worst. The best traders don't stand around and debate the pros and cons of defensive action when they find themselves in trouble. Instead, they act! You should emulate their actions. Let's say you have written calls in anticipation of price weakness and the market goes against you. What do you do? If you have a contingency plan, you'll know. You might take a loss quickly. You might use a stop-loss order. You might then double up and reverse your position. It all depends.

One thing is certain. If you don't have a contingency plan, you'll probably make a mistake. Typically, the convenient, and understandable, thing to do is to watch your position. While you are watching, however, things will probably go from bad to worse. If you have a plan, you can avoid the agony of sitting around waiting. If you are wrong — get out! If not, stay. It is usually when you start thinking too hard and the thought turns to hope that you are inviting trouble. The best traders know what to do under good and bad conditions. You should as well.

Rule 14: Make Money Every Day

Unless you are using the ag options market to hedge (in which case some losses are acceptable if they add to your overall profitability and peace of mind), you want to try to make money every day, even if it is just $25 or $50. As fun as the markets can be, the effort involved isn't worth it unless you are making money. So monitor your position daily — and look elsewhere if the profits aren't forthcoming.

Using a bit of common sense in your trading activities can help you gain a perspective on what to expect. Some examples? Well, let's say you have decided to write out-of-the-money calls to capture time premium. Time-premium income generally increases as expiration approaches. So if you write the option for 10¢ with four weeks to expiration, you may capture a penny or two the first week, 3¢ or 4¢ the second week, and the bulk of the premium in the remaining days to expiration. The rate at which the premium income will be realized will increase as the option approaches expiration.

Another example? Know that when the profits aren't arriving on schedule, you are probably in the wrong trade. It is better to lose a few dollars than many. Above all, don't allow yourself to escape into a world of unreality by saying that next week things will be different. Most profitable trades become profitable almost from the outset. If you aren't making money every day, you are doing something wrong.

Rule 15: Protect Your Trading Capital

The day you run out of trading capital, you'll be politely asked to stop trading, no matter how much your broker enjoys your company. So if you make a minor killing in a good market, don't go out and overextend yourself in the belief that an endless stream of similar profits is inevitable in the future; it probably isn't. In fact, if history is of any value, the likelihood is that a sizable winning streak will be followed by a period of adversity. You have to protect yourself against such adversity by building up a cushion of trading profits. It is the rare trader who won't need these profits at some time during his trading career to offset a losing streak.

As a rule, too many traders take on too much risk for their capital base. When the inevitable adversity hits, they are wiped out, despite the fact that the setback was only temporary. This is especially true if you are a trader who aggressively tries to get back the day's losses by doubling up and reversing. If, for instance, you start with four contracts and you double up and reverse, you have to take on eight; if you are wrong again, you are now trading sixteen. Can you take such financial pressure? If not, start with one contract and trade within your means.

Rule 16: Know When to Plunge

This is part of being a knowledgeable risk-taker. First, a little-known fact: chances are you can't make any serious money trading just one contract at a time. Sure, you will have your share of winners; everyone does. But over time, factoring in trading losses and commissions, the single-contract option player has the percentages working against him. For this reason, the knowlegeable options traders will bide their time and then plunge when the circumstances are right. The profits on just one good trade can see you through literally dozens of small losses. There is a well-known futures and options trader in Chicago who has earned over $100 million trading in the markets in the past four or five years — starting with virtually nothing. He maintains he makes all his profits on just 5 percent of his trades. He rides the winners and exits the losers. The key is knowing when you're right.

Rule 17: Never Give Back a Profit

Professional floor traders are sore losers; they hate giving back a profit. Their attitude is one to be emulated. It might be characterized, to borrow a phrase that President Kennedy once used about the Soviets, as follows: "What is mine, is mine; what is yours, is negotiable." Take this attitude, and you will never have to apologize for losing your profits.

You will often hear floor traders and others talking about having a great morning but a disastrous afternoon. This is because they didn't take this rule to heart. Sometimes good fortune is short-lived. So your first strategy should be to hold onto what you've already won. One method of guaranteeing a profit once won is to take on smaller and smaller positions after you've achieved your daily or weekly or monthly profit goal. By doing so, you will be protecting your profits while allowing yourself an additional windfall.

Rule 18: Strive to Be Delta Neutral

Delta is a term used to measure the percentage response of an option when the underlying futures contract moves by 1 point or 1¢. Thus, an option with a delta of 1 would move point for point with the underlying futures. Unless the option is deep in the money, it won't have a delta of 1. More likely — and this is especialy true of out-of-the-money options — the option will have a delta of considerably less than 1, such as .50. If the option's delta is .50, you know that for every 1-point move in the underlying futures, the option will move by .50 points. For example, if an out-of-the-money live-cattle call with a strike of 66 has a delta of .50 and is trading at 2.00 when futures are at $60 per hundredweight, a 1-point move in the futures to $61 should move the call to 2.50 in value.

The concept of delta neutral, therefore, tells you how many calls you need to hedge a move of x points in the underlying futures and achieve a one-to-one offset in value. With a delta of .50, two calls would be required to hedge one futures contract. Let's say you are short in cattle futures and you want to hedge by purchasing call options. To be delta neutral, you would need two calls for every underlying future when the option's delta is .50.

What determines the delta? The delta, or delta factor, is established by a complex mathematical formula that takes into account the distance between the option's strike price and the underlying futures prices, time left until expiration, and, significantly, the volatility of the market, commonly called "implied volatility." In most delta software programs, the user of the program can type in any implied volatility he wishes, and the program will print out the delta for each option as well as a value for each option. That is, of course, a theoretical value; there is no guarantee that actual options will trade at that price. But option traders rely on these "option valuation tables" to know when to buy and sell option contracts. When the market places a higher price on an option than the theoretical value, traders will sell the options; lower actual option prices will cause traders to purchase the undervalued options in hopes that the price will rise to its theoretical option value.

Let's look at an actual example. On Tuesday, February 5, 1985, a trader on the floor of the Chicago Board of Trade ran a copy for the theoretical values of the five near soybean option trading months, March 1985 through January 1986. The options on the March contract had just four trading days left prior to expiration. So we'll look at the May 1985 contract, which had 67 days left to expiration. The implied volatility was 17.8 percent, and the table for the calls was as in Table 2.

On the date shown, May soybean futures closed at $6.13¾, up 7¢ on the day. Since the data in the table were printed out during the trading day, the bullish influence on the day may not have been reflected in the theoretical premiums. First, let's make sure we know how to read the table. Reading across the top of the table, you'll see four strike prices —575 through 650 at 25¢ intervals. Since May soybean futures are in the $6.13 area, the two lower-strike calls will be in the money and the two higher-strike calls will be out of the money. Reading down in the left outer column, you will see hypothetical futures prices—600, 602½, 605, 615, and so on. The designation "Hdg" below each price refers to the "delta" of each call. Therefore, if we want to know the theoretical value of the 625 call when May soybean futures are trading at $6.00 on a particular day, we look in the table and see that the theoretical value is 8⅝¢ and the delta is .31. This tells us that we need approximately three calls to hedge each futures contract in this particular option at this particular time.

Since the May beans didn't trade at $6.00 per bushel on February 5, 1985, let's look at a slightly more realistic example and then compare the theoretical option value with the actual closing price on that day. We'll look at the in-the-money May 600 call. The table tells us that the May 600 call should have a value of 25¼¢ when May futures are at $6.12½. Since the May futures closed just about 1¢ higher, let's look at the actual closing price of that call. The May 600 call closed at precisely 27¢ on the day shown. If we add 1¢ to the theoretical value of 25¼¢, we get a theoretical value of 26¼¢. As you can see, the actual value and the theoretical value are quite close, less than 1¢ apart. At the same time,

Table 2. Sample option valuation table for May 1985 soybeans (date: February 5, 1985).

	575 Strike	*600 Strike*	*625 Strike*	*650 Strike*
Futures Price	Calls — Implied Volatility 17.8 percent			
600.00	32.75	18.00	8.62	3.62
Hdg	.72	.51	.31	.16
602.50	34.62	19.37	9.37	4.00
Hdg	.74	.53	.33	.17
605.00	36.50	20.75	10.25	4.37
Hdg	.76	.56	.35	.18
607.50	38.37	22.12	11.12	4.87
Hdg	.77	.58	.37	.20
610.00	40.25	23.62	12.12	5.37
Hdg	.79	.60	.39	.21
612.50	42.25	25.12	13.12	5.87
Hdg	.80	.62	.41	.23
615.00	44.25	26.63	14.13	6.50
Hdg	.82	.64	.43	.25
617.50	46.37	28.25	15.25	7.12
Hdg	.83	.66	.45	.26

Source: The Options Group, 50 Broadway, New York, NY 10004.

the delta is .62, suggesting that for every 1¢ gain in the futures, the call will increase in value by $\frac{5}{8}$¢, or about 62 percent.

How can you use the tables? Professional traders make it a practice always to sell inflated time value. Let's look at one more example. On Tuesday, February 5, 1985, with May futures at 613¾, the out-of-the-money May 625 call changed hands at 15¢ per bushel. The theoretical value of that call at $6.15 would have been about 14⅛¢ per bushel. Therefore, even if the market had been higher in price, the theoretical value of the call would have been less. If the theoretical value for the call at the actual market price of 613¾ had been available, it would have been something like 13¼¢ to 14¢. Yet the 625 call was selling for 15¢. This was a genuine opportunity for the option writer to sell calls and capture the declining time premium.

As it developed, there was an additional favorable influence at work: the bean market was weak. In the following weeks, May soybeans fell to 576½ by March 1, and the May 625 call, with still a month left to expiration, declined to just 1½¢. The point is, the call option was over-valued to begin with. The declining market, of course, made the writing of the calls that much better an investment.

In practice, the would-be option buyer can avoid situations like this by concentrating on options that are trading below their theoretical value. By concentrating on undervalued options, he can then be certain he has at least received a fair price, regardless of the subsequent direction of prices.

Rule 19: Continually Test Yourself in the Market

All the theory in the world isn't going to help you unless you apply yourself to an actual hands-on trading experience. Moreover, some of the best-intended theories neve seem to work out in practice. So make it a point to be an active trader and continually test and refine any trading strategies you are interested in. It won't make a bit of difference in your trading account if you don't put your knowledge into practice. Only then will you understand whether you are accomplished at the task of trading agricultural options. Casey Stengel said it best: "Knowing how to do something and doing it are two different things."

Rule 20: Use Options in Combination with Futures

There's a good reason why ag options are traded alongside their futures counterparts. The two similar, yet different, contracts are designed to complement each other. The most sophisticated traders use a combination of futures and options, although there is no rule that you can't trade just options.

Options can make futures trading safer and more profitable — often both. Moreover, options can be used to enhance profitability in the futures. It all depends on your particular trading strategy.

For the commercial hedger, the difference between futures and options is that whereas futures permit the hedger to lock in a particular price, options permit the same hedger to lock in a particular price ceiling or floor. You might say that futures are the proverbial double-edged sword, whereas options are single-edged swords. You can save yourself a significant amount of money using a futures contract; on the other hand, you may also lock out a significant profit by hedging with futures. Options, however, offer the best of both worlds. Because an option is a unilateral instrument, the buyer can use its profit-making features through exercising the option. If it isn't profitable to exercise the option, on the other hand, the buyer can simply walk away. The choice is his alone.

What are the strategies that employ both futures and options? There are many. And we've covered quite a few. But the most popular among floor traders is known as *ratio writing*. This means you purchase or sell futures and write calls or puts against the position. The "ratio" refers to the number of calls and puts you write relative to the underlying futures position. If you write on a one-to-one basis, you are considered fully covered. But to enhance profitability on the position, traders often use other ratios.

Let's look at an example. With May beans trading at $5.80, let's say you *sell* one May soybean futures contract and write five out-of-the-money May 575 bean puts against the position for a premium of 9¢ or $450, each. The May 575 puts will have intrinsic value at expiration only if May soybeans are trading below the strike price of 575. Above that price, the writer of May puts will retain the premium income. Since you wrote a total of five puts for $450 each, the total premium income will be five times as much, or $2,250.

Now consider the possibilities. If soybean prices rise, you will have a loss on the short futures position. But this loss will be offset in part by the premium income you received for writing the five puts. In fact, you are protected all the way to $6.25, or $5.80 (the level of entry on the short position) plus the 45¢ in writing income. The maximum profitability on the position is at the strike of 575. There, you will have a 5¢ gain on the futures, plus you get to keep the premium generated by the five puts. The total profit at 575 at expiration of the put: 5¢ futures profit plus 45¢ writing income, or 50¢. Should prices plummet, however, you had better take some defensive action, such as "rolling down" the puts (selling more lower-strike puts) or selling more futures. The point is, a combination of futures and options can be tailored to suit your particular style of trading. Remember, this is just one popular strategy used by floor traders. There are many more.

Don't Forget Murphy's Law

Murphy's Law says that whatever can go wrong, will. It probably wasn't made with the futures and options market in mind, but it might have been. The guy who claimed that Murphy was an optimist probably was an ag options trader. The "safety" of options trading ultimately rests with the user of the option — not the brokerage house, not the exchange, but the user. How you use the new options will determine how "safe" they prove to be.

What can go wrong when you're trading options? Better stated, what can go right? Just about everything can prove problematical if you aren't aware of the risk involved. If you aren't aware of an upcoming report, for example, your whole strategy can suddenly go awry when a report comes out that is extremely bullish or bearish. There is, by the way, a strategy that traders use to "fade"—or trade against—government reports. Since most traders try to second-guess soon-to-be-released reports, they often take positions to capitalize on the news. More often than not, however, their analyses prove inaccurate and the market suddenly reverses.

What's the clue that a hidden opportunity exists just prior to the release of a government crop report? Look for an anticipated bullish report to be issued amid bullish expectations. Then watch how the market reacts. If it can't rise, it's a sure sign of a good *selling* opportunity. You'd be surprised how often this counter-trend strategy works.

Many of the market pitfalls can be avoided with a minimum of planning. Any time an option is in the money, the seller is in danger of an exercise. Let's say you are a writer of soybean calls. Are you prepared to have short positions at the strike? If not, better take action by buying back your calls when they go into the money. Certainly, there is a defensive strategy available, no matter what the problem. But human nature being what it is, many of us would prefer to put off dealing with the problem. In general, this is a mistake. When you are on the wrong side of the market, things tend to go from bad to worse. Someone once said that the key to success in the market is dealing with the losses; the profits will take care of themselves. In short, learn to take losses quickly.

More than one trading fortune has been lost by an individual who refused to deal with a market mistake in its early stages. One only has to look back at the silver debacle in 1980. In that situation, many well-financed silver traders went broke because they refused to believe it was a runaway bull market. Not that the market manipulation by the Hunts helped matters. But the point is, alternatives to losing a great deal of money are available. Learn to pay up quickly when you are wrong, and Murphy's Law won't come back to haunt you.

4

Option Strategies for the Commercial Hedger

Let no one underestimate the tragedy of agriculture in recent years. Declining farm-land and commodity prices coupled with persistently high interest rates, a strong dollar reducing exports, and huge budget deficits have hurt farming and farmers in the most severe way possible. Their very ability to survive is being threatened. Indeed, few people in the Middle West need to be told of this tragedy.

The Options and Futures Markets Aren't the Villains

Despite the problems currently being experienced in the agricultural markets — we all know farmers can't make a living on 2.70 corn or 3.60 wheat — the futures and options markets are not the culprits, as some in the farming community think. Prices are not set in some diabolical scheme on the floor of the futures exchanges, only "discovered." And the market forces at work are far, far larger than even the best-capitalized speculator. If anything, speculators, by providing market liquidity and a fair price, are the friends of farmers.

What about selling short? Isn't it the short selling that drives down prices? Hardly. First, there has to be a buyer for every seller. If farmers wanted to do away with the futures markets entirely and have prices quoted on a transaction-by-transaction basis between producers and users, there would be real dislocations in the markets. Despite the occasional windfall due to adverse weather conditions and a shortfall of supply, during the harvest the bottom would fall out of the market and risks would be magnified many times beyond their current levels. Second, it is the underlying supply-and-demand conditions that have resulted in low farm prices. Until the economic machinery finds a way to make our markets more attractive to foreign buyers and put a lid on interest rates at home, the agricultural sector will be at a disadvantage to other industries.

The trading community would like to see high prices as much as the farmer. During periods of rising prices, speculators pour into the markets, generating commissions as well as additional opportunities to profit from volatile prices. In addition, with this influx of new business, the price of membership seats on the exchanges rises. Since 1980, some of the memberships on the leading futures exchanges have declined by as much as 50 percent. This is hardly a situation with which the professionals can be pleased. Like the farmer, they would like to see higher grain and livestock prices.

Why, then, don't futures traders simply purchase contracts and push up the price of grain and livestock? They would if it were profitable to do so. But acting in concert with Adam Smith's "invisible hand," speculators operate in a manner which they believe will earn them profits — and their actions benefit all. In the last few years, the short sellers have gained the upper hand, since the forces of supply and demand have dictated lower prices. But just as the darkest night gives way to the bright sunshine of morning, the trend will change in the agricultural market — if for no other reason than the wholesale destruction of our agricultural community, which will result in fewer farmers and fewer farms, the classic lower-supply situation. If the present decline of the American farm continues, there's a good chance we'll be paying substantially higher prices to encourage people to *take up* farming in years to come; after all, *someone's* got to produce the food we all need to survive.

Hedging Possibilities Have Come a Long, Long Way in Recent Years

Despite the low prices affecting farmers in recent years, there are better alternatives available today for commercial hedgers than ever before. Studies have shown that only 10 percent of all farmers use the futures market to hedge their crops. In part, this is understandable, since the futures markets have some disadvantages that often complicate a marketing program. For instance, a farmer who placed a short hedge to ensure himself a fixed selling price was often met with margin calls when his timing was less than perfect. On paper, his cash crop was gaining in value, but the futures position required additional margin funds, money that the farmer often didn't have or didn't want to risk. Then, too, many farmers complained that they didn't have time to both farm and watch the market.

With the introduction of the new options on futures in the grain and livestock commodities, a new world of possibilities has opened for the commercial farmer or processor. Now, for the first time, a commercial can ensure himself a price and still have an opportunity to benefit if the market continues in his favor. With futures or forwards, this possibility didn't exist. So the introduction of options offer a new prospect that might be of interest to a great many farmers and commercials who weren't comfortable with the open-ended risks associated with the futures market.

What are these new alternatives? We've already covered the basics of a number of them, but we'll now look at the key strategies designed specifically with the hedger in mind.

What's My Risk?

Farmers learn to live with risk. There are the risk of drought, the risk of foreign imports pricing domestic farmers out of the market, the risk of a politically inspired embargo drying up demand, the risk of crop failures, and the risk of high interest rates cutting off the flow of capital. Most, if not all of these high risks are unavoidable — well beyond the control of the individual farmer or grain-elevator operator. But there are other real risks with which the commercial *can* deal effectively. These are the risks we want to identify here.

When it comes to the marketing of commodities, there are two kinds of price risk: so-called *basis risk* and *market risk*. For hedgers, basis risk constitutes the difference between the price one sells at in the futures market and the price one actually receives at home. The basis is defined as the difference between the nearby futures price and the cash price available in one's home location. Hence, variables such as transportation costs, interest rates, and storage and handling costs in your particular area will determine your basis. The grower who markets his grain in Topeka, Kansas, for instance, won't have the same basis as the grower who sells in Sioux City, Iowa. What's more, the basis at the same and different points will change over time. You might lock in $3.70 per bushel of wheat in Chicago, while your cash price locally is $3.50. In this case, your basis is 20¢ under. By the time you are ready to lift your hedge, however, futures may have risen 15¢ to $3.85 per bushel and the cash commodity only 5¢ to $3.55. In that case, the basis would have *widened* from 15¢ to 30¢. Your risk, of course, is that the basis moves against you while you are hedged.

What can you do about basis risk? Very little. Yet hedging is designed to cope with a much more dramatic risk, namely market risk. Market risk, as the name suggests, is the risk that prices will fluctuate considerably in an adverse manner during the time you are net long or short in the cash commodity. For example, if you have soybeans growing in the field, you are long in cash soybeans. Your risk is that soybean prices will decline from the time you grow them until the time you offer them for sale in the cash market. The futures market is a vehicle that enables you to sell your soybeans for future delivery nine or ten months down the road. In theory, if not in practice, by selling futures contracts, you establish a viable selling price that you can live with *regardless* of subsequent price movements. You might say the hedger hands the risk associated with fluctuating prices to the speculator. He says, in effect, "Here, you take the risk—I've quite enough of my own out on the farm."

The advantage of the traditional selling hedge in futures is that it guarantees the producer a price he can live with. But there are drawbacks. Guaranteeing that price may not be as easy as simply selling futures. You have to margin the futures position. This could result in tying up a lot of money, not to mention the possibility of losses. Moreover, if, in response to higher prices, you decide to "lift," or liquidate, the hedge prior to the harvest and sale of the soybeans, you stand unprotected against market adversity. You could, in this scenario, lose on the futures hedge and subsequently lift the hedge only to have prices decline and sell your cash beans well below your intended selling price. So it is not as simple and risk-free as it might seem.

On the other hand, we know that agricultural options permit the hedger to establish a price floor for his sales and a price ceiling for his purchases—all for a fixed, predetermined, one-time premium payment. This is a genuinely new development for the potential commercial hedger, one he should investigate before he writes off the futures and options markets entirely. It may just solve a few of his financial problems.

Alternative Strategies for the Commercial Hedger

The most common problem faced by commercial hedgers is what hedge, if any, to place and when. Now that farm options are available, the task is somewhat more complex in the sense that a greater number of strategies are available. On the other hand, a variety of option hedges provides a greater degree of flexibility to the commercial hedger.

To illustrate the principles involved, we'll consider just one side of the hedging process, the selling side. To the wheat farmer, who is a producer of grain, declining prices represent the real risk. A precipitous decline in wheat prices can wreak havoc with the wheat grower's marketing program. The traditional hedge for such a grower has been the so-called futures *selling hedge*. In this strategy, the short sale of the futures establishes a selling price. As the futures contract matures, the wheat farmer either gives delivery against his futures contract or simply offsets his futures position at a profit — or a loss — and sells his grain in the cash market.

In either instance, assuming no change in his basis, the hedger receives the price he contracted for in the futures market, either by gains in the futures market (if prices decline) or gains in the cash market (if prices rise).

Now, with the introduction of farm options, the hedger has at least two other alternatives to implement his hedging program: buying puts and writing calls.

To illustrate the pros and cons of each of these three key strategies, let's look at an actual example and compare different results.

Example: During midsummer, December wheat futures are trading at $4.00 a bushel, the December 400 put is priced at 17¢, and the December 400 call is available for 18¢. The commercial grower is a wheat farmer who is looking to lock in a price for his wheat crop or, at least, establish a price floor or profit cushion for his wheat.

The question is: Which is the best hedge? And how will each hedge react to various price changes?

Strategy 1: The short futures hedge. This traditional approach to hedging against price declines, which involves selling futures short, has the benefit of locking in the selling price but the drawback of locking out potential gains in the event of a price rally. Moreover, the short hedge has the real drawback of requiring the hedger to post margin. Thus, in the event of higher prices, the hedger will be forced to post additional margin to finance the paper losses on the short position — despite a corresponding rise in value of his cash crop.

Strategy 2: The long put hedge. In this strategy, the commercial hedger might decide to buy a December at-the-money 400-strike put for the premium of 17¢ per bushel. The drawback to this approach is that the hedger must overcome the cost of the put in the market. That is, if prices stay stationary, the 17¢ premium will be entirely lost. Hence, the net selling price will not be $4.00 a bushel at all, but rather $3.83 a bushel. Below $3.83, the put will provide protection. On the up side, of course, the advantage of the put is that it can be abandoned. As a result, the hedger can participate in the rise in wheat prices and sell his commodity at the now higher value — an opportunity that is not available to the hedger who uses a short futures hedge.

Strategy 3: The short call hedge. The commercial who *sells a call* to hedge his long cash crop provides himself with a cushion of safety by virtue of receiving the premium income. This strategy will prove beneficial if the price of wheat remains within 18¢ (the premium received) of the striking price, but could prove problematic if prices were to fall dramatically. The reason? By writing the call, the hedger provides himself only with a margin of safety. If, for instance, the losses on the cash crop are larger than the offsetting premium income, the hedger will have a real loss.

On the up side, the hedger who uses this strategy finds himself faced with the same problem facing the short futures hedger. He must post margin on a marked-to-the-market basis. As a result, he not only has a financial drain by posting margin but effectively locks out profits above the call's strike price.

In Table 3, you will find the net results of the three strategies listed side by side. You should remember that the hedger owns the cash crop. Hence, he is long in wheat. Upon harvesting his crop, he will be selling it in the cash market for what it will bring. The purpose of the hedge is just to provide added income in the event that cash prices move lower.

Table 3. The selling hedge: three alternative hedging positions.

	Gain or Loss		
Hypothetical Wheat Prices (per bushel)	*Strategy 1: Short Dec. Wheat Futures @ 400*	*Strategy 2: Long 1 Dec. 400 Wheat Put (Premium = 17¢)*	*Strategy 3: Short 1 Dec. 400 Wheat Call (Premium = 18¢)*
$5.00	(1.00)	(.17)	(.82)
4.80	(.80)	(.17)	(.62)
4.60	(.60)	(.17)	(.42)
4.40	(.40)	(.17)	(.22)
4.20	(.20)	(.17)	(.02)
4.00	0	(.17)	+.18
3.80	+.20	+.03	+.18
3.60	+.40	+.23	+.18
3.40	+.60	+.43	+.18
3.20	+.80	+.63	+.18
3.00	+1.00	+.83	+.18

Table 3 shows the gain or loss on the hedge alone. Table 4 shows the net gain, taking into account the hedger's cash crop position. The example assumes the cash crop is valued at the same prices as the nearby futures at expiration.

The traditional short futures hedge in Strategy 1 returns a fixed selling price, regardless of the subsequent move in wheat prices. The at-the-money December 400 put purchase locks in a somewhat lower selling price, yet allows for a steady growth in profitability should prices rise. Lastly, the short call position in Strategy 3 results in a somewhat higher selling price near the strike price, but locks out profit should a dramatic rise occur. Also, it offers only limited protection in the event of a decline in prices.

In summary, if you are certain of lower prices, you'll probably just want to sell wheat futures and use the short hedge. If you are uncertain about the future direction of prices but suspect a sharp rally might occur, use Strategy 2 and purchase a put. And if you anticipate steady to slightly higher or lower prices, you'll probably want to use Strategy 3, writing an at-the-money call.

The Buying Hedge

The *buying hedge* is undertaken by someone who is short in the cash commodity. The risk he is hedging against is that prices might rise between now and the time that he will eventually purchase the underlying commodity. An example would be the processor of soybeans. He

Table 4. Net selling prices for the three hedging strategies (assuming cash crop is sold at same price).

Price	Strategy 1	Strategy 2	Strategy 3
$5.00	$4.00	$4.83	$4.18
4.80	4.00	4.63	4.18
4.60	4.00	4.43	4.18
4.40	4.00	4.23	4.18
4.20	4.00	4.03	4.18
4.00	4.00	3.83	4.18
3.80	4.00	3.83	3.98
3.60	4.00	3.83	3.78
3.40	4.00	3.83	3.58
3.20	4.00	3.83	3.38
3.00	4.00	3.83	3.18

uses soybeans in his processing operations and therefore is net short in the cash commodity. His risk: that soybean prices might rise. To offset the risk associated with being short in the cash market, he generally purchases futures contracts to establish a buying price.

To establish the buying hedge, therefore, the processor will purchase soybean futures contracts. In the event of a rise in prices, he will profit on the futures — hopefully, enough to offset his higher cost in the cash market. Should prices decline, however, the buying hedge will lock out the windfall gain the processor might have otherwise had. His futures losses, in that case, will be offset by the lower prices he will eventually be able to purchase the beans for. One other problem: should bean prices fall after he places the hedge, he will have to maintain margin on his position.

The simplest and most straightforward alternative to the futures buying hedge is the buying hedge using call options. Instead of futures, the processor now purchases calls. Should soybean prices rise, the hedger can either sell the calls for what they will bring in the market or exercise them and take on the long futures at the strike price. He can then either take delivery on the futures contract or sell the futures for a profit.

The risk associated with this strategy is the cost of the calls. Unlike in the buying hedge using futures, the processor must earn back the cost of the calls in the market. If he doesn't, he will simply view the cost of the calls as a sort of insurance policy that he didn't have to use. By substituting calls for futures, he also limits his risk to the downside. After all, the farther soybean prices fall, the more money the processor saves on his cost of doing business. This, in turn, can translate into a higher profit margin. Using futures as a buying hedge, the profit margin is more or less established at the outset because his buying price is known; with calls, however, only the cost of the hedge is established at the outset. A sharp decline in prices can result in a real windfall.

The buying hedge can also be implemented in a limited fashion by writing puts. The writing of put options on the underlying commodity used in the hedger's operations will have the effect of generating a cash flow to offset any small rise in prices. For example, with soybeans trading at $6.00 a bushel, the commercial hedger might write at-the-money puts for a premium of 30¢ per bushel. Should bean futures prices subsequently rise (meaning the cost of the hedger's cash beans will rise as well, increasing his expenses), the puts will remain out of the money and unexercised. The income generated by writing the puts, therefore, will offset the higher cost of cash soybeans — up to a point. Beyond that point, of course, the hedger will have to take additional action.

What if prices decline? If prices tumble, the put will be exercised, and the put writer will receive a long futures contract at the strike. This will enable him to purchase soybeans at a price that he initially found would result in a tolerable price for his end product. Hence, everyone is well served. The hedger is able to buy soybeans at a price he can live with in his commercial processing operations, and the purchaser of the put receives a profit — or at least something back, as long as futures remain below the strike at expiration. The only drawback to writing puts as a buying hedge is that the protection to the up side is limited and one must forgo an opportunity profit should prices fall. Also, the short puts must be fully margined, just like a futures position.

Like the commercial grower seeking protection through the selling hedge, processors and other users of commodities have several alternatives in placing an effective hedge. Let's look at a specific example and see how different hedging strategies will affect the outcome over a range of prices.

> Example: A meat packer, looking to lock in the cost of live hogs, is exploring different ways to establish a purchase price for two to three months in the future. At present, June live-hog futures are trading at $50 per hundredweight. The June 50 call option is available for a price of 1.60 points ($480) and the June 50 put option is available for a price of 1.70 points ($510).

For simplicity, we'll leave out the questions of basis and a favorable or negative basis change in this example. We'll assume that the meat packer can make a reasonable profit if he purchases live hogs at today's June futures price of $50. His risk: that live-hog prices will rise substantially over the next two or three months.

Strategy 1: The long futures hedge. When live-hog prices rise, a processor who must eventually purchase live hogs stands to have his margins affected if he must pay higher prices. To protect his cash position (which, prior to the purchase of the live hogs, is short), the processor will want to purchase futures. Traditionally, this was the only hedging vehicle the meat packer had available to him prior to the introduction of options on hog futures. Rising prices, of course, will mean this strategy protects the hedger. With declining prices, the purchase price still stands — his cost will be established by the price he paid for the long futures, or $50 in our example. The drawbacks are that he must margin the futures contract and will miss out on the ability to purchase hogs at lower prices.

Strategy 2: The long call hedge. Let's say that, as an alternative to the long futures hedge, the meat packer purchases the at-the-money live-hogs June 50 call for 1.60 points, or $480. This allows him to purchase live-hog June futures at the strike price at any time prior to expiration of the option. In the event of higher prices over the time he holds the option, he will either sell the call to take profits or exercise the call and take on the long June futures position. In either case, the option hedge will serve to offset any higher price he will eventually have to pay in the cash market. One advantage over the long futures buying hedge is that he will not be forced to purchase at $50. Should prices fall to $45, he will simply abandon his call and buy hogs at $45 — a $5-per-hundredweight savings. His cost: the premium cost, or $480.

Strategy 3: The short put hedge. By selling puts, the commercial provides himself with a cushion of safety equal to the writing income. For each at-the-money live-hogs 50 put sold for a premium of $510, the commercial provides himself with the same amount of safety to the up side. That is, he will break even at a price of 51.70, because at that price he will lose exactly the amount he gains from writing the put, or $510. Also, by writing, he lowers his purchase cost in the event the puts are exercised. Now, instead of purchasing hogs at a price of $50, his cost falls to $48.30 — or the strike price (at which he must be willing to purchase hogs by virtue of having been given a long futures) *minus* the writing income ($510), which is his to keep. The short put hedge offers only limited up-side protection, but it is typically a better strategy than not hedging at all, unless you anticipate sharply lower hog prices.

Table 5 lists the results of these three strategies. As you can see from the hypothetical results, each offers its advantages and disadvantages at different prices.

As you can see, some strategies work better than others at different prices. Assuming stationary prices, writing the June 50 put is the best strategy, since you take in the writing income and are still able to purchase hogs at $50. At moderately higher prices, the long futures hedge offers the best protection. At $54, for example, the long futures hedge will ensure you a cost of $50. The long June 50 call will return only $2.40 after the $1.60 premium cost is taken into account. And the writing of the 50-strike put will offer only limited protection — you'll end up paying $52.30 for the hogs.

When you look at the lower hog prices, you begin to see the advantages of the call. Whereas with the futures you are committed to $50 hogs no matter what happens, with the call you have to pay out only $1.60 in a $44 market. Thus, your net purchase price is $45.60 per hundredweight. When you use Strategy 3, writing the June 50 put, you are committed to $48.30 hogs when prices decline. The bottom line is,

Table 5.   The buying hedge: three alternative hedging strategies.

	Gain or Loss		
Futures Price	Strategy 1: Long June Live-Hog Futures @ $50	Strategy 2: Long 1 June 50 Live-Hog Call (Premium = 1.60)	Strategy 3: Short 1 June 50 Live-Hog Put (Premium = 1.70)
$60	+10.00	+8.40	+1.70‡
$58	+8.00	+6.40	+1.70
$56	+6.00	+4.40	+1.70
$54	+4.00	+2.40	+1.70
$52	+2.00	+.40	+1.70
$50	0	(1.60)	+1.70
$48	(2.00)	(1.60)	(.30)
$46	(4.00)	(1.60)	(2.30)
$44	(6.00)	(1.60)	(4.30)
$42	(8.00)	(1.60)	(6.30)
$40	(10.00)*	(1.60)†	(8.30)

* This is the loss on the futures position. The net price will still be $50, since the hedger will be able to purchase cash hogs at the lower price of $40.
† The net purchase price will be whatever the cash price is at the time of purchase, minus the cost of the call.
‡ The net price will be whatever the hedger pays for the cash hogs, minus the premium he takes in for writing the put.

the hedge to use depends on the market you are in. After all, at the lower prices, the would-be long hedger is better off doing nothing. The problem comes with predicting prices.

In Table 6, I have listed the net purchasing prices for the three strategies.

Starting a Call-Writing Program

Commercial hedgers have an added edge on speculators when it comes to writing calls: they have the product. A speculator who decides to bet against higher prices by writing calls has no choice when his judgment proves wrong except to buy back the short call or take on a short futures position with a built-in loss. The farmer, however, is in a much more enviable position. In fact, should the calls become valuable to the buyer, the farmer can take one of several routes. Like the speculator, he can buy back the calls at a loss. But that isn't the end of the transaction — at least not as far as the farmer is concerned. With higher prices, he can then sell his grain or livestock in the cash market for what it will bring. If he is exercised against and receives a short futures position at the strike price, he won't necessarily be forced to liquidate the short position. Because he owns the grain or livestock, he can deliver against the short futures at maturity and pocket the option premium as an offsetting gain. Lastly, because he can make good on his commitment, he is in a better psychological position to ride temporary market rallies if he wishes. He may even wish to sell a portion of his cash crop on short-term strength in the market. In short, his alternatives are many.

Depending on the type of market one is trading, 60 percent to 75 percent or more of all calls will expire worthless. Therefore, the percentages favor the writers. For the commercial hedger, moreover, a comprehensive writing program should provide a steady stream of profits. Why does one write calls? One reason: *to earn premium income.* Since most farmers are net long in the underlying commodities they raise and grow, writing calls should be the strategy of choice. Upon exercise, they will have a fixed selling price through the short futures they will acquire. If the calls aren't exercised, on the other hand, they will generate a cash income that will serve to partly offset soft commodity prices.

For the commercial hedger, writing calls shouldn't be a one-shot affair. The market being as unpredictable as it is, chances are the first two or three writing attempts will prove less than satisfactory. What if you write a call just as a bull market is beginning? You will earn a little and miss out on a lot. But if you begin an aggressive campaign to write calls steadily and consistently, not only will you achieve a steady stream

Table 6. Net purchase prices for the three hedging strategies (assuming cash commodity is purchased at same price).

Futures Price (Live Hogs)	Net Purchase Price		
	Strategy 1	Strategy 2	Strategy 3
$60	$50.00	$51.60	$58.30
$58	50.00	51.60	56.30
$56	50.00	51.60	54.30
$54	50.00	51.60	52.30
$52	50.00	51.60	50.30
$50	50.00	51.60	48.30
$48	50.00	49.60	48.30
$46	50.00	47.60	48.30
$44	50.00	45.60	48.30
$42	50.00	43.60	48.30
$40	50.00	41.60	48.30

of writing income, but you will find the percentages working in your favor as you collect on most of your short options and lose on the minority.

Writing calls is not for everyone. Unless you are prepared to monitor your call positions and put up some cash for margin, you are probably better off leaving the short side of the options market alone. Remember, as a writer, you are settling for a fixed, predetermined premium in advance. This is the most you can take in. On the other hand, the liability associated with writing calls is unlimited. You can indeed lose many times what you put up. The good news, of course, is that on average the writer makes the money and the buyer loses his bet.

Writing calls is for people who anticipate steady or slightly lower prices. If you foresee a market collapse and are seriously concerned about the price you will receive several months from now in the cash market, you are better off selling futures short. But if you are relatively neutral on the market, you might well begin an aggressive call-writing campaign.

Now let's assume you are a cotton grower and you expect relatively soft cotton prices through the harvest period. You can write at-the-money calls and profit to the full extent of the premium received if the calls remain below or at the strike price at expiration of the options. Let's say you receive 1.50 points per call. In cotton, that translates into $750 on the 50,000 lb contract. If you write 100 such contracts, you immediately increase your revenue by $75,000. Another way of looking at this strategy is as a means of providing some "cushion" should prices decline slightly. In this case, the premium income would offset the decline in revenue that you will ultimately achieve by selling your cash crop.

A dynamic hedging program will require periodic adjustments in your hedge. Hence, if you write calls and you find prices easing upward, it may pay to buy back the calls and "roll up" to the call with the next-higher strike price. The reason? It raises your ultimate selling price. By staying with the lower-strike calls, you permit the buyer of the calls to profit — in effect, you lock out your profit. By rolling up, however, you are saying that your selling was a bit premature and now you would prefer to take a small loss (depending on the strike price of the calls) and create a new opportunity by selling the higher-strike calls.

There's a trade-off involved here, however. Higher-strike calls will have lower premiums. If you sell calls that are deeply out of the money, the income you'll receive may not be worth the potential risk.

For example, if you write a call that is deeply out of the money, you may receive only 3¢ or 4¢ in writing income on a grain option. Should a runaway bull market develop, that call may increase in value twentyfold or thirtyfold. Thus, the ratio of what you stand to gain versus what you stand to lose may be too high. Since the leverage of at-the-money calls is much lower (although the probability of exercise is higher), the risk/reward ratio is probably more inviting for the would-be option writer.

Like the speculator who writes uncovered calls, the commercial grain farmer or livestock rancher will want to have a contingency plan to deal with all situations. We know that the commercial hedger, in this example, is undertaking a somewhat safer strategy, since he is, in effect, covered against the call option. If he must, he can always deliver against the short futures that will develop upon exercise.

We've mentioned "rolling up" the calls. What if prices decline? Well and good, you say, because the call premiums will likewise decline and the hedger will have a profit on the calls. Yes, but you must understand that the out-of-the-money calls will tend to have a lower and lower delta as prices decline. This means that as long as prices remain below the strike (and the call remains out of the money), the decline in the futures will not be matched dollar for dollar by the decline in the call.

One solution is to make the hedge delta neutral at all times. Therefore, if a delta of a given call is, say, .50, you will write two calls for every futures position you would like to hedge. But if prices fall farther, the delta is also going to fall—say, to .25. Now you'll need four calls to remain delta neutral. Because the options will retain *some value* no matter how far prices fall (remember, every option retains some time value until expiration), you are probably better off buying back those deeply out-of-the-money calls and "rolling down" to lower strike calls. That means you will write the new lower-strike calls for their time premium. By doing so, you may be able to match the potential losses in the cash market with new and steady writing earnings in the call options market.

Lastly, as a commercial farmer who wishes to hedge by writing calls, you'll want to be on the lookout for promising writing opportunities. We know that most options will retain their time premium value until just before expiration. Prior to that time, however, there should be some erosion in time value. But once the expiration comes in sight, you should start thinking about capturing new time value by "rolling out" your calls in the next adjacent month. This will enable you to keep the steady stream of writing earnings in the pipeline while waiting for the last few pennies on those soon-to-expire calls. As an alternative, having taken the lion's share of profits out of the calls, buy them back and simply concentrate on the next maturity series.

By constantly adjusting your hedge in this fashion, you can fine-tune your strategy to achieve its maximum potential. At the same time, you give yourself the maximum *ceiling price* for your grain or livestock. For instance, if you write 600-strike soybean calls, that's the maximum you can expect as your selling price. But if you "roll up" to the 625-strike calls, you've just given yourself a new ceiling price. What's more, you are always taking in your premiums, which, of course, add to your overall net selling price.

> Example: With heavy supplies overhanging the market, a grower of corn is neutral to slightly bearish on corn prices over the next seven or eight months. The September corn futures contract is trading at $2.80 per bushel, with the September 280 call available for 6¢. To generate income, he decides to write 100,000 bushels (20 contracts) of September 280 calls for 6¢ each, or a total of $6,000 on the 20 contracts. At the mid-August expiration of the calls, September corn is trading at $2.97 per bushel, and the 100,000 bushels are "called away" from him at the strike. What price did he actually receive for his corn?

Assuming the farmer did nothing, his net selling price was $2.80 (where the call was exercised) plus the 6¢ writing income, or $2.86 per bushel. Since the futures went to $2.97 by expiration (and assuming no change in the basis), he locked out some profit by staying with the calls. On the other hand, he made more money than he might have had he simply shorted futures at $2.80 or forward-contracted for the sale of his corn.

But, during the time he held the calls and they remained unexercised, he had alternatives available to him. For example, when he sensed corn prices rising, he might have taken defensive action by buying back the 280s and rolling up to the 300-strike calls. Let's say the 280 calls, which he had initially written for 6¢ each, were trading at 6½¢ when he decides to roll up. Why only 6½¢? For one, despite higher prices, the time value would have most certainly worked in the *writer's favor*. With two months taken out of the options, even with higher prices — say, $2.82 per bushel — the call might very well be trading for just 6½¢. The result would be a net loss of ½¢ per option (commission costs aside) — or about $500 in losses.

Not too bad. Remember, he *received* $6,000 for writing the calls; if he buys them back for 6½¢ each, he will pay $6,500 on the 20 contracts or 100,000 bushels. Having done so, he is unhedged. He may want to do nothing and simply watch prices rise. But let's say as September corn futures approach $3.00 per bushel, they show signs of stalling out. Now a new writing opportunity presents itself. For the farmer might now want to write the September 300 calls.

Let's say the September 300 calls are trading at 8¢. Remember, suddenly the market has become more volatile and more bullish. Call buyers are willing to pay more for a call that shows a real possibility of proving profitable. So the commercial corn farmer instructs his broker to sell 100,000 bushels of September 300 calls for 8¢ each. He takes in $400 per call, or $8,000 for 20 calls. Prices rise and fall and remain choppy. But at expiration of the calls, the September futures settle at exactly $2.97 and the calls expire worthless. The aggressive call writer gets to keep the full $8,000 minus commissions and the $500 on the 280 calls, for better than $7,000 in writing income; in addition, he gets to *sell* his cash crop for a significantly higher price than it was worth just several months earlier.

Obviously, not every hedging scenario will prove to be quite so promising, but the example shows how working with a hedge can allow the commercial farmer to move his price ceiling higher while still collecting income from his writing activities — all the while remaining fully protected in an essentially covered writing situation.

Any time you write calls, you must ask yourself what will happen at different prices in relation to the strike. For example, what happens when futures prices close below the strike price of the call at expiration? Nothing happens. The options expire worthless. And you, the writer, get to keep the entire premium. What happens when futures trade *above* the strike price is another matter, however. When futures are above the strike at any time prior to the expiration of the option, you stand to have them "called away" as the call is exercised against you. This means you will have a short position placed in your account, with a built-in paper loss. We'll assume that once the call is exercised, you have your broker liquidate the short futures position you will receive at the strike. At the same time, we'll assume you sell your cash crop. In that case, your net selling price will amount to the strike price plus the premium (minus your local basis).

Let's say you have written a soybean call with a strike price of 625 for a premium of 35¢, or $1,750, when futures are trading at $6.25 per bushel. If soybean futures rise to $6.30 prior to expiration, your short call will be exercised against you, and you will receive a short futures position at the strike of $6.25 per bushel. You could then offset your short futures by buying one soybean futures and sustain the 5¢ loss. But having taken in 35¢ for initially writing the call, you will earn a profit of 30¢ on the call.

The next step will be to sell your soybean crop. Assuming a local basis of 25¢ under, you will receive $6.05 per bushel. You add to this the gain on the writing of the calls, and you achieve a net price of $6.35

per bushel — 30¢ per bushel better than you could have achieved by doing nothing at all.

The calculations are as follows:

$6.25 strike price
− .25 basis
+ .35 option premium
$6.35 total return

Hedging with Options in a Stationary Market

If you have some idea of the market action to expect in the future, you can follow a few guidelines in regard to option strategy selection. As some of the preceding examples suggest, *option writing,* as opposed to option buying, is the best strategy to follow when prices are stationary. The writer gains the writing income in full if the options remain unexercised. The buyer of an option, however, must gain back his premium through market action.

In fact, put and call buying remains the least attractive strategy for the farm hedger when prices are stationary. The futures hedge, the forward contract hedge, the option writing hedge — all will show better returns in a stationary market.

Nevertheless, you might want to consider buying an option as a form of inexpensive insurance. The reason? For one, you don't know for sure that prices will in fact remain stationary. And if they have moved sideways over the past several months, chances are the premium cost will be relatively small compared to the protection you'll receive. Moreover, option buying turns the limited-potential-gain/unlimited-potential-liability equation of option writing on its head: now the *writer* stands to lose an unlimited amount while you, the hedger, are risking only the cost of the put or call premium.

Consider the advantages of buying options as a hedge. If you purchase a put to protect against declining prices, you are free to sell at substantially higher prices in the event of a bull market. By contrast, with a futures or forward contract, you are locked into the selling price — that is, short of lifting the hedge. And you have to pay only the put option premium for virtually the same protection you'd achieve with the short futures hedge. Thus, the short futures hedge prevents you from profiting from a price *increase,* whereas you can get the same protection from buying puts and still have the opportunity to sell at higher prices.

There is an example that compares the two strategies. Suppose you are a corn grower with a current $2.80-per-bushel market. Your risk is that corn prices will decline between now and harvest. You can use the short futures hedge by selling at the current market price. This will establish the present market price as your selling price, basis considerations aside. As an alternative, you can purchase put options with strikes at $2.80 per bushel for the going market price of 6¢, or $300 per 5,000 bushels. Should corn prices soar between now and harvest time, you can simply abandon the puts and absorb the costs from your higher cash market price. On the other hand, should prices tumble, you can always exercise the puts and receive $2.80 per bushel. The premium costs should be viewed as the cost of your price ''insurance.''

Now, if prices remain stationary throughout the life of the puts and through to the harvest, you are going to incur some additional expenses—namely, the cost of the puts. But what was the alternative? To remain unhedged? What if corn prices at harvest were only $2.50? Could you have earned a profit on your farming operations at that price? Probably not. There will always be the case when the decision to remain unhedged becomes the intelligent decision—with 20/20 hindsight. But if you lack that hindsight, options provide an intelligent choice to hedge your bets against lower prices.

In summary, keeping in mind that a put provides its holder with the right to *sell* a futures contract of the underlying commodity at the strike price, the would-be seller of a commodity might want to investigate the use of puts in his hedging program. The purchase of puts establishes a *minimum selling price* for the hedger's commodity. At the same time, it does *not* preclude the possibility of achieving a *higher price* in the cash market. The holder of the option alone decides whether to exercise the option and sell the underlying futures at the strike price.

Coping with Yield Risk

In the real world of agriculture, crop yields are rarely known in advance. As a result, a farmer is often reluctant to hedge 100 percent of his expected crop, for fear that his yield will come in low and any losses in the futures market will not be offset by comparable gains in the cash market. When looked at from the standpoint of a potential variable yield, therefore, options become even more attractive as a risk management tool. Since the ''risk'' on a put or a call, at least from the buyer's standpoint, is limited to the option's premium, the commercial hedger using options can afford to hedge without concern that low yields will upset his risk management program. For a low crop yield and higher crop prices will result only in the abandonment of the long put hedge, not a one-for-one lockout on a futures hedge that was set up with a higher crop yield in mind.

When looked at in this perspective, buying and selling puts and calls may well be a preferred method of hedging, since it is apt to return a *higher average net selling price* over time when yields vary.

The principles involved here are best illustrated by an example. In the real world, lower yields typically mean higher prices. So we'll assume that our hypothetical wheat farmer, who is representative of the wheat market in microcosm, has a set of variable yields, all with different cash market prices. In addition, for the sake of simplicity, we will assume a basis of 15¢ under, which is steady through the period studied.

Table 7 shows the returns to the wheat farmer with variable yields if he does not hedge. The numbers show that as production declines and prices rise, the net overall sales tend to decline. The average cash sales amount to $144,000.

In Table 8, we will assume that the farmer anticipates an average of 40,000 bushels in his yield and that he hedges for half this amount. At 5,000 bushels per contract, the hedge will require a total of four contracts to fully hedge 20,000 bushels. In addition, we'll assume the following for the three different hypothetical yield situations: in the first example, wheat prices *decline* by 10¢ after the short futures hedge is placed at $4.05 per bushel; in the second example, wheat futures *remain unchanged* at $4.05; and in the third example, wheat futures *rise* by 30¢.

Because the market movement was relatively small, and because the rise in prices on the lower yield crop resulted in $6,000 in losses on

Table 7. Hypothetical wheat harvest prices and production, and returns for unhedged cash sales.

	$3.80/bu.	$3.90/bu.	$4.20/bu.
Cash price	$3.80/bu.	$3.90/bu.	$4.20/bu.
Futures price	$3.95/bu.	$4.05/bu.	$4.35/bu.
Production	45,000 bu.	40,000 bu.	25,000 bu.
Unhedged cash sales	$171,000	$156,000	$105,000
Average net return on cash sales	$144,000		

Table 8.   Impact of short futures hedge on the example in table 7, assuming the wheat farmer sells four futures contracts.

Cash market	$171,000	$156,000	$105,000
Futures return	+$ 2,000	0	−$ 6,000
Net return	$173,000	$156,000	$ 99,000
Average net return on hedged positions	$142,666		

the short futures hedge, the overall return from hedging with futures was somewhat lower than the completely unhedged position shown in Table 7. Now let's substitute the purchase of put options selling for a premium of 6¢. Remember, we'll be purchasing four puts at a strike of $4.00. Table 9 shows the results.

While the unhedged position remains the most profitable of the three strategies for the prices shown, you can see that the put hedge was slightly more profitable than the short futures hedge. This is because in the third example it locked out only $1,200 (the cost of the puts) instead of the full 30¢ move from $4.05 (where the short futures hedge was originally placed with four contracts) to $4.35, where the short futures hedge was subsequently lifted. In the first example, however, where futures prices declined by 10¢, the short futures proved to be the best hedge, returning $2,000 compared to a loss of $200 on the put hedge. Why? Because the short futures begin making money as soon as prices decline from the entry price.

The put options also begin making money below the strike price. But in the example shown, the puts were 5¢ out of the money to begin with, and the subsequent 5¢ gain on the puts returns only $1,000 against an initial premium cost of $1,200. (Each 6¢ put cost $300; since we purchased four puts, the total cost was $1,200.)

Table 9.   Impact of put purchase on the example in table 7, assuming the wheat farmer buys four put options.

Cash market	$171,000	$156,000	$105,000
Put return	+$ 1,000	0	0
Put premium	−$ 1,200	−$ 1,200	−$ 1,200
Net returns	$170,800	$154,800	$103,800
Average net return on hedged positions	$143,133		

We've looked at this example in terms of using no hedge, selling futures, and buying puts. Now let's try one more hedging strategy, writing calls. Let's assume we write four calls on wheat with a strike of 400 when the underlying futures are trading at $4.05 a bushel. We assume the premium is 10¢ per bushel, or $2,000 for the four calls. The results are shown in Table 10.

By writing calls, we improve the results when the underlying wheat prices stay more or less stationary, but we don't do quite so well when yields decline and prices move higher. On average, however, the call-writing hedge outperforms both the purchase of puts and the short futures hedging strategy. The do-nothing strategy, in this example, continues to outperform any of the hedging strategies.

The real differences in the strategies would become more evident if the underlying commodity prices moved significantly higher or lower. If prices were to soar, you would soon begin to wish you had opted for the put-purchasing hedge or no hedge at all, since you would much prefer to sell your wheat at higher prices. In the event of significantly lower prices, you would wish you had placed the short futures hedge to maximize your net selling prices on your wheat crop. Finally, unchanged prices would reveal that the call-writing strategy would be the most productive one to follow.

In the case of a low crop yield, you would profit the most from remaining entirely unhedged, since the higher prices could immediately be captured at harvest time by selling for cash. If you anticipate low yields and correspondingly higher prices at harvest, the tables suggest you would do best shying away from any short futures hedge. Similarly, in a high-yield/low-price situation, look to place the short futures hedge or at least write calls to maximize your net selling price.

Table 10. Impact of writing four calls as a hedge, for the example in table 7.

Cash market	$171,000	$156,000	$105,000
Call premium	+$ 2,000	+$ 2,000	+$ 2,000
Futures (if exercised)	0	−$ 1,000	−$ 7,000
Net return	$173,000	$157,000	$100,000
Average net return on hedged positions	$143,333		

Selecting the Strike Price

For the commercial hedger who is looking to *buy* options as a hedge against his cash position, the selection of the strike price will depend not only on his market outlook but also on his attitude toward risk and what he is willing to pay for price "insurance" in the options market. For the farmer who raises hogs for a living, the ability to purchase put options on hog futures can provide sufficient peace of mind to allow him to forget the futures market entirely and concentrate on his farm operations. What is such price protection worth? Three hundred dollars? Six hundred dollars? Obviously, it depends on precisely what you are buying with that put contract.

At-the-money options tend to offer the best profit opportunities for both buyer and seller. The participation is greatest in the at-the-moneys, which are therefore most likely to give you a fair market price. Moreover, from the buyer's standpoint, he isn't tying his cash up in purchasing intrinsic value. Nevertheless, just as one might wish to purchase car insurance with a large "deductible" in return for lower premiums, the commercial hedger might be willing to sustain the first couple of dollars' loss should prices decline and only want to "insure" against catastrophic losses by purchasing deeply out-of-the-money options.

Obviously, the "deductible" one selects in purchasing an option will be reflected in the premium price. For example, with September corn futures trading at about $2.70 a bushel, you can purchase the out-of-the-money September 260 put for about 4¢. That's just $200 for an option with four or five months left in time value. But it won't be worth a dime at expiration unless corn futures lose 10¢ per bushel first. Want more protection? Maybe you can't make money at a guaranteed $2.60 a bushel. The at-the-money September 270 put is available for about 9¢. But that's more than twice as much money. Understandably, it gives you another 10¢ in protection by guaranteeing you a price of $2.70 a bushel. For another 7¢, you could opt for the in-the-money September 280 put, trading at 16¢, but these in-the-money options are rarely a good buy. That leaves the at-the-money 270 or the out-of-the-money 260.

Your decision should be based on the selling price you *must* have to turn a profit on your operation and your willingness to take risks. A high risk-taker who doesn't think he'll need the insurance provided by the puts will probably purchase the out-of-the-money option. By spending less on insurance, he stands to make more on his eventual sale of his corn. Of course, you might ask, "Why hedge at all? Can't you save even more money by not hedging?" Absolutely. But could you survive if corn prices fell to $2.00 a bushel?

A Put-Buying Example with Fixed Crop Yields

When you're shopping around for an option to provide you with price protection, you want to consider a number of factors. What is the option premium? What protection does it provide? What will be the outcome under a number of different circumstances?

Let's assume a soybean farmer in June is expecting to harvest about 30,000 bushels in October. Anticipating a basis of 65¢ under the November futures contract, the farmer is looking for alternative methods of hedging against lower prices. At present, the November soybean futures are selling at $6.00 a bushel. By selling six November futures contracts (covering 30,000 bushels), the farmer can lock in a cash price of $5.35 a bushel. If futures decline to $5.00 a bushel (and cash to $4.35), the short futures hedge will ensure the net price of $5.35 per bushel, sufficient to return a profit on his farming operations.

As an alternative to selling futures, now let's consider what will happen if the farmer buys puts to hedge his crop. The at-the-money November 600 put is available for 17¢ a bushel. Thus, the total premium for six contracts will amount to $5,100. In return for paying this premium, the farmer will be assured of a net cash price of $5.35 ($6.00 on November futures minus the basis). As an alternative to buying the November 600 puts, the farmer might consider the November 575 put trading for 10¢ or the in-the-money November 625 put trading for 35¢. The 575 put will cost $3,000 for six, but will provide less protection than the higher-strike puts. The 625 put will cost $10,500 for six.

At the outset, the farmer will know that the average net return from selling futures is greater than that from buying put options. The reason? Buying puts requires an initial premium payment, selling futures does not. But under certain circumstances, buying puts proves the more sensible choice.

Let's consider the impact of the hedge over a range of prices. We'll assume futures could drop to $5.00 on the down side but could rise to $12.00 on the up side. One important factor must be taken into account: what exactly is the potential for an explosive move to the up side versus the down side? If there is a high probability of higher prices and a relatively small chance of prices declining, you may very well be better off with the option hedge. Why? Because selling futures as a hedge establishes your selling price no matter what happens. With a put hedge, the farmer is free to participate in any upward movement.

For example, let's assume he purchased the out-of-the-money 575 puts for 10¢ a bushel and prices rise to $9.00. He simply abandons the puts (who would want to sell soybeans for $5.75 if he could get $9.00 in the market?) and sells at his cash price of $8.35 per bushel. His net price is $8.35 (the cash market price) minus the cost of the option, or 10¢ a bushel—which comes to $8.25. Had he taken the more traditional route of selling November futures, however, he would have locked in his $6.00-per-bushel selling price and ended up with $5.35 per bushel net in the cash market. Actually, he would have sold his cash beans for $8.35. But the $3 loss on the short futures position would have lowered his price to the initial $5.35 he contracted for— assuming, of course, that there is no change in the basis.

At lower prices, the futures hedge proves the best alternative. For example, at $5.75 in November futures, the selling hedge would have returned 25¢ per bushel to offset losses in the cash market, but the November 575 put would expire entirely worthless. A stationary market, by the way, is the only situation in which buying an option is the least attractive alternative. Indeed, at $5.75 a bushel, the futures hedge returns 25¢ while the put hedge would *cost* 35¢ —the 25¢ you lost on the market decline *plus* the 10¢ per bushel you paid for the put. Nevertheless, the cost of the option premium is a small price to pay for insurance against an adversely volatile market.

The real payoff for the put option hedger is to the up side. If soybean prices rise to $12 per bushel at expiration of the puts, the futures strategy still returns $5.35 (taking the 65 under basis into account), whereas the put-buying strategy yields a net return of $11.25 per bushel. The $11.25-per-bushel net figure is arrived at by taking the November futures price of $12 and subtracting the basis of 65¢ and also the cost of the puts, which is 10¢ each.

If you are expecting substantially higher prices over the period prior to the harvest, you might be well advised to choose the put-buying hedge over the short futures hedge. One way to make this decision is to review the history of your commodity. Over a number of years, has the price of the commodity tended to increase more often than it declined? If so, you might be a good candidate for put option hedging.

There is another consideration involved here. Option buying is strictly for cash. You pay your premium and receive your put. With futures, you have to deal with the daily mark-to-the-market requirements. Are you prepared to meet margin calls all the way up from $6 to $12 a bushel, if necessary, to ensure protection of your crop? If so, you had better keep a lot of cash on hand. And if you lift your hedge? Remember, if you liquidate the futures hedge at a loss rather than meet margin calls, and prices *retreat* downward, you stand to lose on the hedge as well as in the cash market.

When Do You Sell Your Puts?

With the put hedge, if prices rocket upward, you aren't committed to writing off the entire expense as a cost of doing business. On the contrary, you can sell the put in the options market for whatever it will bring. For instance, let's say you purchased the November 575 soybean puts for 10¢ each. Well, as prices move up, the put premiums will decline, so don't expect a profit. In fact, as the puts become far out of the money, you'd better forget about selling them for much more than ¼¢ or ⅛¢. With soybeans trading at $9 a bushel, who is going to pay much for the privilege of selling them at $5.75? But at $6 to $7, the 575 puts may still retain a substantial amount of their premium as long as they haven't expired. Thus, having purchased the puts for 10¢ each, you might be able to sell them for 6¢ or 7¢ several months later if they aren't

Table 11.   Hedging soybeans at three different prices, using either futures or puts.

Cash price	$4.35/bu.	$6.35/bu.	$9.35/bu.
Futures price	$5.00/bu.	$7.00/bu.	$10.00/bu.
Production	30,000 bu.	30,000 bu.	30,000 bu.
Cash net return	$130,500	$190,500	$280,500
Average net return	$200,600		
Sells six futures contracts at $6.00			
Cash market	$130,500	$190,500	$280,500
Futures return	+30,000	−30,000	−120,000
Net return	$160,500	$160,500	$160,500
Average net return	$160,500		
Buys six Nov. 575 puts at 10¢ each			
Cash market	$130,500	$190,500	$280,500
Option return	+22,500	0	0
Option premium	−3,000	−3,000	−3,000
Net return	$150,000	$187,500*	$277,500*
Average net return	$205,000		

* Assumes puts are held to expiration and expire worthless. Return would be greater if puts were sold prior to expiration.

trading too far above the strike. The drawback, of course, is that you would have then lost your down-side protection; but by that time, you either see a bull market on the horizon or you don't, and, besides, for 4¢ or 5¢ you have achieved an important degree of protection. Now that time has passed, you can sell the puts.

Notice how different this is from the short futures hedge. With the short futures hedge, you begin *losing* money immediately on the futures position as prices rise; with the put option hedge, you *gain* back part of your initial expense when you sell your options. Remember, there is no rule that you have to hold a put option hedge. Not only can you sell the puts in the market and earn back part of your expense, but you can "roll up" your put options and *guarantee* yourself a higher selling price. For instance, having purchased the November 575 puts for 10¢ you can then sell them for, say, 1¢ or 2¢ and buy the higher-strike 650s and 675s as bean prices rally. By doing so, you guarantee yourself a higher selling price no matter what happens in the market.

The decision to sell your puts must be based on expectations concerning the price of your commodity. The advantage of selling is that it enables you to recapture part of your cost. Obviously, since you want to achieve the best possible price for your puts, you should wait until futures make a decline. Since the future direction of prices is uncertain, there is no way of telling for sure when the best time to sell arrives. But, having sold your puts, don't be afraid to buy them back should you again need the down-side protection. Trading in-and-out of the market is second nature to professional futures and options traders; the professional hedger should likewise recognize that occasionally his judgment will be wrong and he should again take on the hedge. The liquidity of the new options markets makes this an easy task.

One method of deciding when to "lift" the option hedge is to use a percentage rule in the premium cost. For example, having paid 10¢ for a put, you might make it a rule to sell it when it loses half of its value, or 5¢. By doing so, you will really pay only 50 percent of the option premium, not the full cost. Of course, you must always be on guard against a potential tumble in the market. But remember that no matter how far out of the money an option is, it will command some value in the options market. Why not get back something on your investment, especially after it has served its original purpose?

In Table 11, you will see the results of a soybean hedge for 30,000 bushels at three different prices. In the first case, the farmer uses futures; in the second, he uses options.

5

Options and Futures Together

We've looked at some of the more elementary uses of puts and calls on agricultural futures. Now let's consider some of the more sophisticated strategies. The maximum benefit from the new agricultural options will be derived by the strategist who is highly creative. What could be more creative than futures and options together?

Even the most advanced option strategy is nothing more than a combination of simpler strategies. So don't be put off if a given technique appears overly complex at first. In this chapter, we are going to explore the uses of options and futures together. If you don't understand a strategy at first, look at the impact of the futures position alone; then, after understanding one part of the strategy, look at how the options position affects the trade.

Ratio Writing

Ratio writing is nothing more than writing a certain number of options against an underlying futures position or other options. For our purposes in this chapter, we'll concentrate on ratio writing in which you write options against the underlying futures position.

Ratio writing is a strategy that permits you to profit within a range of prices. Nevertheless, ratio writing is not without its drawbacks. So let's consider the pluses and the minuses.

Ideally, the ratio write is established with a particular market in mind. After all, if you are anticipating a runaway bull or bear market, why fuss with options at all? Ratio writing, unlike buying or selling futures or simply purchasing puts or calls, is a strategy that can be "played" to reflect changing market conditions. One side or the other can be tipped in favor of the changing balance in the market — a sort of see-saw arrangement. The real art of ratio writing is knowing when to favor one side and when to favor the other.

The strategy itself is relatively simple. You write so many calls against so many long futures positions. Of course, the reverse, writing puts against short positions, is also an acceptable strategy. This is just another way of saying that ratio writing can be accomplished on a "buy-and-write" or "sell-and-write" basis. The net result of a ratio write is a combination of covered and uncovered options positions.

The 2:1 Ratio Write

The most popular ratio write is known as the 2:1 ratio write. In this strategy, you write twice as many calls or puts as you hold underlying positions. For example, a 2:1 ratio write in soybeans might involve purchasing a long May soybean futures contract and writing two May 575 soybean calls. Depending on where May soybeans are trading at the time you initiate the position, you will have a position that enables you to profit from a rise in soybean prices on the one hand, and, at the same time, profit if prices stabilize or decline slightly. The key to the success of the trade is knowing how to handle the respective options and futures. Should futures soar, what should you do? What if prices break?

Let's look at a hypothetical example. With June live-cattle futures trading at $67.35 per hundredweight, the out-of-the-money June 68 calls are available at a price of $1.30 each. To set up the 2:1 ratio write, you purchase one futures contract and write two calls. The net result will be an immediate gain of the writing income, which in this example will amount to 1.30 points multiplied by 2, or $1,040 (260 points at $4 a point). The profit area of the strategy will exist at the entry level of the futures minus the amount of the writing income on the down side, and the strike plus the writing income on the up side.

Since the 2:1 ratio writer is "covered" on only half his position, a sharp rise in futures prices will result in losses. On the down side, the safety cushion provided by the writing income will protect the long futures position only to the extent of that writing income, and no more. As a result, substantially lower prices will likewise result in losses. The

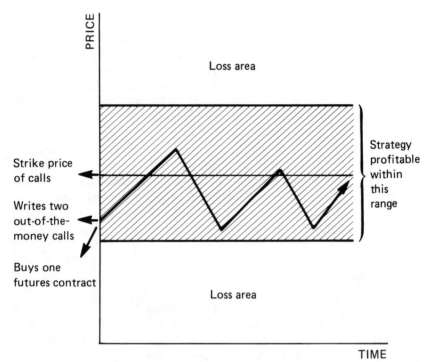

Figure 8.   The 2:1 ratio write.

2:1 ratio writer, therefore, anticipates that prices will move within a relatively narrow range. Should the calls expire while prices are within that band, the strategy will prove profitable. (See Figure 8.)

Now let's calculate precisely at which prices at expiration of the June 68 call the strategy will return a profit. Remember, at initiation, the strategy resulted in a new inflow (commission costs aside) of $1,040 when two out-of-the-money 68 cattle calls were written against the purchase of one June cattle futures contract at 67.35. Table 12 shows some of the outcomes of such a strategy.

As you can see, the point of maximum profitability for the 2:1 ratio write will exist at the strike price of the short calls. At the price of $68, the two calls will expire worthless, enabling the writer to keep the full premium of $1,040. In addition, the modest rise in prices will result in a .65 point gain on the long June cattle futures, another $260. Hence, the maximum profitability on the strategy will be $1,300 if the futures are trading at precisely $68 at expiration of the calls.

Where does the strategy reach the breakeven point? With a total of $1,040 in writing income generated from the sale of the calls, the breakeven point will exist at precisely $64.75 on the down side at expiration. Why at $64.75? Because at that price the loss on the long futures will exactly offset the gain from the writing income. At a price of $64.75, the long futures, which were purchased at $67.35, will have a loss of exactly 2.60 (67.35 − 2.60 = 64.75). Since the writer took in 2.60 points for writing the calls, the gain on the calls exactly offsets the loss on the futures—hence the breakeven at $64.75 per hundred-weight.

On the up side, the breakeven point will exist when the loss on the two short calls exactly equals the gain on the long futures. That price will be $68.65 per hundredweight. At that price, the long June cattle futures, which were purchased at $67.35, will have a profit equal to precisely 1.30 points. At expiration of the calls, however, the two short 68 calls will also have a value of .65 points each. Hence, the gain on the single futures contract will precisely offset the loss on the two short calls. Above breakeven, of course, the situation will become progressively worse for the 2:1 ratio writer.

Above the strike price, the loss on one 68 call will be offset dollar for dollar by a corresponding gain on the long futures position. Since the 2:1 ratio writer sold two calls, however, the other call will continue to gain in value (lose money for the writer) as prices rise. Therefore, the profit range for our example is between $64.75 on the down side and $68.65 on the up side at expiration. Given no change in volatility, such a range could be a pretty good bet, considering cattle prices hadn't moved more than $4.50 in volatility over the entire life of the June contract. With just two months to expiration, the 2:1 ratio write provides an inviting trade to the option strategist.

Table 12. Example of a 2:1 ratio write using cattle calls and long futures.

June Futures at Expiration of 68 Call	Gain (Loss) on June Futures	Gain (Loss) on Two June 68 Calls	Net Gain (Loss)
64	(3.35)	2.60	($300)
65	(2.35)	2.60	$100
66	(1.35)	2.60	$125
67	(.35)	2.60	$900
68	.65	2.60	$1,300
69	1.65	(2.00)	($140)
70	2.65	(4.00)	($540)
71	3.65	(6.00)	($920)

Protecting the 2:1 Ratio Write

In calculating breakeven points and points of profit and loss, one must remember that the numbers in our example refer to values *at expiration* only. Prior to expiration, the value may differ markedly. For example, should volatility increase during the life of the option, chances are both puts and calls will increase in value *even if* prices are trending in just one direction. Under normal conditions, one would assume that lower prices would increase the value of puts and decrease the value of calls. But, in reality, *both* are likely to increase in value. Enhanced volatility may result in larger price swings and, hence, a greater chance for both types of options to increase in value.

No matter how reasoned your analysis of the market, there will come a time when you will want to take defensive action. Indeed, the possible adversities should be part of your initial trading plan. What will you do if prices rise sharply? Or if prices break? You'll want to know the answers to these questions before you engage in writing options against futures positions.

First, let's look at a price break. The down-side protection, provided by the sale of the calls, will be limited to the writing income. As long as you hold the long futures, however, your potential liability to the down side is virtually unlimited. What are the alternatives? In the event of a price tumble in cattle futures, you can exit the entire position. This will involve selling the futures position and buying back the calls. Depending on a host of unknowable circumstances, the call premiums may be higher or lower.

Even if prices decline, however, there is no guarantee that call prices will decline at the same time. Depending on the delta of the calls, their value may rise or fall. Moreover, there is another factor to consider: time premium will decrease at an unequal rate. With two months left before expiration of the calls, the options may give up their time premiums grudgingly. This tendency for time value to dissipate slowly, together with the likelihood of increased volatility, translates into higher premiums for all options, which may pose a difficult problem for the 2:1 ratio writer.

One thing is certain. A decline in futures prices will result in losses on the long futures position. Having taken in only 2.60 points in writing income on the two calls, you cannot withstand much adversity on the down side at any time before expiration of the calls. So a sharp decline in prices will probably result in losses on the 2:1 ratio write if you don't liquidate the position at the first sign of adversity.

Let's say prices drop a point to $66.35. With considerable time left to trade in the calls, their premiums might decline to .90 points, down from 1.30. This will translate into a .40-point paper gain on each option or a total of .80 points on the two, or $320. We'll assume you buy them back at this price. At the same time, the long futures you purchased at $67.35 per hundredweight will be off a point at $66.35, a loss of $400. Factoring in commissions, you have lost over $100 on the trade. Actually, this is not bad, considering the real liability you face if prices decline further. So, clearly, exiting the entire position is one alternative you'll want to consider.

What are the other possibilities? There is always the "do-nothing" strategy. By standing firm, you may indeed profit should prices again rise and the trade is closed out in the profit area. But you run the risk of standing firm and having more damage done to your position. As time passes and prices decline, the calls will inevitably lose their value, resulting in a greater and greater paper profit; but at the same time, you will be faced with greater margin requirements on the long futures position—perhaps even a margin call. Are you prepared to deposit more money? Will you continue to hold the position if the bottom drops out of the market? Chances are you'll want to try another strategy.

Fortunately, the versatility of options enables you to fine-tune your trading strategy—even in such a situation, where all the alternatives are clearly painful to some degree. We've looked at liquidating the entire position and doing nothing. Apart from this all-or-nothing strategy, however, there is a middle path. What if you sold more calls to increase your writing income? This strategy, known as "rolling down," involves buying back the higher-strike calls and simultaneously writing lower-strike calls. The reason? The lower-strike calls will provide more writing income and greater protection to offset the losses on the futures position.

For example, having written 68-strike calls for 1.30, you might buy back the 68s and sell two June 66 calls. Let's say you are able to capture 1 point per call on the 68s and received $800 in income. This will offset a drop of 2 points in the underlying June futures, or offset your losses to $65.35, 2 points below the original position. Now, to generate additional cash, you write the lower-strike June 66 calls. With the 66 calls now out of the money (June futures = 65.35) and less time to expiration, the June 66 calls might be selling for only .60 points, or $480 for two. You write two calls and receive the $480 as income. Now you have a greater cushion of profits to offset still further declines in prices on the underlying futures. The trade-off, of course, is that you've lowered the price at which the strategy will prove profitable to the up side. But remember, this is a strategy for a declining market.

There is no rule that says having initiated a 2:1 ratio write, you have to stay with this ratio. You may feel more comfortable varying the number of calls per underlying futures contracts. You may want to write four calls for every futures contract, or six or even nine calls. By increasing the size of your position of short calls, you again increase your writing income — but at a price of higher risk.

The trade-off will be more income in return for substantially higher risk in the event of a rally. If you write calls for every long futures position, you run the risk of having five short positions given to you at the strike price in the event of exercise. To avoid this possibility, monitor your position carefully and be prepared to buy your calls should prices threaten to rise above the strike. Remember, whenever prices rise above the strike, the call may be exercised against you. Ask yourself if you are prepared to assume a short futures position at the strike price. If not, you are better off exiting the trade by covering the position and buying back the calls.

The 2:1 Ratio Write Using Puts

The 2:1 ratio write works with puts as well as calls. The only difference is that you write puts instead of calls and that the underlying position involves a short sale of the underlying futures contract. In all other respects, this strategy is the mirror image of the 2:1 ratio write using calls.

Let's consider an example. With May soybeans trading at $5.85 per bushel, you write two May 575 puts for a premium of 6¢ each and simultaneously sell short a May futures contract at $5.85. Remember, with May soybeans at 585, the 575-strike puts are out of the money. Hence, the puts wouldn't prove profitable to their buyers unless soybean prices fall below the strike at 575. The writing income amounts to a total of 12¢, or $600. Like the 2:1 ratio write using calls and a long futures contract, the 2:1 ratio write using puts sets up a profit zone near the strike price. Hence, a sharp decline in prices will result in losses, as will a sharp rise in prices. The profit zone, however, will exist around the strike. Table 13 shows some of the profit/loss possibilities for this theoretical example.

As you can see, the 2:1 ratio write using puts and a short futures position achieves its maximum profitability at the strike price, where the strategist profits by 10¢ on his short futures position and earns the full 12¢ writing income on the two puts. The same rules are used — in reverse — to calculate the profit/loss zone on the strategy. This strategy would be used if the investor anticipated a modest decline in futures prices.

Table 13.   Example of a 2:1 ratio write using soybean puts and short futures.

May Futures Price at Expiration of 575 Puts	Gain (Loss) on May Futures	Gain (Loss) on Two 575 May Puts	Net Gain (Loss)
525	60¢	(100¢)	($2,000)
550	35¢	(50¢)	($750)
575	10¢	12¢	$1,100
600	(15¢)	12¢	($150)
625	(40¢)	12¢	($1,400)

Variable-Ratio Writing

Variable-ratio writing involves writing a multiple of options against each futures position. Depending on the number of options you write, their premium value, and the relationship of the futures to the respective strike prices, you will have potential profits and, perhaps, losses over a wide range of prices. Also know as the *variable hedge*, or *variable hedge writing*, this strategy can be very flexible and tailored to fit virtually every market situation. The ability to add and subtract short put or call positions in response to changing market conditions makes this one of the most versatile strategies available to the agricultural options trader.

In setting up the variable hedge, you want to decide how many options to write against each futures position. The number will be determined by your outlook on market prices and a host of other factors, some of which we've just mentioned. Let's look at a hypothetical situation.

The first step is to determine your outlook on the market. Are you bullish or bearish? Very bullish or very bearish? Mildly bullish or mildly bearish? Obviously, you have no way of being certain about your market outlook, but an educated estimate can go a long way in helping you determine your particular stance. Let's say you are bearish on soybean prices, but only mildly so. May soybeans are trading at $5.85 per bushel, and you expect a decline of 5¢ to 7¢ over the next month or so. With two months left to expiration in the May soybean options, you decide to set up your variable-ratio hedge by selling May soybean futures and writing May 575 puts. With a strike lower than the market, the May 575 puts are available for 6¢ each ($300). Being an aggressive trader, you decide to write ten May 575 puts for $300 each. At the same time, you sell short one contract of May soybeans at $5.85.

Having set up the variable-ratio write in this fashion, you'll have established a 10:1 ratio write — essentially a naked put-writing position, since you are "covered" on only one short put. Your risk is that soybean prices may fall below the strike price, making the puts profitable for their buyers to exercise. Should exercise occur, you will find yourself long nine contracts at the strike — all of them with paper losses. The other contract, which you have shorted at a price of $5.85, 10¢ above the strike, will have a $500 profit, but this will hardly be sufficient to offset the losses on the naked puts. On the up side, you will have a total of $3,000 in writing income, or a 60¢-per-bushel protection on the single short May soybean futures position. The maximum profit will exist at the strike price of the ten short puts at expiration, or $5.75 per bushel. At that price, you will receive a 10¢ profit on the short May futures, together with the entire writing income of $3,000 on the ten puts.

Why not write calls in this situation? You might have written calls. But a mildly bearish market would have resulted in a loss on the long futures position that you would have purchased in the 10:1 ratio write. By writing puts against a short position in futures, you stand to profit on both options *and* futures.

What are the strong and weak points of this strategy? As long as the decline in bean prices over the near term is modest and not sharp, the strategy should return profits. The maximum profit, by the way, is $3,500, namely, $3,000 in writing income plus $500 in profits on the futures. But the risk, should prices decline sharply, is also considerable. With nine uncovered puts, you would owe a total of $45,000 if bean prices dropped $1 per bushel by expiration of the puts. There is also risk on the up side, but only once prices rise more than 60¢. Table 14 shows the hypothetical results at expiration on such a 10:1 ratio-writing strategy.

There is no requirement to maintain the 10:1 ratio at all times. As prices change, the puts will vary in price, and you may wish to take advantage of a temporary price rise to offset some of your short put positions. For instance, with prices 10¢ above the strike at initiation, the puts might be trading at 6¢. But five or six weeks later with, say, just days to expiration and higher bean prices, the puts won't be worth much at all, perhaps $\frac{1}{4}$¢ or $\frac{1}{2}$¢. You can take advantage of the situation by buying back the puts and pocketing your profits. By doing so, you lessen the risk should prices subsequently tumble and the puts suddenly appear likely to become profitable. You won't gain the last penny or half-cent per bushel, but since when did greed make a sensible trading strategy? Strange things have happened just prior to the expiration of

Table 14. Example of a 10:1 ratio write: Write ten May 575 soybean puts and sell one May futures contract.

May Futures Price at Expiration of 575 Puts	Gain (Loss) on May Futures	Gain (Loss) on Ten 575 May Puts	Net Gain (Loss)
550	35¢	(250¢)	($10,750)
575	10¢	60¢	$3,500
600	(15¢)	60¢	$2,250
625	(40¢)	60¢	$1,000

option contracts. Just ask some of the hapless stock-index call writers who severely regret holding soon-to-expire option contracts.

A more aggressive strategy, which is the mirror image of the "rolling down" strategy used to defend the 2:1 ratio write using calls, is to "roll up" the puts. With rising prices, you will have declining put prices. This means paper profits for the writer. Why not play the market by buying back the May 575 puts and writing the May 600 puts? The decision to undertake such a strategy must be based on market action, however. And there is significant risk involved. Let's say prices rise to a point where the May 600s are at the money. What's to say prices won't soon break back to the 570 area? In that situation, if you've written the 600-strike puts, guess what will happen? Everyone of them will be exercised against you, and you will be left with long futures at $6.00 a bushel in a $5.75 soybean market. The result will be big paper losses, with the likelihood of still greater losses ahead. Being aggressive is fine, but you must know what you are doing.

The more practical strategy is to use a flexible-ratio write strategy. Write just four or five calls or puts against each futures position, and take them off or add to the position as the market dictates. But don't place yourself in a position where you could be severely hurt in the event of price adversity.

Striking a Balance

The 2:1 ratio write using options and futures is popular because it consists of one covered and one uncovered option. In the event of price adversity, the futures position will offset any loss on one option, leaving just the single other option as a potential problem. As you add multiple short option positions, however, you greatly enhance your profit possibilities. There is only one drawback: you also enhance your liability. The ideal is to strike a balance between risk and potential reward.

One technique that many traders rely on is to establish a writing program. Instead of engaging in a variable hedging strategy on a haphazard basis, the would-be variable-hedge strategist reasons that despite occasional losses, over time, a regular variable program makes sense. Hence, he buys futures and writes calls, or shorts futures and writes puts, on an ongoing basis. So many calls against futures in the May contract, so many in July, and so on right around the calendar year.

A word of caution here. You don't want to become overly mechanical. If you have reason to believe a big move is coming in either direction, it's better to abandon a buy/write program for the short term. But given choppy, directionless markets, a variable writing strategy should churn out the profits month in and month out.

How do you set up such a buy/write program? Simply by deciding which commodity to specialize in and then tracking the market. Upon expiration of the near-term options (or sooner), you will roll into the next active contract month. By the way, it pays to keep the buy/write program separate from whatever else you are doing in the market — hedging, spreading, or whatever.

How do you know the future direction of the market? You don't. No one does. The buy/write strategy is based on playing the percentages, however, which over time should prove you a winner. The point is, you must keep at the program and take a businesslike approach. For instance, let's say you want to implement such a program in soybeans. You are committed to writing out-of-the-money calls against long futures positions in a ratio of 6:1 — six short calls against each futures position. Assuming you concentrate on capturing time value on the nearby months, you might be able to write the calls for about 6¢ each, or about $1,800. You can probably use the strategy at least four times a year.

The Option Hedge

Are you strictly a futures trader who wants to use options for their insurance qualities? Are you a hedger who doesn't welcome a cash drawdown in the futures market even if you are growing cash-rich out on the farm? Do you want to avoid margin calls once and forever?

Well, you might want to look at options as a cheap insurance policy on your market activities. If you can admit that you are occasionally wrong in the futures market — and are tired of paying the price in horrendous losses — perhaps it is time you purchased options to safeguard all your futures positions.

It works like this. If you are long in futures, you purchase a corresponding put option; short sellers will purchase calls. The options, of course, will be for the same commodity and the same delivery month as the long futures. This is a particularly suitable strategy for the futures trader who takes long-term positions. The greater the potential reward of a position, the greater your interest in protecting the position with a call or a put. And you won't ever have to worry about losing more than you can afford. The purchase of the put or the call makes the risk predetermined.

How much risk are you willing to withstand? The answer to this question will determine which strike price to buy. Let's say you are a short seller in futures, looking for a substantial decline in prices. Your protective stop in this strategy will be the strike price of your call. Once above the strike, the call will have intrinsic value, which will mirror any loss on the futures. But the question is: Which strike? Let's consider the alternatives.

One strategy is to purchase the call after the futures have moved down in price. At this stage, you have a profit on the futures, and you wish to protect the paper profit. In this strategy, you are using the option as a stop — a strategy we'll discuss in greater detail shortly. One way of doing this is to purchase a call at the prevailing market price. Buy the call, and your profit is assured.

Another strategy is to purchase a deeply out-of-the-money call against the short futures. The advantage of this strategy is that the call will be relatively inexpensive. You can buy out-of-the-money soybean calls that still offer some measure of protection for 2¢ or 3¢ per bushel. The drawback to this strategy is that you're probably throwing money away. The call will probably never prove profitable — nor, for that matter, would you want it to. But, just in case, it might be worth the investment. Another problem is that the loss on the short futures would be quite high by the time prices soared above the strike price, and you may not wish to lose that amount. The deep-in-the-moneys don't make much sense either, since you are paying primarily for intrinsic value — needlessly purchasing value that might otherwise be leveraged. And that leaves the at-the-money options, which are perhaps the best buy, since you receive protection while paying just for time value.

Let's look at an example. Anticipating a decline in live-cattle prices, you sell short June live-cattle futures at a price of 66.50 and simultaneously purchase a corresponding number of live-cattle June 66 calls for a premium of 1.80 points, or $720 each. The June 66 calls are

Table 15. Example of an option hedge using short cattle futures and a long call.

June Futures Price at Expiration	Gain (Loss) on June Futures	Gain (Loss) on June Call	Net Gain (Loss)
64	2.50	(1.80)	$280
66	.50	(1.80)	($520)
68	(1.50)	.20	($520)
70	(3.50)	2.20	($520)

slightly in the money when June futures trade at 66.50, so even with stationary prices, you'll get back .50 points, or $200, on each call. Should prices break as you anticipate, the calls will be abandoned. Should prices rise, however, the futures will be bought back at a loss. The net loss will be the cost of the call minus whatever intrinsic value it contains at the time of purchase. The bottom line is: your risk is precisely $720. Table 15 shows the respective gains and losses for this strategy, assuming just one long call for each short sale of futures.

In the example, the call is used strictly as insurance lest prices move higher. Since the call had some intrinsic value at the time of purchase, this cash value ($200) is realized should the call be exercised or sold upon expiration. Figure 9 shows how purchasing a call against a short sale in futures protects the investor against unlimited loss to the up side while reducing profits to the down side by no more than the cost of the premium.

The option hedge is equally effective in providing insurance for the futures trader who is bullish on the market. Only in this instance, the investor purchases a put to protect the long futures position instead of purchasing a call against the short futures position. Assuming the strike of the put is identical with the entry on the long futures, the total risk is the premium cost. No matter how far futures prices fall, the investor using an option hedge will be liable only for the cost of the put option.*

Let's consider an example. With live-cattle futures for June delivery trading at 65.72, the in-the-money June 66 put is available for 1.70. The bullish cattle trader purchases one June futures contract and buys one June 66 cattle put for a premium of 1.70 points, or $680. The total

---

* This does not mean that the investor will not be required to post margin against the long futures position should prices decline. He will have to keep the position fully margined at all times. However, the paper profits on the put will, in part, offset any losses on the long futures position. Upon expiration of the put, the investor will receive the cash value the option retains through exercising the option or selling it.

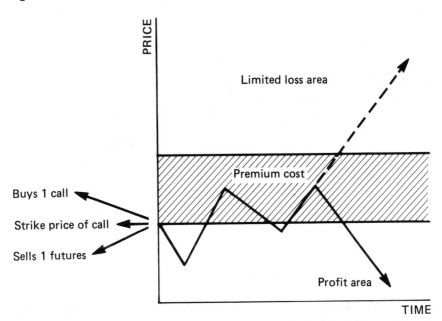

Figure 9.   Example of an option hedge — buying a call against a short futures position.

risk on the trade is $680. At the same time, the trader can earn virtually unlimited profit should futures prices soar. Table 16 shows the theoretical values at expiration.

Once again, look at the maximum loss on the trade. If you purchase a put as protection for a long futures position, your risk is limited to the cost of the put. If you anticipate substantially higher cattle prices, the put provides cheap insurance. If, however, you anticipate steady to moderately higher prices, you may want to forget about buying the insurance protection, since the cost of the premium must be overcome in

Table 16.   Example of an option hedge — long cattle futures and a long put.

June Futures Price at Expiration	Gain (Loss) on June Futures	Gain (Loss) on June Put	Net Gain (Loss)
64	(1.72)	.30	($570)
66	.27	(1.70)	($570)
68	2.27	(1.70)	$230
70	4.27	(1.70)	$1,030

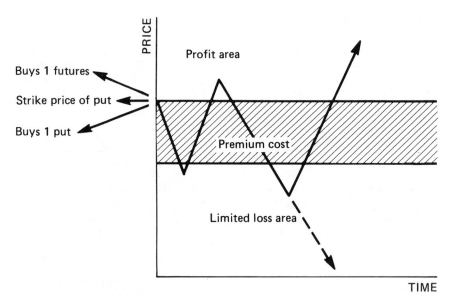

Figure 10. Example of an option hedge — buying a call against a long futures position.

the futures market on the long position. Figure 10 illustrates the concept of buying a put against a long futures position for protection.

To use an insurance analogy, you can cut down on your costs in the option hedge by increasing your "deductible." To do this, simply purchase options that are deeply out of the money. The further the options are out of the money, the lower their cost. However, in the event of an adverse market move against your futures position, these out-of-the-money options can provide enormous leverage should the market make them profitable. The actual cost of each option will depend on a variety of factors, such as the relation of the strike price to the market price, the volatility of the market, the price outlook for futures, and even interest rates. But even a glance at the futures tables can give you a clue to how inexpensive this type of price insurance can be.

Let's say you are a bull on corn futures prices and are looking to provide price insurance for the long positions you presently hold. You'll want to investigate the put option prices, since you want to be able to "put" the long futures at the strike to achieve a fixed floor price. At recent price levels, December corn futures, with more than nine months left to expiration, are trading in the $2.60 a bushel area — a low price by historical standards. Nevertheless, you may still want down-side protection.

So you scan the options tables, and here's what you come up with. The at-the-money December 260 put is available for about 9½¢ per bushel, whereas the December 250 put is available for just 4½¢ — 5¢ cheaper. If you are willing to risk another 10¢ decline, you can still assure yourself a floor price of $2.50 per bushel by purchasing the December 250 put. Your cost is $225 versus $475 for the at-the-money puts. That's a full eight months of insurance (remember, the corn puts expire a month before the futures) with a total risk of 10¢ per bushel (the difference between entry and the strike) for just $225. Having paid 4½¢ per bushel for the puts, you only need a rally of that magnitude in nine months to repay their cost.

Another feature of this strategy is that you need not risk even the full 4½¢-per-bushel premium cost. Let's say prices rise as you expect and the long futures have profits. Chances are the out-of-the-money December corn puts, falling still further out of the money, will lose value. As long as time value remains, however, the puts will be worth something. When they were only 10¢ out of the money, they served as a floor and provided the trader with peace of mind. Now that the bull trend is under way, however, their usefulness begins to vanish. So you can sell the puts for what they will bring in the market — say, 2¢ per bushel. This will limit your cost to just 2½¢, or $125, to protect a contract valued at more than $13,000. If you wish, you can always purchase some higher-strike puts — say, the 280s — to ensure a new floor for your hard-won futures profits.

This brings us to yet another use for the options hedge — as a protective stop-loss mechanism to ensure profitability on a futures position. Let's say you are a futures trader who has held a position for two or three months, and the market is behaving favorably. What is your risk? That prices might move against you. You could, of course, simply place a stop-loss order and exit the market by using some sort of trailing stop — that is, a stop that is moved up or down to "trail" the market. But this strategy has its drawbacks. You might well be "stopped out" on a modest, and somewhat meaningless, gyration in futures prices. You might well have been correct in your original analysis. Why risk being stopped out and perhaps having to chase prices when you can purchase options that will establish a price floor or ceiling (depending on your position) no matter what happens? Used in this manner, options can guarantee you a pre-established price.

For example, let's say you saw the enormous bear market in grains coming some months and years ago, and you shorted corn futures when they were $1.00 a bushel higher. Seeing the bear market as a relatively long-term move of several months duration, you may be reluctant to liquidate your position, because you anticipate still further declines. One method of ensuring a profit on the short futures is to purchase out-of-the-money calls. With December corn futures at $2.60 a bushel, you might purchase December 280 calls for 4¢ per bushel. Again, this is cheap insurance that not only provides you with a certain amount of peace of mind but also guarantees you profit resulting from the difference in price from where you originally shorted the futures and the strike price of the calls.

The advantage of such a purchase over stops is that you can wait to the expiration of the option to see whether it will prove profitable or not. That is, corn prices might rally above $2.80 momentarily, only to collapse later. As the holder of December 280 calls, you don't have to worry whether the rally will continue or not. Instead, you can watch the rally and hold onto the futures position. If prices subsequently break, fine — you are still short. If prices soar back above your original short sale price, no problem — you have the right to purchase the futures at the 280 strike. In either event you can't lose beyond the cost of the call plus the difference between today's market price and the strike price. It is a strategy tailor-made for an individual who likes to capture the big trend but doesn't want to risk giving back his paper profits.

A variation of this strategy is to hedge the futures with calls at different strikes. This will give you a guarantee of so much return on one portion and so much on another portion. In the preceding example, let's say you were short a total of 50,000 bushels of corn, or ten contracts. With December corn trading at 260, you might want to purchase three calls with a strike of 260, three calls with a strike of 270, three calls with a strike of 280, and one 290-strike call. The trade-off will be the premium you pay for each call versus the potential reward. Are you willing to pay, say, 10¢ or 11¢ per bushel for an at-the-money call when you can have the out-of-the-money, higher-strike call for half that amount, or even less? The decision, of course, is yours. By purchasing calls to hedge a short futures position in this manner, you are agreeing to establish an average price guarantee on the position. As always, the cost will be the premium expense — the same sort of expense you have to ponder whenever you purchase insurance.

Getting Your Hedge to Be Delta Neutral

You won't always be able to hedge your futures position with an option whose strike matches the market price. In order to achieve a hedge that protects the futures completely, you will want to be delta neutral. Delta measures the change in an option's value for a given change in the underlying futures. The futures price, by definition, always has a value of 1.00. Hence, an option with a delta of 1.00 would move one to one with the futures. For a variety of reasons, most options have a delta that is considerably less than 1. For puts, which increase in value as prices fall, delta is expressed as a negative number.

For instance, with soybeans trading at 580, the 600 calls aren't going to have a delta of 1.00. Why should a 1¢ move in the soybean futures from 580 to 581 translate into a 1¢ move in the 600 call, which is still far out of the money? For obvious reasons, the call wouldn't move on a one-to-one basis; hence its delta would be considerably less — perhaps only .05.

Now, suppose you wish to hedge a futures position in a manner that completely protects you against a move in the futures. To do so, you would need a position that is *delta neutral* — that is, one that moves one to one with the futures. Hence, if you lose 5¢ in futures, you would gain 5¢ in options. To make your position delta neutral, you need to take on enough option positions to protect yourself on a one-to-one basis. Therefore, if an option has a delta of .50, you would need exactly two options to offset the losses on the futures; if the option's delta were .25, you would need four options; and so on.

This concept of delta neutrality is important, because it helps you fine-tune your strategy to avoid needless losses. In general, the rule is that you should strive to be delta neutral. When you are, a move one way or another will be completely offset by a comparable move in the other instrument.

Knowing how many options to use to hedge a futures contract is just one function of delta. Another function is to know how much an option's premium should rise or fall given a 1-point move in the underlying futures. Yet a third function of delta is to determine how many options are needed to hedge another option. When hedging options with options, use similar thinking. An option with a delta of .25 will be delta neutral against an option with a .50 delta only when you have twice as many of the former.

Writing Covered Options

If you write an option and own the underlying position, you are considered a "covered" writer. This is in comparison with a so-called "naked" writer, who doesn't have a position in the underlying futures. You can write options either covered or uncovered. The main difference between the two strategies is that naked writing is far more risky, since you stand to have a short position at the strike price should you write a call, or a long position at the strike should you write a put. By writing "covered," you already have the underlying position.

Keep in mind that covered writing is a strategy designed to capture declining time value. You might take a long futures position and write a call against it. The opposite tactic is to take a short position and write a put.

Let's look at the advantages and drawbacks of covered writing, starting with the short seller who writes puts. Let's say you sell one August live-cattle futures short and write an at-the-money August 66 live-cattle put for a premium of 1 point, or $400. Your account is credited with the $400, and this income is yours to keep, regardless of the subsequent movement of futures prices. If prices stay where they are until expiration (an unlikely event), the put will expire worthless and the futures will be neither a gain nor a loss. The net result will be a $400 gain minus any commission costs. Should prices decline over the life of the option, the put will gain in value and ultimately be exercised against you. However, since you are already short August live-cattle futures, having a long position at the strike will only result in the profits on the short futures being transferred to the account of the owner of the put. You will have an opportunity loss on the futures. But you still get to keep the $400 in premium income.

The only real risk is that prices may rise. This would result in losses on the short futures position that are greater than the income derived from writing the put. Above the strike, the put will prove worthless to the buyer. Hence, you will receive the full $400 income. But what if prices rise, say, 3 points, to $69 per hundredweight? If this happens and you don't take defensive action, you will have a net loss of 2 points (3 points lost on the futures, partly offset by a 1-point gain in the put writing income).

Figure 11 shows how the writing income from the put provides a small cushion of profit above the strike. While it effectively locks out profits on the short position should cattle prices decline, it does give the writer the premium income. Thus, it is profitable over a wide range of prices — from just above the strike down to zero. The covered write is a conservative strategy that results in steady profits *if* the covered writer is quick to take defensive action in the event the market rises while he is writing puts and selling futures.

Buying futures and writing calls has a profit potential similar to that of selling futures and writing puts. The only difference is that in the case of the covered call, the risk will exist on the down side. If the market

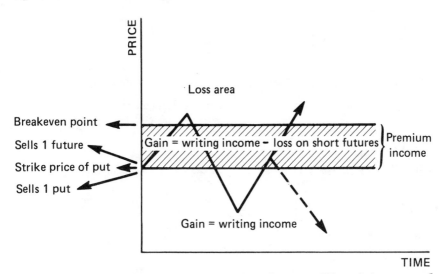

Figure 11. Example of a covered write—selling futures and writing puts.

tumbles more than the value of the call, the covered writer will sustain a net loss. Using the example of the at-the-money August 66 live-cattle calls, one could purchase August cattle futures and write a corresponding number of calls against the position. The result would be total safety on the up side. As long as the calls remain in the money, chances are they will be exercised and the long position called away. If fact, what happens is that a short position is given to the call writer at the strike. Hence, having purchased one August live-cattle futures at 66 and having a short position given to him by virtue of exercise, the trader will end up with a position that is a wash. Nevertheless, the writer gets to keep the premium income. On the down side, the writing income provides a cushion of safety equal to the value of the call. Below that point, losses on the long cattle futures will exceed the writing income, and the covered writer will have a loss. The strategy is illustrated in Figure 12.

Let's look at an example of a covered write. Anticipating steady to lower prices, you might decide to write an August 66 live-cattle put for a premium of 1.70 ($850) against the sale of the underlying August live-cattle futures at 65.75. Don't let the fact that the put is slightly in the money bother you. For our purposes, the August 66 put is the at-the-money option when the August futures are trading at 65.75. One must assume that the cash portion of the option—the area between the strike price and the market—really belongs to the buyer. So expect to

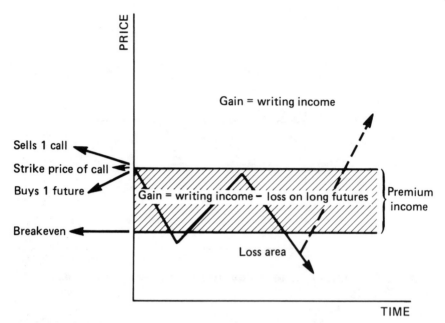

Figure 12.   Example of a covered write — buying futures and writing calls.

repay him this amount should the option prove profitable to exercise. Your real writing income, therefore, is somewhat less than the premium. As long as prices don't soar upward (in which case you'll find yourself in a loss position) or plummet dramatically (locking out profits on the short futures), you stand to profit from this covered-writing strategy. A list of potential returns on the covered write is shown in Table 17.

Selecting a Good Covered-Writing Opportunity

Now that we've looked at the principles involved in covered writing, it's time to see whether we can select an actual option to write against futures in the daily futures and option quotes in your newspaper. What's the best relation of market to strike price? How do you decide on the proper duration to write? No doubt you are aware that some options offer far better profit opportunites than others. Did you know there are options you should never write, no matter how inviting the prospects for profit? Why should you haphazardly write options when there are clear-cut signs that some options are better writing candidates than others?

If you're worried about selecting the wrong option to write, a few simple guidelines should help you choose, if not the best ones, at least not the worst options. In the first place, covered writing is a relatively safe practice. As long as you control the underlying futures, nothing dire is going to happen. Second, accept as inevitable that a number of your covered writes will be exercised against you. That is, if you write calls and buy futures, a rise in the market will result in the call being exercised and your long futures being "called away."

When the call is exercised, your account will be treated as having sold one futures position. Since you are already long on futures, the transaction will result in the long being sold at the strike price — hence, you will have no position. If you purchased the futures below the strike of the call, you'll even have a profit — but you will miss the move above the strike. Such is life. The real risk, remember, exists on the other side of the equation, where market adversity means you might lose more on the futures than you stand to earn on the short put or call. So be prepared for the eventualities — namely, that occasionally you'll make less by covered writing and sometimes you'll even have a loss.

Selecting the proper put or call to write against a position in futures is relatively straightforward once you understand a few simple rules. First and foremost, always make it a rule to write an out-of-the-money option. You want to capture time value, not cash value. An in-the-money option will result in a larger net inflow, so it will *seem* that you are making more — but you won't necessarily be making more in reality. Why? First, assuming the market stays steady, you'll have to pay back the cash value to the buyer at expiration or upon exercise. Second, in-the-money options can be exercised anytime — even the day after you write one. Third, because you have to margin short options, you're going to needlessly tie up money you could use for more productive purposes, such as writing additional out-of-the-money puts or calls.

Another rule is that you want to avoid soon-to-expire options. The time value in such options isn't sufficient to justify the risk involved. Not

Table 17. Example of a covered write — sell cattle futures and write a put.

August Futures Price at Expiration	Gain (Loss) on August Futures	Gain (Loss) on August Put	Net Gain (Loss)
64	1.75	(.30)	$580
66	(.25)	1.70	$580
68	(2.25)	1.70	($220)
70	(4.25)	1.70	($1,020)

only will commission costs make writing such options uneconomical, but sudden and unexpected volatility in such options can wreak havoc with your writing program.

Finally, you want to stay away from options that have a long time left to expiration. That means options with six to nine months left to run. Why? Here again, you want to follow the middle path. Options expiring in five or six days don't make sense for off-the-floor traders, for the reasons explained. If the option is trading at only $\frac{1}{2}$¢, how are you going to make money if you are paying commissions? You won't. On the other hand, the option that retains six or nine months in time premium isn't going to lose that time premium tomorrow. In fact, it will lose its time premium at a very, very slow rate, increasing in speed only when the maturity date appears on the horizon.

The bottom line is, you want to concentrate on options that are "close to the money" but not in the money and that have a month or two left to expiration. The problem with deeply out-of-the-money options is that their premiums are too small. On the other hand, in-the-moneys, while they may contain a substantial premium, have the wrong kind of premium — cash premium — as opposed to the eroding time premium, which the writer will capture no matter which way the market moves.

Now that we've looked at some of the guidelines, let's consider an actual options table. The time is mid-March, and live-cattle futures are trading at $62.00 for April delivery, $65.25 for June delivery, and $64.90 for August delivery. Table 18 lists the prices for options on live-cattle futures.

One factor you'll have to contend with in scanning the options and futures prices is that the futures price represents the settlement price on the day, whereas the option price quoted in the newspaper represents the last trade of the day, which might have occurred 30 minutes prior to

Table 18.   Sample price quotes for options on live-cattle futures (quotes in cents per lb, for contract size of 40,000 lb).

Strike Price	Calls — Last			Puts — Last		
	Apr	June	Aug	Apr	Jun	Aug
62	0.57	—	—	0.57	0.40	0.55
64	0.07	2.20	—	2.05	0.95	1.20
66	—	1.20	1.15	4.00	1.95	2.22
68	—	0.57	0.60	6.00	3.27	3.62
70	—	0.27	0.27	8.00	5.00	—
72	—	0.12	0.12	10.00	6.82	7.15
74	—	0.05	—	—	—	—

the close. There is no guarantee that you, or anyone else, will obtain the actual prices quoted here under real market conditions.

To begin our writing selection, let's just concentrate on calls for a moment. Remember, the covered write will involve purchasing live-cattle futures and writing calls. Since it is already mid-March, the April options can be eliminated entirely. Options on futures expire the month *prior* to expiration of the futures — so, at best, you are looking at six or seven days to expiration in the April contracts. That leaves June and August options. In a few days, when the April contracts expire, the October contracts will start trading. As a writer, you will probably want to concentrate on the June options, because they will lose their time value faster than the August options. This selection of the June options, however, is based on your stance in the market. If, for instance, you were a buyer of live-cattle calls, you'd probably want to purchase the August contracts because of the greater time left to expiration.

Next, consider the relationship of the market price of the underlying futures to the strike of the call. With June futures trading at 65.25, you will probably want to write the out-of-the-money June 66 call for a premium of 1.20 points, or $480. Why not the June 68s? They are trading for .57 points, less than half as much. It actually depends on how bullish you are on the market. If you are genuinely bullish on cattle futures, the June 68s are a better deal. Not only do you stand to capture the .57 points in writing income, but the long futures can capture the entire profit on the difference in price between the market price of 65.25 and the strike price of 68.00. The 66 calls will limit the upward potential on the futures to just .75 points.

One call you will want to avoid is the in-the-money 64 call. Too much cash value. Also, you probably want to forget the 70- and 72-strike calls. Not enough writing income, and a sudden surge in cattle prices could result in paper profits on the short calls that you might want to avoid even if you are long in the futures. In the real world of futures and options trading, a sudden increase in prices and higher volatility will cause the 70-strike call and the 72-strike call to increase rapidly in price — even if futures prices remain well below 70. For the $48 to $108 in total writing income, you don't need the headache of knowing that those options are now worth 30 or 40 times that amount. That leaves the 66- and 68-strike calls.

Which to choose? Again, it depends on your analysis of the market. For a stable to slightly bullish market, the lower-strike June 66 call is the best. If you anticipate substantially higher cattle prices, sell the 68 call. You also have to take into account the amount of down-side protection each call offers. If you purchase June futures, the 66 call gives you precisely 1.20 points in down-side protection (to 64.05), whereas the higher-strike 68 call gives you less than half the protection. All things considered, you are probably better off with the June 66 call.

It is time to take the trade. Assuming that you are able to purchase the June live-cattle futures at 65.25 and simultaneously write the June 66 call for a premium of 1.20 points, your account will immediately be credited with the $480 in writing income. Your breakeven on the down side (commission costs aside) will be 64.05 (the entry level on the futures) minus the premium income on the call. Maximum profitability for the covered write is at the strike price of 66 — a total of $780 before commissions. That's the profit on both the call (which will expire worthless at that price) and the profit on the long futures. By the way, that profit will exist at expiration at any point higher than the strike as well. The real risk on this covered write exists when prices decline. There is no rule, of course, that you have to hold the short call until expiration. However, the call will retain some value as long as it has not expired. If you want to capture the entire writing income, you therefore have no choice but to hold the call and allow it to expire worthless.

One alternative that many option writers rely on is a formula for closing out winning short option positions once the bulk of the writing income is derived. For instance, with just days left to expiration and little chance of the 66 call ever proving profitable to its buyer, the premium may fall to .10 or .20 points. Why not buy back the option at that point? You have already earned at least 85 percent to 95 percent of the potential profit. The advantage of buying back options in this situation is that it allows you to look elsewhere for writing profits. With maturity of the June contract on the horizon, you might want to start looking at the August contracts for potential time value.

As you can see, the real advantage of covered writing is that it is fairly safe and that the market doesn't need to move much for you to make money. Indeed, this is a welcome strategy in the grain and meat markets of recent years. These markets have proved frustrating to countless futures traders who've bought and sold futures in hopes of some volatility entering the market. With this strategy, you need only sit back and let the profits develop slowly over time — and at very low risk!

Table 19 shows some of the hypothetical gains and losses on this covered write at expiration. As you can see, the strategy achieves its maximum profitability at the strike price or higher. You can achieve greater up-side potential by writing the higher-strike 68 call, but only at the cost of lessening your down-side protection.

Table 19. Example of a covered write using long June cattle at 65.25 and a short June 66 call at 1.20.

June Futures Price at Expiration	Gain (Loss) on June Futures	Gain (Loss) on June 66 Call	Net Gain (Loss)
62	(3.25)	1.20	($820)
64	(1.25)	1.20	($20)
66	.75	1.20	$780
68	2.75	(.80)	$780
70	4.75	(2.80)	$780

Use Low-Delta Options in Covered Writes

As a measure of the rate by which the option premium changes relative to a change in the corresponding futures, delta is a helpful indicator of a good writing opportunity. If you concentrate on writing out-of-the-money options, you shouldn't have too much problem on this score — an option's delta will approach 1.00 only when the option is in the money. But when selecting among several different options, look for one with low delta. Remember, as a writer of an option, you want the value to decline to zero by expiration. If it does, you profit by the entire premium. Delta is not a static measurement, however; over time, an option's delta will change. So expect change in this number. As long as the delta remains low, you can expect a positive movement in your futures position to translate into a modest negative change in your position. This is the situation that will prove profitable to you.

Writing Options Against Actuals

A strategy akin to covered writing in which the risk is strictly limited is available to commercial hedgers who have a potential long or short futures position by virtue of their position in the cash market. A grower of soybeans, for instance, has a potential short futures position, since the time will come when he will harvest his crop and want to sell his soybeans. Likewise, the commercial user of grain or livestock products will be a potential long hedger, since he will eventually want to take delivery of the cash commodity. One means of doing this, of course, is through the futures market. But whether the commercial grower or user uses the futures market in his marketing activities is immaterial to his actions in the options market. In that market he can write options for income, knowing that exercise will result only in a futures position—one which, he knows in advance, he can use in his marketing program. The bottom line in this strategy is that the writer either has the product to deliver or the willingness to purchase the commodity of the underlying futures contract.

Let's look at an example of a processor of soybeans who must take delivery of beans. His risk is that a soaring soybean market will increase his expenses. To hedge this risk, he would normally purchase soybean contracts, or be what is known as a "long hedger." By purchasing bean contracts, he establishes a purchasing price for soybeans. In the event of higher soybean prices, the profit on the long futures offsets the rise in the cash market. Declining cash prices would mean losses on the futures, but offsetting gains in the cash market. This is the classic hedging example.

Now let's look at the same processor, who is short soybeans and willing to take on a long futures position. Given this market stance, why not write put options with a strike price that might result in a long futures position for the writer if exercise occurs? First, if the option is not exercised (that is, prices stay above the strike), the writer will receive the writing income—funds to offset the higher cost of soybeans, which he'll eventually want to purchase. The other alternative is that soybean prices decline. If they fall below the strike, chances are the put option will be exercised and the soybean processor will receive a long futures position at the strike. This is precisely the position he wanted in the first instance—although he would wish, no doubt, to be long at a slightly lower price. The point is, he *is* long at a slightly lower price, since he received the writing income. If he receives 10¢ per bushel for writing each put, and the put is exercised and he is now long at the strike, his actual entry price on the long futures is the strike minus 10¢. If this is a price he can live with in his hedging activities, he has made a good trade.

Now let's turn the situation on its head. You are a farmer who needs $6.25 per bushel on his soybeans, but you would like a better profit if possible. You would like to be able to sell soybeans at 625. But you are reluctant to sell futures because of the finality of the decision. Once the futures are sold at $6.25 per bushel, that's the maximum you will receive. Let's say you decide, as an alternative, to write 625-strike calls against your cash position. Depending on market conditions, you might receive 25¢ per bushel for each call. Now you've created a range of prices over which you will achieve at least 625 and perhaps 25¢ more per bushel.

Assuming futures are at precisely 625 at expiration, the calls will expire worthless and you'll get the 25¢ writing income. Below 625, the calls will again be worthless; but you will have a 25¢ cushion of profit, giving you the target 625 even if futures trade as low as $6.00. Above 625, the call will be exercised. As a result, you will be given a short futures position at the strike price of 625. In addition, the original writing income of 25¢ is yours to keep. Hence, you have a potential maximum selling price of the strike plus the writing income, or 650. The only real risk is that prices may plummet more than 25¢. In that case, the loss in the market will offset any gain achieved by writing the options.

In summary, to write against actuals, you must first establish a price at which you would be willing to take on a long or short position in the futures market. You then write a put if you are willing to be long futures (that is, if you are short the actual commodity); conversely, you write a call if you are willing to be short futures (that is, if you are long the actual commodity). Stated another way, short futures hedgers (growers, livestock raisers, and so on) should write calls, and would-be long futures hedgers (processors, packing firms, and the like) should write puts.

> Example: A wheat farmer, willing to sell his crop at $4.00 a bushel, writes 400-strike September calls for a premium of 30¢ per bushel. His immediate gain is $1,500 per 5,000 bushels of wheat. If exercise occurs, he is prepared to be given a short wheat futures at $4.00 and subsequently provide delivery to the buyer. His risk is that the wheat market may collapse between the time he writes the call and expiration. Should this occur, he stands to lose more than the 30¢-per-bushel writing income. This may mean he will not achieve his selling price of $4.00 per bushel. However, he will have at least 30¢ per bushel more than if he had not hedged at all.

Typically, this approach will be taken when wheat prices are below $4.00 a bushel. By writing the call, the wheat farmer boosts his current income. Even if prices don't move higher, and the call isn't exercised and the farmer doesn't receive a short futures position at the strike, *the writing income provides sufficient additional revenue to establish a profit.* For instance, let's say the cash market price for wheat is $3.80 a bushel when he writes the 400-strike call. The writing income will provide him with the price he needs to earn over $4.00 a bushel *even if prices stay below $4.00 a bushel throughout the time he holds the short call.* Indeed, prices may stay under $4.00 after the call expires and the futures goes off the boards. Thus, one way to obtain a $4.10 selling price in a $3.80 market is to write calls.

Now suppose that, in our last example, wheat futures are trading above $4.00 a bushel. Another approach in that case is to write calls that are in the money. The writing income will then provide a cushion of profits should prices decline. Let's say prices on September wheat futures are $4.20 a bushel. By writing the call, whose intrinsic value will be at least 20¢, the farmer can ensure himself of some down-side protection and capture the declining time premium as well. With $4.20 September futures, chances are the 400-strike call will have some time value, if only 5¢ or 6¢. All things being equal — which, of course, they never are — if the option expired at precisely $4.20, the writer would receive the strike price ($4.00) plus the cash value component of the premium ($.20) plus the time value (say, another 5¢). Thus, the total price per bushel with futures selling price and writing income will amount to $4.25 a bushel — better than if he simply sold futures short at the market price of $4.20.

What about the commercial hedger who wouldn't mind receiving a long futures position? His posture on the market would be to write puts. In the event of exercise, he'll be long futures and, hopefully, fully hedged and prepared to take delivery if necessary. Here's an example that shows how it works.

> Example: A meat packer engaged in the wholesale trade with large retail chains requires box cars of live cattle. The wholesaler's risk, of course, is that rising prices of cattle will lower his profit margins. As long as he can purchase the live cattle at a price of $60 per hundredweight, he stands to earn a favorable return on his investment. He would prefer to be able to purchase cattle at $56 per hundredweight; but, this being the real world, he is willing to settle for $60 per hundredweight. He knows that if cattle prices rise above $64 per hundredweight, his operation will only break even. To hedge himself, therefore, he writes put options with a strike price of $60. With August live cattle trading at $60, he writes 60-strike August puts for a premium of 2.00 points ($800) each.

The writing of the puts ensures the meat packer a favorable price on his cattle within a given range. First, if prices stay steady, he effectively purchases the cattle at $58 — the $60 market price plus the $2 he receives in writing income. If prices decline, however, he still keeps the $2 in writing income, but he'll be able to purchase cattle, by exercising the long futures, at a price of $60 — still all right, since the net price stays $58. Finally, if prices rise, he is protected at least as far as $62. At $62, the put will expire worthless, since no one will want to sell cattle at $60 through exercise of the put if he can more profitably sell cattle in the market at $62. To the packer, however, $62 in the market will translate into a real price of $60, since he received $2 in writing income ($800 per car of cattle). Thus, the only real risk exists at higher prices, where the writing income won't offset the higher cost.

Writing Straddles in Conjunction with Futures

Straddle writing is a neutral trading strategy designed to capitalize on declining time premium. (See Appendix I for additional discussion of straddles.) The straddle writer gains his maximum profit if futures trade right at the strike upon expiration of the put and call. But let's add another position to the straddle-writing equation and see how the situation changes. What if you wrote an at-the-money straddle and simultaneously purchased the underlying futures? If we pull apart the components of such a trading strategy, you'll see that the call will be covered (if exercised, you have the long position, which will be offset by virtue of selling a contract at the strike) and the short put will be uncovered. Therefore, your risk will exist on the down side. Should prices decline, not only will your long futures lose you money, but the put will be exercised and you will find yourself long another contract at the strike price. In summary, you'll be short two contracts, both of them with losses.

Purchasing the long futures contract in conjunction with writing straddles involves a slightly more bullish outlook than outright straddle writing.

What if you sell a futures position short at the strike upon writing an at-the-money straddle? Your short put would be covered, but in the event of a rally, you'd find yourself short two contracts — one short sale taken upon initiation of the short straddle and the second due to exercise. The only protection you have in such a situation is the premium you receive for writing the straddle. This premium will be welcome in minor rallies — you may even emerge with a profit. But if you walk into a rip-roaring bull market, look out. Write straddles in conjunction with short futures when you are neutral to slightly bearish.

Writing Strangles in Conjunction with Futures

If there were ever a "have-your-cake-and-eat-it-too" strategy, this might be it. For when this strategy is properly applied, you stand to profit all around — on the short put, on the short call, and on either the long or short futures. Let's look closely at the strategy. First, the strangle consists of an out-of-the-money call and an out-of-the-money put.

Since you will be writing the strangle, both put and call are sold. Thus, you take in two premiums — and you'll be asked to perform only if the futures price rises *above* the call's strike or *below* the put's strike. (Chances are, only one option will be exercised). As long as prices remain *between* the two strike prices, however, you stand to gain 100 percent of both premiums.

To illustrate, let's say soybeans are trading at $6.30 and you write the out-of-the-money 650 call. This will give you one premium. Then you write the out-of-the-money 600 put for another premium. Now you have two premiums and considerable leeway to take defensive measures if prices rise or fall. But let's add to this equation a short-term point of view on the market. Let's say you are bearish on the near-term prospects for soybean prices. In addition to writing the strangle, therefore, you sell futures short at the market price of $6.30. Now, as prices fall, you stand to gain on the short futures. In fact, if, at expiration, prices trade *exactly* at the lower strike of the put at 600, you will achieve maximum profitability on the strategy. You will gain 30¢ on the short futures as well as pick up the premium for writing the call and the premium for writing the put, since both options will expire worthless. And if prices trade still lower and the put is exercised? In that case, the long futures that you, as a put writer, will be given at the strike will simply offset your short futures position — and you will still gain the difference between the initial sale of the futures and the strike price.

Obviously, this example has a bearish outlook. If you were more bullish, you might have purchased the underlying futures. The risk, of course, is that the potential liability on the futures is greater than the potential writing income. If you take in only 13¢ for writing the strangle and you end up losing more on the futures, you will have a net loss. But the advantage of this strategy is that it allows you to profit over a relatively wide range and the writing income serves to offset any loss on the futures. All in all, when intelligently applied, this can be an effective strategy for a neutral to slightly bullish or bearish market.

Writing Puts to Acquire Futures

There are many reasons, as we've seen, for writing options against futures. But what about writing options to *acquire* futures? One popular strategy is to write puts in order to acquire a long futures position below the current market price. Let's say you are fundamentally bullish on prices. You want to buy futures, but you also would like a somewhat better price than is available in the market right now. One alternative, of course, is to simply stand by and wait. Perhaps futures will trade lower, perhaps they won't.

The put writer who wishes to take on the long futures does so with a particular idea in mind. First, he knows that he doesn't want to buy at today's price. Second, he would like some income while he is waiting for prices to reach a support level (that is, a price where buyers are willing to purchase futures and support the market) — somewhere below the present market. Third, he is quite willing to miss the futures move entirely if prices don't retrace first and simply move higher. Given these conditions, he willingly writes puts.

What are the benefits of put writing to acquire futures? Well, there's the income, of course. When you add the income to the lower price at which you will acquire a long futures position if the put is exercised, you get an entry price that's below the market. You also achieve writing income if the market moves higher and the put remains unexercised. As a writer, you get to keep the premium. Your only real risk is that the market might move down and you are exercised against, meaning you acquire a long position at the strike — and then the market plummets. But what would you do if you didn't write puts and simply purchased futures? You would sell your long futures at a loss and run. That's the only sensible thing to do. With put writing to acquire a long position, you have the writing income to lessen the loss or enhance whatever profit exists.

At the time of this writing, an interesting opportunity exists to acquire futures positions by selling puts. Corn futures are trading just a couple of cents off their life-of-contract lows. The December corn futures, with some nine months left to expiration, are particularly attractive. December corn futures are in the $2.62-per-bushel area, and the December 250 puts are available for 5¢, or $250 each. What if you were anticipating weaker corn futures over the near term, with a very real possibility of higher prices five or six months from now? What's more, what if you see a lot of buying in the $2.50-per-bushel area for corn? Writing the December 250s would prove a very attractive opportunity. On the one hand, the options are a full 12¢ out of the money. You'll need a break in the market below life-of-contract lows for the 250 puts to ever have any intrinsic value. So there's a good chance the puts will expire worthless and you'll pick up the full 5¢ premium on as many as you write.

But what if prices decline? Wouldn't you find corn futures at $2.50 a bushel an attractive buying opportunity? The down-side risk, after all, is minimal. Moreover, your real price of entry at expiration won't be $2.50 anyway. The actual price will be the 250 strike price *minus* the 5¢

writing income, or $2.45 a bushel. So the strategy is this: you write puts, take on the long futures position if necessary, and hold the position. If corn futures don't tumble further, you should emerge from the trade in healthy financial shape.

Synthetic Futures

Synthetic futures are proxies for outright net long or short positions created by using options alone. *Synthetic long futures consist of a long call option and a short put option with the same strike.* Generally established at modest cost (the writing income of the short option tends to offset the cost of the long option), synthetic futures tend to have similar profit/loss characteristics as the outright futures position for which they are a substitute.

For example, instead of buying November soybeans, you want to establish the synthetic long futures by purchasing the at-the-money November 600 call for 10¢ and writing the at-the-money November 600 put for 9½¢. Your cost will be the difference between what you take in and what you pay out, or ½¢ ($25 per contract). As long as soybean prices rise, the call will match the rise dollar for dollar at expiration above the strike. Declining prices, however, will result in losses on the position, since the put option (which you sold) will be gaining in value for its buyer. This, of course, would also be the situation if you had gone long November beans and the market had declined. The risk is the same.

Synthetic short futures consist of a long put option and a short call option. Like the short futures position, synthetic short futures give you profits as prices decline. An at-the-money put will gain dollar for dollar below the strike at expiration. Hence, the only cost of synthetic short futures is the cost of the long put, minus the writing income you receive on the short call. The liability on the position will be similar to that in selling futures short. As the call gains in value (when prices rise), the writer is liable to the holder. An example of a synthetic short futures position would be the purchase of a May 65 cotton put and the simultaneous sale of a May 65 cotton call when the underlying futures are at 65.

For additional discussion of synthetic futures, see Appendix I.

Conversions and Reverse Conversions

Although these terms are used in football, conversions and reverse conversions refer to option strategies as well. If you understand what synthetic long and short futures are, you'll understand these two strategies, since they involve just the addition of a futures contract. First, the *conversion* is the combination of a long futures contract and a synthetic short futures position (selling a call and buying a put at the same strike price).

Let's take an example. You establish the synthetic short futures by writing a May 65 cotton call and purchasing a May 65 cotton put. Then you purchase a May futures contract in cotton. The conversion is essentially an arbitrage strategy that locks-in the initial credit when the conversion is established. Since you are fully hedged against all eventualities, whether the market moves up or down is of little consequence to you when you use the conversion or reverse conversion strategy. For the conversion, the payoff at expiration is equal to the strike price of the options minus the current futures price, plus the call premium minus the put premium.

As the name suggests, the *reverse conversion* involves just the opposite of the conversion. In the reverse conversion strategy, you short a futures contract against a synthetic long position (buying a call and writing a put). Taking its component parts, you might first establish the synthetic long futures by purchasing an at-the-money May 575 soybean call and simultaneously writing an at-the-money May 575 soybean put. To establish the reverse conversion, you then sell short May soybean futures. Like the conversion, this is an arbitrage strategy whose payoff is equal to the current futures price minus the strike price of the options, plus the put premium minus the call premium. When established at an advantageous price, this strategy results in a risk-free profit that will be gained regardless of the subsequent price movement. Since the potential profits of conversions and reverse conversions are relatively small, it is important to take into account the impact of commission costs. Normally, this type of risk-free arbitrage is used only by professional traders, who do not pay commissions.

6

Option Spread Strategies

You can't trade options for long without recognizing the potential for sophisticated and potentially profitable spreading strategies among options on the same and different commodities. Spreading means essentially purchasing an option of one strike and duration while simultaneously selling another of different strike and/or duration. It can be an important source of revenue for both aggressive and conservative options traders who understand what the various strategies involve. As with any market strategy, it helps to know in advance precisely what you are looking for in a trade. Moreover, it helps to know what to do when you are wrong—when to take defensive action.

I've already indicated that a number of strategies were designed to cope with specific market situations—bull markets, bear markets, stationary markets, and so on. Then we looked at combining futures and options. But what about combining options with options? Aren't there profitable techniques in which you buy and write options together? There are, indeed. And in this chapter, we are going to look at the most popular ones to see whether a particular strategy will fit our trading needs.

Capitalizing on the Option Trade-Off

Why trade spreads? Aren't they more complicated than simply buying a put or call? Or, for that matter, writing a put or call? True, option spreads are somewhat complicated, because you are dealing with two or more options that are bought and sold at different strikes or have different durations, or both. On the other hand, option spreads can make an options play even safer—and lower in cost!

Spreading options enables the investor to capitalize on the inevitable trade-offs. What are these trade-offs? Well, if you are a seller of options, you have an unlimited risk, just as in futures trading. If, on the other hand, you are a buyer of options, you must pay a nonreturnable premium, which you must recover in the market if you are going to profit. The advantage of option spreads, however, is that it can lessen the risks associated with writing while simultaneously cutting down on the key disadvantage of option buying — namely, the premium cost. In short, under certain circumstances, option spreading allows the best of both worlds — the ability to profit within a range of prices at very low cost. In fact, option spreading, when used properly, can prove a powerful tool in your portfolio. That's why it is so popular among professional floor traders, who are always looking to hedge risk.

How can you capitalize on the option trade-off by using spreads? One method is to use option spreads instead of outright net buying positions. For instance, let's say you can purchase an at-the-money October 64 live-cattle call for 1.85 points, or $740. What would you say if I told you that virtually the same trade could be accomplished by purchasing a cattle spread for just .80 points, or $320? That's less than half as much. In the second instance, you wouldn't be buying exactly the same thing, of course. But you would be obtaining meaningful leverage and better downside protection.

Here's what we are talking about. Let's say that instead of purchasing an at-the-money October 64 live-cattle call for the prevailing price of 1.85 points, you purchased the same call and simultaneously *wrote* the higher-strike October 66 call for a premium of 1.05 points. Now you are spread as follows: bought one October 64 call for 1.85 and sold one October 66 call for 1.05. Your cost is the difference between what you paid (1.85 points) and what you received for writing (1.05 points), or just .80 points, equal to $320. For this modest investment, you stand to earn the difference between the lower strike and the higher strike, or 2.00 points, a profit of 250 percent if October futures trade at or above the higher strike at expiration.

The Vertical Bull Call Spread

In the vertical bull call spread, the most you can lose is the initial debit, or the difference between the amount you pay and the amount you receive. The strategy consists of buying a lower-strike call and writing a higher-strike call for the same duration. Having established the spread, you have the same profit/loss possibilities as a call buyer. But there is one key difference. The cost is lower, and the profit possibilities are limited to a predetermined profit range.

In our last example, you could have accomplished placing the vertical bull call spread for just $320, compared with a cost of $740 to purchase the lower-strike call option alone. In return for this saving, you must be prepared to give up the profit above the higher strike. Here's how it works. The higher-strike call enables the *buyer*— remember, you are the seller— to purchase a live-cattle futures contract at the strike price. That means that you, the seller, must perform on that call option if it is called away from you. That's the drawback of the strategy.

And the advantage? The risk of having the higher-strike short call exercised against you is covered because you own the lower-strike call. If the short call is exercised, you simply give up the additional profits *above* the higher strike. In the meantime, you capture all the profits between the two strikes—in this example, 2 points, or $800. As you can see, the option spread strategy enables you to profit within a specific range of prices.

The key advantage of the bull spread strategy is that within its parameters, the spread is *more profitable* than outright call buying. After all, ask yourself: With just two months left to expiration, what's more likely—a 2-point rise in cattle prices or a 10-point rise? If you have selected the former, you are better off bull-spreading. By bull-spreading, as in this example, you lower your initial cost of entry while enabling yourself to profit from a *modest* rise in prices.

One way to look at the spread is in terms of its maximum profitability versus its maximum potential risk. This gives us a percentage return. The maximum profit in this example is $480. Where did that figure come from? First you take the maximum return on the lower-strike call and then you subtract the initial cost of the spread. The lower-strike call can gain 2 points, or $800; above the 2-point gain, the lower-strike call's gain will be exactly offset by the higher-strike call's loss, resulting in a wash. From this maximum profit, you subtract the initial net cost, or $320. The result is $480. Now, let's go a step further. If you pay just $320 and have the potential to get back $480, the potential return is 150 percent! And that's on a modest rise in prices over two months' time. On a percentage basis, therefore, the return is quite good.

Now let's compare the risk involved in the bull spread with that involved in call buying. Which amount of money would you prefer to risk— $320 or $740? The answer is obvious.

When you look at the spread in terms of what is likely to happen, the bull spread also makes sense—again, within given guidelines.

Eliminating the possibility of a bull market, consider what will happen if you purchase just the lower-strike call for $740. Even if the market rises 2 points, the return will be just $800, hardly enough to pay commissions. And, of course, if the market goes down instead of up, you'll lose the entire $740 call premium cost. Arguably, a 10- or 12-point move in cattle prices would offer a substantially higher return on the call buying position. But when was the last time you got such a sharp run-up in prices? And when was the last time you got the run-up in two months' time? Obviously, you've got to be enormously lucky to catch such a move.

The argument for options is that while they won't allow you to capture the big moves, they are low in cost and, as a result, are more likely to allow you to earn profits *consistently* over time. That, in a nutshell, is the option trade-off advantage.

A Bull Spread Example

The whole purpose of the bull option spread is to enable the investor to profit from a rise in prices at a bargain-basement cost. By definition, since you will always be purchasing the lower-strike option and selling the higher-strike, the bull spread will always be placed at a debit when you use calls. If your debit on the spread is 8¢, that's the cost you'll have to overcome in the market, or your maximum risk. The two strikes *minus* the initial cost will constitute the maximum possible profit. The bull spread will lose money at the lower strike and below, while it will earn some return above the lower strike, although breakeven won't be reached until it earns back the initial debit.

The maximum possible profit will exist at the higher strike and above. Thus, in summary, we have three zones: total loss at the lower strike and below; partial loss or partial gain between the two strikes; and maximum gain at higher strike and above. Remember, we are talking about calls on the same delivery month on the same commodity here. With puts, the situation is different. Let's now look at an example in which we compare the purchase of the bull spread with the purchase of the lower-strike call alone.

Let's say you can purchase an at-the-money July 600 soybean call for a premium of 15¢ per bushel. At the same time, the out-of-the-money July 625 soybean call is available for 6¢. To place the bull spread, we buy the lower-strike and write the higher-strike. Our initial debit is the difference between what we pay and what we receive from the sale of the July 625 call.

In this example, the cost is 9¢. At the time the bull spread position is established, its maximum potential gain and loss can also be established. The breakeven point will be the lower strike plus the cost of the spread, or $6.09 per bushel. In Table 20 I have compared the different returns of the bull spread with the outright purchase of the July 600 call.

As you can see in Table 20, *as soon as the upper strike is reached, the spread achieves its maximum profitability.* It can earn no more profit, regardless of how high prices trade. This is because the gains on the lower-strike call are matched by losses on the short call above the higher strike. The inference to be drawn is that bull spreading is *not* for a runaway bull market but rather for a mildly bullish one. On the other hand, because it costs *less* than the outright call position, the bull spread achieves its profitability sooner — in this example, at $6.09 a bushel compared with $6.15 a bushel. But, significantly, within a small range of prices, the bull spread outperforms the net call buying strategy. At the upper strike of $6.25, the bull spread is worth $800 in net profits, compared with just $500 for the next call-buying strategy.

The Vertical Bear Call Spread

Known as the *vertical bear call spread*, the spread between calls to capitalize on lower-trending prices involves *buying* the higher-strike options and simultaneously *selling* the lower-strike ones. Since lower-

Table 20. Call buying vs. the bull spread. Investor using the bull spread buys July 600 soybean call for 15¢ and writes July 625 soybean call for 6¢.

Futures Price at Expiration of Options	Return on Bull Spread	Return on July 600 Call
$5.50 per bu	($450)	($750)
5.75	($450)	($750)
6.00	($450)	($750)
6.09	0	($300)
6.20	$550	$250
6.25	$800*	$500
6.50	$800	$1,750
6.75	$800	$3,000
7.00	$800	$4,250

* Point of maximum profitability. No matter how much higher prices trade, the bull spread will not return a greater profit.

strike calls will always be worth more than higher-strike calls, the bear spread in calls is placed with an initial *net credit*. As a result, you will take in funds when you establish the bear spread. The maximum profitability on the spread will exist at the lower strike and lower. At that price, you will earn the total initial net credit, or the difference between your writing income and what you paid for the long higher-strike call. The maximum risk will be the difference between the exercise price of the calls, less the credit received for putting on the spread.

Let's look at an example. In January, you see weaker prices for live-hog futures ahead. Rather than simply writing a call, you decide to place the bear spread by buying an out-of-the-money June 52 live-hogs call option and simultaneously writing an at-the-money June 50 live-hogs call. We'll assume the June 52 call is trading at $.70 and the June 50 call at $1.50. Therefore, having written the June 50 call for a premium of $1.50, you will receive $450 in writing income. At the same time, however, you buy the June 52 call for a premium of $.70, or $210. Your initial net credit is the difference, or $240.

Table 21 compares the hypothetical results of the bear spread with those of the sale of the lower-strike June 50 call alone. Note that the bear call spread, by virtue of being *long* in the higher-strike call, protects against a precipitous *rise* in the market. The writing of the net short call, on the other hand, provides no such protection.

Like the bull spread, the bear spread enables the investor to realize a predetermined modest profit over a relatively wide range of prices — $50 per hundredweight and lower. The bear spread, unlike the net short call-writing position, protects the investor to a maximum fixed loss in the event of higher prices. Note how the investor who writes only the at-the-money June 50 call continues to lose money as prices rise. The call writer who is not spread also realizes a slightly larger profit in the event of declining prices, but this potential gain must be weighed against a substantially higher risk on the upside.

The Vertical Ratio Call Spread

The bull and bear call spreads we've just examined are known as *vertical spreads*. The vertical spread takes its name from one leg being above or under the other, such as a $6.00 strike call being spread against a $6.25 strike call on the same expiration month. In the vertical bull and bear spreads, the two legs are equal. That is, you write one call against another in a one-to-one fashion. Now we turn to ratio call spreading. Just as you can write calls against futures in multiple quanti-

Table 21. Call writing vs. the bear spread — live hogs. Investor using the bear spread writes June 50 call for 1.50 and buys June 52 call for .70.

Futures Price at Expiration of Options	Return on Bear Spread	Return on Short June 50 call
$46 per hundredweight	$240	$450
$48	$240	$450
$50	$240*	$450
$52	($360)	($150)
$54	($360)	($750)
$56	($360)	($1,350)
$58	($360)	($1,950)
$60	($360)	($2,550)

* Point of maximum profitability. No matter how much lower prices trade, the bear spread will not return a greater profit.

ties, you can write calls against calls in the same manner — or, for that matter, puts against puts. When you write a greater number of calls against a lesser number, you vary the ratio of short and long positions. This is known as a *ratio call spread.*

The most popular of the ratio call spreads is the *2:1 ratio spread.* The 2:1 involves selling twice as many calls at one strike as you purchase at another. For instance, you might write two May 600 soybean calls for a premium of 12¢ each and purchase one May 575 soybean call for a premium of 32¢. The two short May 600s will generate 24¢ in income, against a cost of 32¢ for the single May 575. Hence, the net cost of the spread will amount to the difference, or 8¢ per bushel.

By selling twice as many calls as you write, you establish a relatively low-cost position that will prove profitable over a range of prices. As a rule, the two premiums you receive for the call you sell will nearly or totally offset the cost of the call you buy. Your objective should be to place the spread with as little cost as possible and with an acceptable risk.

Compared to the standard bull spread, however, the ratio spread is a bit riskier. For you no longer have a covered short position. In fact, you have one covered short position and one uncovered short position. Your risk, therefore, is that prices may soar upward and the unprotected short call may lose money. You can also lose with the 2:1 vertical spread if prices decline in this example. But the down-side risk is limited strictly to the initial cost of the spread. Having paid 8¢ for this spread, you can't lose more than that on the down side. After all, what will happen if prices decline? The two short calls will expire worthless, and you will keep the writing income of 24¢. However, the lower-strike call will also expire worthless, and you will lose the entire 32¢ premium. As a result, you will end up where you were at the beginning — namely, paying the cost of the spread.

We know then, that you will lose if prices go too high and if they decline too sharply. But what if they rise slightly? This is the profit area on the spread. In fact, the point of maximum profit is at the higher strike. At that price, you will collect the entire writing income as well as an additional 25¢ on the long May 575 call. In our example, you will collect 24¢ in writing income on the 600 call at $6.00 per bushel at expiration. Moreover, the 32¢ you paid for the 575 call will return 25¢. The total net profit, therefore, will be 49¢ in income minus 32¢ in cost, for a profit of 17¢, or $850. This compares with a profit of just 7¢, or $350, if you had sold only one call against the purchase of one call. Why? Because one call would have generated 12¢ in writing income. Against this income, you would have paid 32¢. Hence, the net debit on the bull spread would have been 20¢. Now, assuming futures are at exactly $6.00 or higher at expiration, the spread will return 25¢ against a 20¢ net cost. The difference is just 5¢.

The idea behind the ratio call spread is to have the two premiums received for writing the two higher-strike calls offset the cost of the single lower-strike call. Your objective should be to place the spread at a low cost. The extra premium serves to reduce the down-side risk, since it lowers the overall cost of the spread. The drawback, of course, is that you must endure a slightly higher risk if prices rise. If you are willing to monitor your spread positions closely, ratio spreads offer an alternative to simple bull and bear spreads for coping with modestly bullish and bearish markets.

Let's consider a hypothetical 2:1 ratio spread in cattle. With the June futures trading at $66.87, we could establish the 2:1 vertical call spread by buying one in-the-money June 66 call and writing two out-of-the-money June 68 calls. There's an important reason you would want to select these particular options. For one, you want to write out-of-the-moneys. Why? Because any option trading in the money can be exercised at any time. Having written two calls against one call, you are covered on only one. For the other, you'd end up being assigned a short futures position with a paper loss. As for the long call being in the money, this isn't a problem. Remember, you are the buyer. Hence, you are the only one who can decide to exercise. The seller has no such luxury. For another, you want to write and buy options that are at least near the money. So in this situation, the June 66 and June 68 calls make sense.

Now let's see what they are selling for. The June 66 is available for a price of 2.00 points ($800), and the June 68 is available for 1.00 point ($400). This is the perfect situation, because it means you can establish the 2:1 ratio spread for commission costs alone. Remember, you write two June 68 calls for a total premium of 2.00 points and you simultaneously buy one June 66 call for a premium of 2.00 points. Your cost is commissions.

If the market declines, what have you lost? Nothing, really. But if the cattle market rises and the June futures are trading at exactly 68 upon expiration of the options, you stand to gain 2 points on the long June 66, and also 2 points on the expiring June 68s. Your total net profit, therefore, will be 2 points, or $800 — all for a spread that didn't cost you anything! And with almost no risk, aside from commissions. There is one risk, of course. And that is if prices soar well *above* the higher strike of 68. Then your short call will lose money.

It is important to understand how this spread works. If prices are at 68 upon expiration, the June 66 (for which you paid $800) will be worth exactly $800. Hence, you have a wash on that option. But the two June 68s, for which you took in $800, will expire worthless! There's your $800 profit. The down-side risk is minimal, since you can lose only what you paid for the spread — which, in this case, was the cost of commissions. That leaves the only other alternative, rising prices. You *can* lose money if prices rise significantly, but there is always an opportunity to take defensive action should a runaway bull market occur. In almost every respect, this is as close to a risk-free, sure-thing strategy as you will find. The task is to monitor option prices closely and try to place spreads, such as this one, at little or no cost.

In Table 22, I've listed the value of the respective legs of the vertical ratio call spread. For a spread that costs only commissions to place, this one offers a pretty wide range of profitability — just above $66 to $70. You could do a lot worse in the options market than selecting attractively priced 2:1 ratio spreads.

The Horizontal Spread

The *horizontal spread*, also known as a *time* or *calendar spread*, is the purchase and sale of calls or puts in the same commodity with the same strike price but *different* contract months. For instance, you might place a horizontal call spread by writing a July 575 soybean call and

Table 22. The vertical ratio call spread. Investor buys one June 66 live-cattle call for 2.00 and writes two June 68 live-cattle calls for 1.00 each.

Futures Price at Expiration of Options	Return on 1 June 66 Call	Return on 2 June 68 Calls	Net Gain (Loss)
$64	($800)	$800	0
$66	($800)	$800	0
$67	($400)	$800	$400
$68	0	$800	$800
$69	$400	$400	$800
$70	$1,600	($1,600)	0
$71	$2,000	($2,400)	($400)

simultaneously buying a November 575 soybean call.* In general, option spreaders who use the horizontal spread *sell the nearby month and purchase the more distant month.* The reason: the horizontal spreader hopes to capitalize on declining time value. The nearer month will lose time value quickly, while the longer-term option will hold its time value somewhat longer.

Of course, this approach to the market, while theoretically sound, has its drawbacks. For example, if you are putting on a horizontal spread between two crop years, the two different months might trade almost like two different commodities. Whereas the fundamentals of the old crop may be pretty well known, the imponderables of the crop that is still unharvested remain vast. A miscalculation, therefore, could prove costly, and the would-be horizontal spreader is urged to exercise caution.

Let's look at an example of a horizontal spread. Let's say it's April 1 and you are considering placing a horizontal spread in cotton. The July futures are trading at $66.50 and the October futures at $65.50. Since you want to avoid exercise on the short call, you concentrate on the out-of-the-moneys, the 68-strike calls. Both the July and the October 68 calls are out of the money, with July at $66.50 and October at

---

* Please note that such an intercrop spread involves a complicated analysis, since the fundamentals for each crop year must be taken into account. Moreover, since the underlying futures trade at different price levels, the relationship of the two futures to each other, as well as the relationship between the strike price of each option and the price of its underlying future, must be considered. Because horizontal spreads in futures involve futures trading at different levels, they are considerably more complicated and challenging than stock option spreads, where the underlying stock will trade at a given price regardless of the option's maturity date.

$65.50. Let's say the respective premiums for the two are .55 for the nearer July calls and .45 for the more distant October calls. Shouldn't more distant months command higher premiums because of higher time values? A good question. The answer is yes, *if* they were, like stocks, trading at the same level. But the July futures are one point above the more distant October futures. Hence, the lower price in the distant month.

Now, to achieve the horizontal spread, you write the July 68 cotton call for .55 points while buying the October 68 call for .45 points. As long as both options remain below the strike and expire out of the money, you should earn a modest profit on the spread. How much? Well, below 68 at expiration, both calls will expire worthless. Since you wrote the July 68 call for .55, you will keep the entire premium of $275; having paid .45, or $225, for the October 68 call, however, you will lose the entire amount. The profit, therefore, will be just $50 a spread. Depending on what commissions, if any, you are paying, you may be able to make money on this spread.

But we are assuming here that both options *expire at the same time.* And this is clearly not the case. Instead, the July option will expire in mid-June, whereas the October option will continue to trade until mid-September, three months later. There are profitable implications to this difference. Again, assuming the July 68 expires worthless, with the July futures below 68, the spreader will earn the full writing income of $275 per spread on the short 68 call. At the same time, however, the long October 68 cotton call will retain some value *no matter how far out of the money it trades.* Accordingly, the October 68 (which you bought) will retain some value when the July 68 is expired and worthless. Since you purchased the October 68 call for $225, you can recoup part of your investment by selling it upon expiration of the July call in mid-June. How much will it bring? That depends on its relationship to the strike price and its prospects for proving profitable over the next three months. But we know one thing for sure. It is going to be worth something.

For the sake of our illustration, let's say the October 68 call is trading for .20 points, or $100, in mid-June when the July call expires. Having paid $225 for the option, you will now have a loss if you sell it for $100. But you must remember that this was a spread trade. You earned first $275 for writing the July 68 call (in fact, you have *already made* a profit), and now you are going to pick up another $100 for selling the long October 68 call. In other words, you have earned $375 on the spread.

This, by the way, illustrates why, when using horizontal spreads, you want to *write the nearby and buy the distant month.* The nearby month is going to lose its time value more quickly (and hence aid the writer), while the more distant month is going to retain its time value longer (and hence aid the buyer). Sophisticated option traders make it a point to monitor and aggressively trade horizontal spreads.

The Diagonal Spread

There is a third spread that combines the features of the vertical spread (higher-strike against lower-strike spread) with the horizontal spread (nearby month spread against more distant month). Understandably enough, it is known as the *diagonal spread*. What's a diagonal spread? Simply a spread between options having both different strike prices *and* different expiration dates.

We know that the vertical spread, depending upon which month we buy and which we sell, is either mildly bullish or mildly bearish. The horizontal spread, by contrast, is neutral in tone (you can profit from the declining time value if prices remain stationary). Because the diagonal spread in part resembles both types of spreads, it has elements of both: it will help you capture time value while being slightly bullish or bearish, depending on how you set it up.

In looking at the diagonal spread, let's review what we've already learned from the vertical and horizontal spreads. We know that to take advantage of natural time decay, the rule is to sell the nearby month and buy the distant month. This is the thinking behind the horizontal spread. And the rule for rising and falling markets? Buy the lower strike and sell the higher strike to capitalize on rising markets, and do the opposite to profit from falling ones.

Now, how do we use this information to profit from diagonal spreads? First and foremost, you should know that diagonal spreads work best in stable markets. In general, you'll lose the most in a bear market with this strategy, but even then, given the flexibility of options trading, you'll be able to set up a schedule of profit-and-loss decisions and establish upper and lower breakeven points. With the diagonal spread strategy, you use calls when you are mildly bullish and puts when you are mildly bearish. This is the general rule. Assuming futures remain constant at the strike price, therefore, the value of the spread will equal the value of the deferred option, since the nearby month will expire worthless when it is at the money at expiration.

This may be a little abstract, so let's look at an example. Assume corn futures and call options are trading at the following prices:

Futures

July corn futures = $281\frac{1}{2}$
September corn futures = $272\frac{3}{4}$

Options

July 260 call = 20	September 260 call = $15\frac{1}{2}$
July 270 call = $12\frac{1}{2}$	September 270 call = $9\frac{3}{4}$
July 280 call = $6\frac{1}{8}$	September 280 call = $5\frac{3}{4}$
July 290 call = $2\frac{1}{4}$	September 290 call = $3\frac{7}{8}$

Because we know we want to capture time value, and because we know that soon-to-expire options lose their value faster than longer-term options, we will write a near-term July corn option. But which one? With July futures trading at $281\frac{1}{2}$, let's write the at-the-money July 280 call for $6\frac{1}{8}$¢. (You could argue that the July 280 call is in-the-money with the futures at $281\frac{1}{2}$, but this isn't a big problem). By writing the July 280, we immediately gain the writing income of approximately $306. At the same time, we will now buy the September 270 call for a premium of $9\frac{3}{4}$¢, or about $487. The cost of the spread, of course, will be the difference between what we paid and what we received. Commissions aside, the cost is about $181 per spread.

Now we have to factor in the element of time to see how we might profit from this strategy. Let's assume stable prices. Let's say both futures are trading at the strike of the respective options upon expiration of the near-term July call in mid-June. That means that the July 280 call will expire worthless and we pick up the entire $306 in writing income. At the same time, the September 270 call will have lost some of its time value and perhaps a penny or so in its modest cash value. Nevertheless, the September 270 call will still retain some value—certainly its two-month time value prior to expiration in mid-August.

Let's say the September 270 call's premium is now $4\frac{1}{2}$¢, or about $225. That means, having paid $487 for the September 270 call, we can now sell it for $225. The net loss on the September 270 call, therefore, will be $262. Since we received $306 on the short call and lost $262 on the long call, the difference, or $44, will be the profit. Considering that the net cost of the spread was only $181, the $44 return comes to about 24 percent over a two- to three-month period. Annualized, of course, the return would be considerably higher.

Now let's look at a diagonal spread using puts. With June live-hog futures trading at $49 and August live-hog futures at $51, you could place the diagonal spread by writing the out-of-the-money June 48 put for 1.00 point and buying the out-of-the-money August 50 put for 1.50

points. Note that both options will be out of the money, because the strikes will be *below* the prevailing market price. With June futures at $49 per hundredweight, the June 48 put is out of the money, as is the August 50 put when August futures are trading at $51. The cost of the diagonal spread in this example is just .50, or $150.

If there is no change in futures prices, the June put will expire first with no value. Hence the spread will yield the full writing income of $300, or 1.00 point, on the short June 48 put. At the same time, the August 50 put, which was originally purchased for a premium of 1.50 points, or $450, will retain some value, since it still has two months' time value when the June put expires in mid-May. Let's say that at expiration of the June 48 put, the August 50 put is trading at 1.15 points, or $345. One can simply sell the August 50 put for 1.15 points, and gain back $345 on the original $450 investment. The net loss on the long put, therefore, will be just $105, compared to a net gain of $300, or 100 percent, on the premium of the short put. Hence, the return on the diagonal spread will be $195 — better than 30 percent on the original $150 investment.

Since the two options that you spread in a diagonal do not have the same expiration date, one option will always retain some value even if it remains out of the money. Using hypothetical prices, therefore, I have listed in Table 23 how the results of the diagonal spread in our example *might* appear upon expiration of the June put.

Given our hypothetical numbers, you can see that this diagonal spread is most profitable right around the respective strike prices. In

Table 23.   Example of a diagonal put spread. Investor writes one June 48 live-hogs put for 1.00 and buys one August 50 put for 1.50.

June Futures Price at Expiration of June 48 Put	Value of June 48 Put	Gain (Loss)	August Futures Price at Expiration of June 48 Put	Value of August 50 Put	Gain (Loss)	Net Gain (Loss)
$47 per hundred-weight	$300	0	$49	$480*	$30	$30
$48	0	$300	$50	$345	($105)	$195
$49	0	$300	$51	$105	($345)	($45)
$50	0	$300	$52	$60	($390)	($90)

* We are assuming that the August 50 put retains $180 in time value in addition to its cash value when the underlying August futures are trading at $49, making the August 50 put 1 point in the money.

that case, the nearby June 48 put will expire worthless, while the long August 50 put still retains some of its time value. Essentially, the diagonal spreader is looking to pick up the entire writing premium while losing only a small portion of the premium value of the long option, which loses its time value more slowly.

Using Spreads to Adjust Your Level of Risk

Professional floor traders use spread transactions to cope with a changing market and periodically adjust their level of risk. The off-the-floor options investor would do well to do likewise in certain situations. We have seen how substituting a vertical bull call spread for an outright purchase of a call option serves to lower the initial cost as well as the breakeven point. By relying on a variety of spread transactions — or at least being prepared to enter spread transactions — you can significantly enhance the overall performance of your account.

Keep in mind that you always have spreading as an alternative when you hold an options position. Vigilance is the key to success here. A very simple example might be to write higher-strike calls against a position taken by purchasing the lower-strike calls. For example, let's say you are a bull on the soybean market and purchase November 600 calls in anticipation of higher prices. You buy the calls when they are still out of the money, and your judgment is proven correct as November beans move to $6.15 a bushel. But then the market falters and you are pulled in two directions: on the one hand, you fully expect the November soybeans to mount a strong rally above the $6.50 area in the next few months prior to the expiration of the November options; on the other, you have a temporary bear move on your hands.

Why stand by and watch your paper profits disappear? Instead, you might write the out-of-the-money 625 calls, adjusting the position to offset the losses on one by comparable gains on another. This means you must pay attention to the delta of the options. You know by now that an in-the-money call won't have the same delta as an out-of-the-money call. As a result, you may find yourself writing four November 625 calls against each long November 600 call you have. In time, hopefully, the weakness in the market will show signs of ending. You will then cover your short position in the November 625s, having profited from your writing activities. When the bull market resumes, of course, you'll want to hold the long November 600 calls outright.

You should keep in mind that there is no rule saying you have to remain in a net long or short position at any time. You can spread from time to time to cope with changing market conditions. By adjusting your position to deal with the market condition at the time you decide to spread, you put yourself well ahead of others in the market who feel locked into a situation. Thanks to the unprecedented versatility of options trading, you are never locked in. There is always a way to deal with a changing market. Spreading, as most professionals already know, is just one way to cope with risk.

One word of caution is due: spreading as a means of hedging one's risk is a good idea; but spreading to lock in a loss is a different matter altogether. For instance, let's say you are a bull on hog futures and decide to write puts as a means of generating some income in the options market. The strategy makes sense — so far. But then let's say the market plummets, and your puts become profitable to the holder but more and more costly to you, the writer. You might be tempted to buy lower-strike puts as a means of limiting your losses. And, indeed, this tactic might lessen the eventual loss. But the point is, you will finally have to face the day of reckoning in this position when the short put is exercised against you and you are given a long futures position at the strike price. The loss will continue to exist. Upon exercise, you will have a long futures position at the strike of the original short put — say, $50. If you purchased a 48-strike put, the $2 loss from 50 to 48 will eventually have to be paid. It's true, the market may continue to decline, in which case the long 48-strike put will make money — or at least prevent you from losing more money. The profit, remember, will go to the holder of the original put you sold at $50.

The way out of this situation is not to spread to lock in a loss. Rather, you have to deal forthrightly with each situation as it occurs. Having made a bad judgment in writing puts, you should buy them back at a loss and forget the trade. Then, upon analyzing the market further, you might want to purchase puts to capitalize on declining prices. It is psychologically bad to lock in losses. The only effect is to remove you from the market. Better to deal with adversity at the outset and remain free to profit from new opportunites.

The Short Strangle Spread

So far in this chapter on spreads, we've covered long against short positions — buying lower-strike calls against selling higher-strike ones. But just as you can spread one strike against another and one expiration month against another, you can spread puts against calls. One popular strategy is known as the *strangle* or *combination*. The strategy involves out-of-the-money options surrounding the market price. For example, with corn futures trading at $3.30 a bushel, you might write a $3.40 call and a $3.20 put. As long as corn futures remain within the profit area between the strikes, you walk away with both premiums at expiration. You can also buy strangles, of course, by buying the out-of-the-money put and call. But this strategy requires a volatile market to make money. The short strangle, on the other hand, requires nothing more than a continuation of the past—namely, stationary prices.

Appendix I discusses short strangles in some detail. The basic rules involve writing out-of-the-money options and setting up a predetermined profit zone. The options in a strangle tend to have the same expiration dates but different strike prices. The call's exercise price is above the market, whereas the put's is below the market. There is unlimited risk, since the market could move an unlimited amount in either direction, either up or down. But the probability of cashing out the strangle with a profit is also high. The maximum potential profit is known at the outset: it's the initial writing income.

Let's look at an example of the short strangle involving July soybeans. At recent levels, July soybeans were trading at about $6.07 a bushel. With about two-and-a-half months left to expiration of the July options, the out-of-the-money July 625 call was available for 11¢, and the out-of-the-money July 600 put was available for 15¢. That's 26¢ in writing income per strangle, or about $1,300. As long as prices remain between $6.00 and $6.25 per bushel, the seller of the out-of-the-money strangle stands to capture the entire 13¢ premium at expiration. In the meantime, he'll have to maintain margin on both positions, however, and be careful to take defensive action should the soybean market surge higher or tumble lower in the time left to expiration.

The short strangle enjoys popularity among market professionals because of its high probability of success coupled with the fact that most outside investors are purchasers of options as opposed to writers. The traders using the short strangle knows that, over time, despite occasional losses, the percentages are in his favor.

The Short Straddle Spread

The short straddle spread, like the short strangle, involves writing a put and a call. But in the straddle, both put and call are at the same strike price. As a result, the premiums of both options tend to be greater, since one or both have a greater likelihood of being exercised.

From the writer's standpoint, the short straddle involves a greater payment, but this is partly offset by the greater likelihood of exercise. In fact, unless the underlying futures are exactly at the strike at expiration, one of the options will be exercised. Because of the premium payment, however, there is a good chance that the writer will still make money. Why? Because the sum of the two premiums is apt to be larger than the distance that the futures are away from the strike at expiration.

For example, with live-hog futures trading at $50, you might decide to write a June 50 put for a 1.50 premium and a June 50 call for the same 1.50 premium. The total writing income, therefore, will amount to 3.00 points, or $900. Having received $3 per hundredweight for writing the live-hog straddle, the writer will profit at any point within a $3 range of the strike price at expiration. Thus, the writer has, in effect, a $6 range ($3 up from the strike and $3 down from the strike) around the strike price. Why? Because at any point within that range at expiration of the option, the loss on having either the put or the call exercised will be less than the initial writing income.

Let's say the June live-hog futures are exactly at $53 upon expiration of the straddle. The call will be exercised, and the live-hog futures will be given to the buyer of the call at the strike of 50. Looking at it another way, the writer of the straddle will be given a short live-hog futures contract at the strike price of 50. Hence, he will have a $3 loss — the same amount by which he profited by writing the spread. At $53, therefore, he will exactly break even.

At a price of $54, however, the straddle writer will sustain a loss. At $54, he will owe $4 to the call buyer. This loss will be offset only by a gain of $3 received when he originally wrote the straddle. Generally, as a straddle writer, you only have to worry about one option being exercised. By definition, if one option is in the money, the other option will be out of the money and hence remain unexercised at expiration.

The profit zone on the short straddle is the strike price plus-or-minus the writing income. You would write a straddle because you are neutral on a market's prospects.

The Long Straddle Spread

The long straddle spread consists of the *purchase* of a put and a call at the strike price. As the buyer of a put and a call, you stand to profit in a volatile market in which the movement away from the strike price exceeds the price you paid for the straddle. Since you purchase both a put and a call in a straddle buy, you profit from a movement in *either direction* away from the strike. Thus, if you paid 19¢ per bushel for a soybean straddle with a $6.00 strike, you would need a move above $6.19 or below $5.81 in order to earn a profit at expiration.

The maximum risk on a long straddle is the price you paid for the put and the call. In this respect, the risk is identical to that of outright put or call buying: the loss is limited to the premium cost. The objective of the straddle is to profit in a volatile futures market. The key drawback to the straddle is the need to have the underlying futures move sufficiently to overcome the cost of the premium.

Should you purchase near months or distant months in straddle buying? That depends on your near-term outlook on the market. Obviously, the nearer-term options are going to cost less. But you are probably better off buying more time. It is hard enough to buy options that will prove profitable, so you don't want to pick options that have to move within 30 to 60 days. At recent price levels, the at-the-money August live-cattle calls are available for about 1.60 points, or $640. The at-the-money October live-cattle calls with two months more in time value are trading at 1.80, or $720. And the August versus the October live-cattle at-the-money puts are trading only .05 point apart, 1.92 for the August versus 1.97 for the October. Unless you have reason to believe the fundamentals for the long-term October futures are so different that they may result in a completely stationary market, you really have only one intelligent choice in this matter: to buy the October straddle. The extra 60 days in time value that you will be purchasing make the longer-term options the only sensible choice.

If you were to look at the choices here in terms of the weekly cost of buying the straddle, you would see why the October straddle makes sense. Let's say there are 16 weeks left to expiration of the August options and 24 weeks left to expiration of the October options. The cost of the August straddle is $1,410, versus $1,510 for the October straddle. On a *per week* basis, therefore, the August straddle costs $88, whereas the October straddle averages out at about $63 per week for the longer 24-week period. Moreover, for that extra $100, you are buying yourself an extra 60 days in precious time for the market to move in either direction.

Let's look at an example of straddle buying. With July live-hog futures trading at $50, the at-the-money July 50 call is trading at 2.00 points and the at-the-money July 50 put at 1.90 points. Thus, the straddle will cost a total of 3.90 points, or $1,170. Because the straddle is essentially a volatility spread, you will want the price to move away from the strike in either direction. The direction really doesn't matter. But one thing is certain: the farther prices move from the strike, the greater the profit. Table 24 lists the net gain or loss on the straddle at different

Table 24. Straddle buying. Investor buys one July 50 live-hogs call for 2.00 and one July 50 put for 1.90.

Futures Price at Expiration of Option	Value of July 50 Call	Value of July 50 Put	Net Gain (Loss)
$44 per hundredweight	0	$1,800	$650
$45	0	$1,500	$330
$46	0	$1,200	$30
$47	0	$900	($270)
$48	0	$600	($570)
$49	0	$300	($870)
$50	0	0	($1,170)
$51	$300	0	($870)
$52	$600	0	($570)
$53	$900	0	($270)
$54	$1,200	0	$30
$55	$1,500	0	$330
$56	$1,800	0	$630

prices upon expiration of the July options. Note that as you move down from the strike, the straddle gains in value; likewise, as you move up from the strike, the straddle increases in value. The breakeven at expiration will be the premium cost plus or minus the strike, or $53.90 on the up side and $46.10 on the down side.

Spreading Different Crop Years

Intercrop spreading has been popular in the futures market for years. Now, with the introduction of agricultural options, opportunities exist to spread crop years with puts and calls. Perhaps the most popular intercrop spread is that between July and November soybeans, July being the old crop and November being the new crop. The advantage of spreading different crop years in the options market is that the volatility tends to be far greater than the so-called interdelivery spreads between contract months of the same crop year. Of course, the reason for the greater volatility is that different fundamentals for each crop year can make, say, the old crop bullish whereas the prospects for the new crop may be bearish. This means that different futures (and hence different options) of the *same commodity* may move in different directions— November soybeans declining, say, when July soybeans are rising.

If you are going to try spreading different crop years, you should become familiar with the different seasonal patterns that persist in different commodities. (My recent book, *Real-Time-Proven Commodity Spreads*, Windsor Books, P.O. Box 280, Brightwaters, NY 11718, contains a number of seasonal spreads that have proved consistent over the last 7 to 12 years.) As a rule, commodity prices tend to rise prior to the harvest when supplies are short and tend to fall as the harvest time approaches and supplies become more abundant. But this is only a generality. There are other factors involved that can influence seasonal spreads and even produce so-called counterseasonal spread moves. Due to the bearish nature of the commodities market in recent years, the counterseasonals have been particularly profitable.

For the investor who wants to use the agricultural options market to spread different crop years, there are several alternatives. First, you have to decide on the type of spread you are going to use, and then you have to put the strategy into practice.

Commodity spreads tend to conform to what is known as the *general rule*. The general rule, in turn, is based on the notion of carrying charges being higher for distant months. The rule says that in a bull market, the nearby month will rise faster and further than the distant month *when the nearer month is trading at a discount to the distant month*. This is known, by the way, as a *normal carrying-charge market*. Thus, May soybeans might be trading for $6.00 a bushel, July soybeans for $6.09, and August soybeans for $6.10. The difference in prices reflects the greater carrying charges for the distant month.

Now, when bullish forces enter the market, the normal market tends to get *inverted*—that is, the nearby month, which, you may remember, becomes the cash commodity in weeks and even days, is bid up as buyers, ever eager to obtain the cash commodity, compete for the limited supplies on hand. As the market becomes more and more inverted, therefore, the so-called *bull spreaders*—those who purchased the nearby month while selling a distant month—tend to earn profits as their long commodity gains in price faster than the short commodity falls. Hence, the bull spread is also known as the *forward spread*, meaning the front month is purchased and the back month sold. The reverse of this type of spread is known as the *back spread*—long the back or distant month and short the front month. Back, or bear, spreaders make money as inverted markets turn into normal carrying-charge markets.

The idea of spreading is to capitalize on price differentials that occur in the market from time to time. As bullish influences push up prices, things tend to get a little overdone, and the bear spreaders, spotting an opportunity, start buying the undervalued distant months and selling the overvalued nearby months. Their hope, of course, is that prices will once again come back into line.

There is one other thing you have to know about normal carrying-charge markets. The risk, within certain guidelines, is limited for the bull spreader. Why? Because a virtual price floor exists once a spread reaches the cost of full carry. Carrying charges are made up of the costs of holding and storing the commodity from month to month. So the components of carrying charges are the costs of storage, transporation, interest, and so on. Assuming no increase in interest rates — admittedly a chancy assumption to make in today's sensitive interest-rate environment — the nearby month of a storable commodity can fall only to full carry. What do we mean by this? Simply that if, say, full carry for soybeans is 10¢ per month, the May beans can trade at most 20¢ (two months' worth) below July beans. With July beans at $6.10, therefore, the near-term May beans won't trade below $5.90. Were they to exceed the cost of full carry, astute speculators would begin buying up the lower-priced beans and *selling* July futures. Upon maturity of the July contract, they would deliver their soybeans, thus capturing the difference in price that exceeded the cost of full carry.

You really don't have to worry about a commodity exceeding the full cost of carrying charges, because it rarely occurs. However, there is another important implication involved here. That is, if you purchase a delivery month trading near full carry, *the risk is limited to the cost of full carry*. For instance, if beans are trading with the nearby month 13¢ under the adjacent month and the cost of carry for the two months is, let's say, 16¢, the risk is just 3¢ per bushel. Whether you trade futures or options on futures, this is an important piece of information. Sensing the limited-risk aspect of this trade, many speculators, even during bearish times, routinely place bull spreads in hopes of a bull market coming along. They know that the risk to the down side is limited. On the up side, however, the nearer month can soar to any premium it wishes as buyers bid up the price. In other words, it is a one-sided trading affair; they stand to gain a lot while risking almost nothing.

Now we can return to our hypothetical intercrop spread. When you are dealing with an intercrop situation, you have to forget the notion of a limited-risk spread. From limited risk we are turning to high risk. As mentioned before, different crop years can trade almost like different commodities, one rising while the other declines. Of course, the profit opportunities are also great in intercrop spreads.

Let's look at a recent intercrop spread between the old-crop July beans and the new-crop November beans. Old-crop July is trading at $6.09 per bushel, while the new-crop November is at $6.05½ per bushel. What's more, the July 600 call, which is in the money, is trading for 21½¢, while the November out-of-the-money 625 call is trading at the same price, 21½¢. If you were bullish over the near term, here's an opportunity to place a spread at no cost! By buying the July 600 call and selling the November 625 call for the same amount of money, you have a spread that is put on for commission costs alone. Moreover, assuming even stable prices through to expiration of the near-term July 600 call, you would still get back 9¢ in cash value.

The November call, of course, while still out of the money, would retain some time value. Whether or not you had a profit would depend on the amount of time value the November 625 retained. But let's assume a bull market for cash soybeans erupts in the next 60 to 90 days, sending July beans to $6.85 from present levels. The July 600 call would retain the full 85¢ cash premium at expiration. Hence, an option for which you paid just 21½¢ would be worth 85¢ at expiration, a profit of about $3,175. At the same time, let's assume the November soybeans rally only 35¢ to $6.40½. The November 625 call will retain at least its cash value (15½¢) plus whatever time value the market is paying for the option (let's say, another 17¢). Since cash value plus time value constitutes an option's premium, the November 625 call is now worth 32½¢, resulting in a loss of 11¢, or $550, on that leg of the spread. The net profit is $2,625.

As this example suggests, you can use options instead of futures for spreading one crop year against another. But the risks must be acknowledged. In fact, seasonal studies suggest that July soybeans, regardless of overall market conditions, tend to "go off the boards" weak compared to November soybeans. As a result, you might want to reverse positions by writing the nearer-term July call and buying the distant November. Again, the decision depends on your outlook on the market. Ultimately, that will determine your spreading strategy. As I mentioned in the section on the diagonal spread, one strategy is to write options of short duration to capitalize on declining time value. But when you're dealing with bull markets and different crops years, you have to look at the overall market direction if you are going to profit from a spread strategy.

Which Strike Price Should You Select?

We know that the bull calendar, or horizontal, spread consists of a long call and a short call on the same underlying futures at the same strike with different durations — say, July beans spread against November beans. But which strike should you select? Should you be looking at the in-the-moneys or the out-of-the-moneys?

As a rule, you want to spread options that are out of the money but not deeply out of the money. The reason? In spreading two calls on two different contracts, you are looking for two things to occur. One, you want the near-term call to expire worthless and provide you with the writing income. Obviously, if the option is exercised against you, you won't be retaining the premium income. Some or all of the premium will be paid back to the call buyer. Two, you want the longer-term option you purchase to *increase* in value after or before expiration of the shorter-term call. If that happens, both options will return a profit.

By contrast, when you spread two options that are deeply out of the money, here's what is likely to happen. First, you will probably gain the writing income on the first call. But the income will be relatively small, since the option was so far out of the money. Then, too, there is always the risk that the short call will trade in-the-money. When this happens, you have the worst of all worlds. You have written a call for almost nothing, and you have unlimited liability. As for the other leg of the spread, a call that remains out of the money will be worth nothing at expiration. Hence, you will lose the entire premium you paid for the long call. Better to concentrate on options that are either slightly out of the money or at the money.

In sizing up an option spread such as this one, you might be concerned with the option spread's delta. What is the spread's delta, and how is it determined? The delta of a spread, like the delta of an individual call, measures the rate at which the spread will gain in value relative to the underlying futures. The delta of the bull calendar spread will be the delta of the long call minus the delta of the short call. Hence, if you purchase August 66 cattle calls while writing June 66 cattle calls, and the respective deltas are .50 and .25, the delta of the spread will be .25, suggesting that a 1-point move in cattle futures will translate into a .25-point move in the calendar spread. Another way of looking at this, of course, is as a hedge. How many spreads would you need to hedge one futures position? The answer is four if the spread has a delta of .25. Were you using just the long August 66 call with the delta of .50, you'd need two calls to hedge one futures position.

The Box Spread

The *box spread* is a sophisticated arbitrage strategy used primarily by professionals who don't pay commissions. It consists of buying and selling both the bull and the bear vertical spreads at the same strike prices. There are two types of box spreads. One is known as *buying the box* and the other as *selling the box*.

In buying the box spread, you first establish a normal vertical bull spread with calls. That is, you purchase a lower-strike call and write a higher-strike call of the same duration. For example, let's say you are trying to buy the box in corn options. You might begin by purchasing an at-the-money July 280 call and simultaneously selling the out-of-the-money July 290 call. To complete the buying of the box, you would then buy one July 290 put and sell one July 280 put.

As you can see, the box spread consists of equivalent legs — as one gains, the other loses. The buyer counts on buying the box at a discount to parity. This will allow him to profit as the cost of carry declines. A gain on one leg, as we've observed, will be comparable to the loss on another. Hence, the two spreads that comprise the box spread cancel each other, and whether prices rise or fall during the time one holds the box is immaterial. The buyer of the box, therefore, knows his profit at the outset. When put on at the right price, the box spread is a sure trade; unfortunately, the maximum profit on each is severely limited to just $\frac{1}{8}$¢ or $\frac{1}{4}$¢. But as an arbitrage strategy, it has a place in the aggressive trader's portfolio.

When you *sell the box*, you also engage in an arbitrage strategy, which implies a neutral stance on the market. The seller of the box, however, engages in a credit transaction that generates immediate income in his account. Using the same example in options on corn futures, the seller of the box would write a July 280 call while buying a July 290 call. This would create a credit, since the lower-strike call will always be worth more than a higher-strike call for the same duration. In addition, to complete the other leg of the spread, the seller of the box would then sell the higher-strike July 290 put and purchase the lower-strike July 280 put. Both are credit transactions. The total credit will equal the premium received for the call spread plus the premium received for the put spread.

To secure a profit, the seller of the box grants a discount of less than the cost of full carry. He, too, sets himself up in a delta-neutral situation where he is protected completely from higher or lower prices; his profit is equal to the net credit he receives on setting up the spread. You will sometimes hear of box spreads being described as "locked trades." This terminology comes from the fact that their value at expiration is totally independent of the price of the underlying futures.

What Should You Do If a Spread Turns Sour?

Every once in a while even the most carefully selected spread strategy turns bad. You place bull spreads and the market declines. Or temporary strength in the forward months causes your calendar spread strategy to develop losses. One alternative, of course, is to close out the spread as quickly as possible with a modest loss. Few could argue that taking a loss under these circumstances is not a wise choice. But there are alternative defensive tactics that you can employ to cope with a deteriorating market situation.

One popular defensive strategy that we've discussed in previous chapters is known as *rolling*. You "roll" an option up, down, or out to tailor the position to the trend of the underlying futures. The purpose of the rolling is to defend yourself against temporary market reversals. The market may indeed just be in a temporary retracement. And when the time comes, you'll want to reestablish the spread position to fit the original trend. Then, again, the reversal may not be temporary at all. And you will be glad you took the defensive action when you did.

Whether you roll up, down, or out will depend on your initial spread position and what you anticipate will be the new trend. To find the correct way to roll, you have to start with your initial expectations and then shift your position to cope with what the market actually does. For instance, let's take the vertical bull call spread. The idea in placing the spread is to profit from a modest rise in prices. You purchase a lower-strike call and write a higher-strike call. The maximum profit will exist at the higher strike and above that price. Fine. You place the spread and wait. After a while, you realize that perhaps you have misjudged the market, at least temporarily. How can rolling help?

It depends on what the market is doing. Let's assume the market is bullish as you expected, but in time it becomes more than slightly bullish, perhaps very bullish. Having written the higher-strike call, you have effectively locked out profits above that point. Seeing the new bullishness in the market, you might want to "roll up" your calls. That is, you would buy back the higher-strike call and *write a higher-strike call*. At the same time, you would sell your lower-strike call and purchase another higher-strike call. This would move the entire spread up a strike. If the original spread involves a long November 575 soybean call and a short November 600 call, you would roll up to the next higher strike by buying the November 600 call and writing the November 625 call. Now you have another 25¢ in potential profit available to you. In short, you've gone from a slightly bullish stance to a more bullish stance. As prices work higher, you might want to roll even higher.

You can also roll down, of course, to protect yourself against declining prices. Let's say you are long one November 575 soybean call and short one November 600 soybean call when November soybeans are trading at $5.75 per bushel. You stand to profit on a rise in soybean prices, since the November 575 will surely increase in value as prices move higher. But what if soybean prices were to decline? Now you'd stand to lose the entire cost of the spread. To cope with such a situation, you might want to roll down, by *writing* the November 575 and buying the November 550.

Rolling can also help you deal with time spreads prior to expiration. Let's say you write a nearby month and purchase a distant month, anticipating that declining time value will make the nearer month almost worthless while the distant month retains its value. As the near-term option declines in value, you may want to take the profit and then roll into a distant month. The reason? Rather than wait to gain 100 percent of the profit on the spread, you will be taking in, let's say, 70 percent or 80 percent of the potential profit and allowing yourself to sell new time value in a distant month. Be careful, however, to unwind the entire spread and begin anew each time. For instance, let's say you have sold a May 600 call and purchased a July 625 in a diagonal spread, hoping to capture the time value in the near-term May 600 call. As time passes and the time value decreases, you might buy back the short May and sell the long July call. You then sell July and buy November, reestablishing the diagonal spread.

Any time you roll an option as a defensive strategy, you must ask yourself: What is my risk? This is especially true when you write options. When you roll down your calls, for instance, you are saying to the buyer, "I'm willing to let you have the profits above the strike price." In return, you receive his premium money. Is this a trade-off you are willing to make? If not, why not? Are you willing to again take defensive action — perhaps by rolling up — if the downtrend ends and the bull market resumes? These are questions you need to ask yourself.

The same type of thinking is required of those who trade put spreads. When you buy puts, as when you buy calls, the issues are relatively straightforward. You know your maximum risk is limited to the premium. But the writing side of the put spreads involves an uncertain liability unless you hold a lower-strike put to protect you against a short put trading deeper and deeper into the money. As a put writer, are you prepared to take on a long position at the strike price if your put is exercised? Be assured that there is always an alternative to doing nothing. The point is, you want to deal with the issues of risk management *before* you find yourself on the wrong side of a trade.

Let's look at an example of a put spread in which you might want to roll up or down as a defensive measure. You write a higher-strike put and buy a lower-strike put in anticipation of higher prices. This, by the way, is known as *a vertical bull put spread.* As long as prices are at the higher strike or above that price at expiration of the options, you will retain the full net credit, which is the difference between the writing income on the higher-strike put and the cost of the lower-strike put. But let's assume your market outlook is less than perfect. Prices begin to decline, and the higher-strike put begins to go deeper and deeper into the money (remember, you are a *writer* of the option, so this represents a loss to you). What can you do? Roll the spread down. Buy back the losing higher-strike put and sell the lower-strike put. This will get you out of the spread, probably at a loss. You then reestablish the vertical bull put spread by moving the entire spread down one or two strikes. Now, if you get a bounce in prices, you retain the initial net credit and, hopefully, earn enough to offset the losses on the first spread. This is just one example of how rolling can help you in a put spread.

Another way to cope with this situation would be to add to your long put position. For instance, as prices start to decline, you could buy another put at the lower strike. Now, if the downtrend is large enough, you will earn additional income on the second long put. The first put will serve only to offset the losses on the short put *below the lower strike*; the second, however, will earn you profits below the lower strike once the cost of the premium is earned back in the market. For this strategy to work, however, you need a move that is far enough below the lower strike to earn back the premium cost.

Playing the Seasonal Patterns with Option Spreads

Some of the most consistently profitable low-risk trades are spreads based on seasonal patterns. In the agricultural markets, seasonality is an important factor, since supplies are apt to be more abundant during certain times of the year, notably during the harvest period. However, knowing that seasonality exists in the agricultural markets and knowing how to capitalize on that tendency are a bit different.

In 1980, I published a book specifically devoted to pinpointing the most profitable spreads in the grain and livestock markets. (*Computer-Proven Commodity Spreads*, available from Windsor Books, P.O. Box 280, Brightwaters, NY 11718.) In researching the book, I found that the most widely known — and presumably most widely traded — spreads didn't hold up when tested by computer. Nevertheless, there were spreads that provided profits year after year. So consistent were the results that I likened the seasonal strategy to "watching paint dry" — not very exciting but very, very predictable.

The studies were based on the previous five to ten years. But after the book was available for five years, I went back and retested the spreads—and also traded them—and the results were even more encouraging. The updated results are available in a new book, *Real-Time-Proven Commodity Spreads*, also published by Windsor Books.

Briefly, spreads offer a number of advantages not available to the traditional futures trader. For one, in the nonperishable commodities, such as the grains, the so-called "limited-risk" spreads can be placed with a minimum of risk. Assuming the spread is trading near full carry, the full risk is typically only a few cents. On the plus side, the limited-risk spreads offer an opportunity to earn an unlimited amount in the event of a bull market. Even the bleakest markets can provide opportunity to the spread trader looking for a low-risk trade. Few traders would mind risking 3¢ or 4¢ to make 20¢. For another, spreads routinely get "out of line," in the parlance of the market. This means one month occasionally trades at a discount or premium to another month, offering the alert spread trader an opportunity to capitalize on the situation.

Yet another advantage of spreads is the predictability of seasonal events such as the harvest. Moreover, the notion of the "critical" month—a period when one month should trade at a premium or a discount to another—provides a means of "testing" the market. If September corn, let's say, can't gain ground on the more distant December corn during the July–August period, it may be a sign that near-term supplies are abundant and that September will go off the boards weak compared to December, offering a spreading opportunity.

There's a lot more that can be said in favor of spreads, of course, including the ability to make a real killing when a special situation develops. But for now, let's concentrate on some of the more reliable seasonal patterns as proven by computer analysis.

Before we look at specific spreading opportunities, a few observations are necessary. Most spread traders, like most investors in general, are bullish in their outlook. They want the market to rise. And despite the fact that the well-known "limited-risk" spread is a vertical bull spread, the tendency toward bull markets is much *less reliable* than the tendency of the markets to sell off during certain periods of the year. I reached this conclusion, by the way, only after studying the computerized data. So when your broker and other market analysts are all clamoring for higher prices and bull spreads, be patient and await your opportunity to "back-spread" the market by placing bear spreads.

To make money trading these little-known seasonal spreads, you have to precisely analyze the relationships between different contract months. The information that follows should help you in this respect. Remember, the versatility of the new options on futures provides you with several ways to capitalize on seasonal spreads. You can use bull or bear spreads using puts or calls, as well as the more sophisticated strategies such as ratio writing, straddle writing, and the like. For now, let's look at a few of the more reliable seasonal spreads. The specific strategy to use for each spread can be considered later.

1. *Cotton.* Cotton, like a number of other agricultural commodities, has a fairly reliable seasonal pattern: *the nearby July contract expires weaker than the distant December contract.* In the 13 years tested through 1984, July cotton lost ground to the distant December contract a full 70 percent of the time. Although a variety of factors may account for this tendency, the seasonal pattern is clear-cut. Even more impressive, over the past eight years, when the spread was placed during mid-February and held until just before expiration of the July contract, the long December/short July cotton spread lost money only once — in 1981, when the loss amounted to just $30 per spread. Compare this to a profit of more than $1,500 on a single spread in 1978, more than $2,700 in 1979, more than $1,400 in 1980, and then another $1,000 in 1983, and you have a powerful seasonal pattern.

Option spread strategy: There are several methods to capitalize on the seasonal pattern of cotton. One is the traditional time spread, in which you write the nearby July call and purchase the longer-term December call. You can also use the diagonal spread between the July and December calls or puts, using different strike prices. Finally, there are the traditional vertical bear spreads using puts or calls. For example, if you want to use calls, you can write the lower-strike July call and purchase the higher-strike July call — a net credit spread that will reach its maximum profitability at the lower strike. Ideally, place the spread when the higher-strike call is at the money. For instance, if July cotton is trading at 70¢ per pound, buy the July 70 and write a lower-strike option.

2. *Soybeans.* In the world of spreads, nothing compares with the high-flying "old-crop/new-crop" bean spreads — typically, July beans spread against November beans. While the profits can be ample in this spread (in 1977, a single intercrop spread returned more than $11,000 in two months' time), one must exercise caution. The losses can likewise be substantial. On a seasonal basis, soybeans are a complex commodity to trade. This is because there are both normal seasonal and counterseasonal years. During the normal seasonal years, you will want to be bull-spread during the fall and bear-spread during the spring. During counterseasonal years, it is best to stay with the bear spreads.

The really big moves in the intercrop spreads tend to occur about every four years. During 1972 – 1973, the spread had a total move worth more than $25,000 on a single spread; the next big move occurred during 1976–1977, when the spread moved more than $16,000 from one extreme to another. There were also good spread moves in the years 1980–1981 and 1983–1984, when the spread changed in value by more than $10,000.

Option spread strategy: During normal seasonal years, the most consistent pattern is for the nearby July soybeans to go off the boards weak compared to the new-crop November. One means of capitalizing on this tendency is to place a horizontal or diagonal spread, with the nearby July contract as the short month. Another method is to bear-spread the July contract with puts or calls. When July beans sell at a high premium to November, you usually have an opportunity to sell July and buy November and earn profits as the spread moves in favor of November. Here again, the strategy is to sell July and buy November, or position bear spreads in July puts or calls.

3. *Wheat.* Like soybeans, wheat has a consistently downward pattern in that the nearby May contract tends to lose ground relative to the distant month in the two to three months prior to the expiration of the May futures. This seasonal pattern is especially evident when the nearby May contract has a premium 25¢ to 50¢ higher than that of the distant December contract. If you entered the long December/short May wheat spread on January 15 and liquidated at the beginning of the May delivery month, the spread returned profits 75 percent of the time over the past 12 years. In wheat, the old-crop/new-crop spread is represented by the May/July spread, May being the old crop and July the new crop.

Option spread strategy: I did my studies on the Chicago Board of Trade wheat contract, so you had best trade the wheat options at the MidAmerica Commodity Exchange in implementing this strategy (at the time of this writing, the Chicago Board of Trade doesn't offer wheat options). The strategy calls for back-spreading the May/December calls after the first of the year. Typically, you would write an at-the-money May call and purchase an out-of-the-money December call, depending on the prices of the underlying futures. As an alternative, you can purchase out-of-the-money May calls and sell at- or out-of-the-money May calls in a vertical spread. A modest decline in May futures will allow you to keep the entire initial writing premium.

4. *Corn.* Over a 12-year period, the back spreads in corn, as in the other grains, returned profits most consistently — about 67 percent of the time. Although corn has not been a stellar performer in recent years, the winning years in the spreads outpace the losers by a ratio of about 4:1 or 5:1. In 1981–1982, for instance, the spread lost 2¢; during

1983–1984, it made more than 14¢; in 1980, the spread earned more than 26¢. Over time, it has *averaged* about $500 on a single spread position in futures.

Option spread strategy: In good years and bad, look to capitalize on the tendency of the nearby corn futures contract to expire weak relative to its adjacent or more distant back month. Spreads to consider are long (distant) December/short (nearer-term) July corn and long (distant) December/short (nearer-term) September corn. As a horizontal or diagonal spread, the spread can be accomplished by writing the July and buying either September or December calls or puts. If you decide on a bear spread, you can concentrate on writing lower-strike calls and purchasing higher-strike calls — or reverse positions if you are using puts, to place the vertical bear put spread.

5. *Live hogs.* The meat complex has always offered good spreading opportunities, and now, with the introduction of options on futures, the alternatives have been increased about fivefold. One factor you have to contend with as a spreader in the meat complex is the perishability of the underlying commodity. Unlike grain, live cattle and hogs don't readily lend themselves to storage. Hence, although some animals can be held off the market for a short period of time, the underlying supply and demand will ultimately determine prices — often at a surprise to just about everyone. So there is potential risk, but also commensurate potential reward, for substantial changes in the hog and cattle markets.

Live hogs follow a definite seasonal pattern based on the near-term outlook for prices along with the prices of the leading feed grains, notably corn. As a rule, the winter months see a rise in prices, peaking in February. To capitalize on this tendency, spreaders look to sell the near-term April contract during February and spread it against a distant month. In the last five years, this spread has earned about 100 percent of its previous profits over the preceding ten years — an excellent showing.

Option spread strategy: In February, sell April calls and buy distant-month calls. Since the April calls expire during the month of March, this strategy will work only for a limited period of time. Another strategy is to bear-spread the April calls in live hogs by purchasing a higher-strike call and writing a lower-strike call. The net initial credit will be your maximum profit, which you'll realize at the lower strike or below. The bear spread strategy can also be accomplished by using puts.

6. *Live Cattle.* Most futures traders are well acquainted with the June/October live-cattle spread. In the past 15 years, the computer

results show, the long June/short October cattle spread has earned almost $9,000 in profits on a single spread when placed in mid-January and taken off in mid-May, about the time when the June options expire. The seasonality of cattle futures is rather pronounced, with tight supplies typically causing price rises in later winter and early summer. The surest sign of a good opportunity in this spread is if you can find June futures trading at a discount to October early in the year. By April or May, the June contract almost always mounts a rally and trades at a premium to October, resulting in profits on the spread.

Option spread strategy: Unlike the hog spread, the cattle spread involves buying the nearer June contract and selling the distant October contract. This can be accomplished by using the horizontal or diagonal spread with at-the-money calls, or by bull-spreading the June calls (buying a lower-strike, at-the-money call and writing an out-of-the-money call). As the strength of the June futures becomes apparent in the late spring, the long call will gain in value and futures move toward the higher-strike call, resulting in profits.

The Best Spread Strategies

The first step is to make an analysis to determine which way prices are likely to go. Obviously, there is no guarantee that your analysis will prove correct. But try to make the best judgment you can. Then use a spread strategy appropriate for the market condition you expect. You can always change your mind or take defensive action to cope with a changing market condition. The following list will help you find the appropriate strategy.

Strategies for Bull Markets

Vertical bull call spread—buy a lower-strike call/sell a higher-strike call.

Vertical bull put spread—buy a lower-strike put/sell a higher-strike put.

Synthetic long futures—buy a call/sell a put.

Strategies for Bear Markets

Vertical bear call spread—buy a higher-strike call/sell a lower-strike call.

Vertical bear put spread—buy a higher-strike put/sell a lower-strike put.

Synthetic short futures—buy a put/sell a call.

Strategies for Stable Markets

Sell straddle — sell a call/sell a put at the same strike.

Sell strangle — sell a call/sell a put at different strike.

Ratio writes — sell two or more higher-strike calls/buy one lower-strike, or sell two or more lower-strike puts/buy one higher-strike put.

Bull call calendar spread — sell near-term call/buy longer-term call.

Bear put calendar spread — sell near-term put/buy longer-term put.

Butterfly spread — using three different strikes, purchase call (put) at highest and lowest strike/sell two calls (puts) at middle strike.

Box spread — buy lower-strike call and sell higher-strike call/buy higher-strike put and sell lower-strike put.

Strategies for Volatile Markets

Buy straddle — buy a call/buy a put at same strike.

Buy strangle — buy a call/buy a put at different strikes.

7

Nonagricultural Options: Options on Currencies, Interest Rates, Precious Metals, and Equities

Agricultural options represent just a portion of the new options to be introduced in the current options explosion. Indeed, the first wave of options on futures were on such nonagricultural products as U.S. Treasury bonds and gold. So successful has the new boom in options become that today you can buy or sell options on a host of interest rates, foreign currencies, equity averages, and precious metals, in addition to agricultural products.

Some people feel that the options boom has introduced too much too soon. "What's the relevance of a Eurodollar or Deutschemark option to a soybean farmer?" they ask. Given the impact the strong dollar has had on grain exports in recent years, it may indeed be extremely relevant.

While the principles of trading nonagricultural options won't differ significantly from those of trading farm options, their individual uses may be slightly different. Depending on his circumstances, the modern farmer may find the nonagricultural options especially appropriate. For instance, a strong dollar may be the bane of agriculture, but a weakening dollar offers all sorts of opportunities to a knowledgeable user of currency options. As the dollar weakens, foreign currencies will move higher in price, offering an options trader the ability to profit from buying calls, writing puts, or engaging in a half-dozen other strategies designed to profit from appreciating currency prices.

Need a hedge against inflation? You can buy calls on gold futures. Or, if you are bearish on the gold market and think disinflation is here to stay, why not write calls on gold, or purchase puts? The truth is, there are always opportunities in the options market, even if you are just a one-commodity trader.

If you've followed the discussion of trading principles so far, you won't have any trouble understanding the nonagricultural options. They work the same way. Their difference from agricultural options lies with their individual contracts. Now's the time to give these options at least a cursory glance and see whether they are appropriate for your portfolio.

The Equity Options

In discussing nonagricultural options, it's probably appropriate to begin with equity options, for two reasons.

One, the entire concept of listed options began with options on stocks, which had their debut in the early 1970s at the Chicago Board Options Exchange. Although options on stocks had been traded for years prior to that time, the trading was done only through an informal network of options dealers, much as in the over-the-counter market today. A buyer of a call option on IBM shares had to first locate a broker with access to an owner of those shares who was willing to write an option on his stock. The market was fragmented, and there was no continuous trading in a centralized location as there is today. The boom in options trading, moreover, brought a host of imitators and competitors to the scene. Today, options on stocks are traded in New York, Chicago, Philadelphia, and San Francisco.

Two, the second generation of equity options, namely options on stock-market *averages*, has proven to be the most successful in options history. The S&P 100 Index, which is traded at the Chicago Board Options Exchange, is far and away the most popular option in the world.

For most commodities traders, the concept of an index on a stock-market average is a bit difficult to grasp at first. Unlike with traditional commodities, such as soybeans, corn, wheat, or cattle, there is no way to take or give delivery of a stock-market average. You can't truck it to the elevator, store it for three months, and send it to its destination half way around the world via rail car and ship. An average, such as the popular

S&P 500, whose futures and options change hands at the Chicago Mercantile Exchange, is nothing more than a *legal fiction*. That's right. It is just a number based on a basket of stocks. But for anyone who has exposure in the equities market — investors, portfolio managers, insurance companies, underwriters, and the like — the stock-index futures and options market has proven a godsend. For years, managers of large portfolios, who daily purchase and sell millions of dollars' worth of stock, had nowhere to go to hedge against market risks, short of selling their stocks. But with the introduction of the stock-index concept, they, like the farmer, now had the ability to hedge against unfavorable price risks.

Starting with the first stock-index futures contract in February, 1982, the stock-index futures and options markets have mushroomed. Today, there are five major stock-index futures trading in three cities, as well as several minicontracts. Apart from the S&P 100 (an option on a cash index) traded at the Chicago Board Options Exchange, the major futures contracts are: the S&P 500 contract, traded at the Chicago Mercantile Exchange; the Major Market Index, traded at the Chicago Board of Trade; the New York Stock Exchange Composite Index, traded at the New York Futures Exchange; and the Value Line Index, traded at the Kansas City Board of Trade.

The options on the S&P 500 and the New York Stock Exchange Composite Index are traded side-by-side on the floors of the respective exchanges. Major Market Index options, which (like the S&P 100 at the CBOE) are settled for cash, are traded at the American Stock Exchange in New York. The options on the Value Line Index were once traded at the Chicago Board of Trade, but because of lack of public support, the options ceased trading; in January 1985, the Philadelphia Stock Exchange, which recently opened a new options unit, began trading an option based on the Value Line Index, known as the Value Line 100.

As you may suspect, an option on a stock-index average differs in several respects from an option on an agricultural futures contract. The most significant difference rests with delivery. First and foremost, a futures contract on a stock index cannot be "delivered" in the traditional sense. To get around the difficulty, say, of coming up with one share of each of 500 stocks in the S&P 500 average or any other average, the exchanges have created what is known as a *cash settlement* provision. This means that at maturity, the futures contracts for nearby delivery *become identically priced with the cash index price, and all settlement is in cash.* As a result, delivery never takes place. Instead, winners are paid by losers, and the contract ceases to exist. Because of this lack of delivery, the options on the futures *do not* expire one month before the expiration of the futures, as do farm options. Instead, the options may be held until maturity, and all settlement will be in cash.

The options themselves trade much like their cousins, the agricultural options. You can buy them or sell them, or exercise them and take delivery of the underlying futures. Here are the major equity options on futures:

The S&P 500 option. Based on the popular S&P 500 futures, the most widely traded stock-index future, the S&P 500 option has a volume of about one-tenth of the futures. The underlying contract is based on the well-known S&P Composite Index of 500 stocks, which is comprised of 400 industrial, 40 public utilities, 20 transportation, and 40 financial companies. The option, like the underlying futures, is quoted in .05-point increments, with each tick representing a value of $25. The value of the underlying contract is 500 times the quoted price. Hence, a price of 167.25 for March S&P 500 futures would represent a contract valued at 500 times as much, or $83,625. And a quote of, say, 8.60 for the March 160 S&P 500 call (strikes are 5.00 points apart) would cost 500 times as much—or $4,300—to purchase.

The NYSE Composite Index option. Like the S&P 500, the NYSE Composite Index future is valued at 500 times its stated price. The option on the future, like the future itself, changes hands at the New York Futures Exchange, the subsidiary of the New York Stock Exchange. The underlying contract is comprised of about 1,511 common stocks traded on the Big Board. Although the futures and options are not as widely traded as the more popular S&P 500, they are attractive to smaller speculators because of their smaller size. At recent price levels, the NYSE Composite Index futures were valued at approximately $50,000, compared with over $90,000 for the S&P 500.

The Value Line 100 option. This newest entry into the option sweepstakes began trading at the Philadelphia Stock Exchange in January 1985, although the underlying futures are traded at the Kansas City Board of Trade. The Value Line contract is an unweighted, geometrical average of prices for nearly 1,700 stocks listed on all major exchanges. The Value Line average tends to be the most volatile of all the stock-index averages and often leads the market in advancing or declining. The Value Line 100 is unique in the sense that it is the only unweighted index option on the market. Unlike the Value Line futures traded in Kansas City, the Value Line 100 options are valued at only 100 times their quoted price, not 500 times the quoted price like the futures.

Apart from the wide speculative appeal of equity options, they offer participants in the stock market an opportunity to hedge against risk. The most common strategy among investors who own stock is to place a sort of selling hedge using futures or options on stock indexes. Assuming one's portfolio moves up or down in similar fashion to the major averages, one can hedge by either selling futures or buying puts against an anticipated market decline. Should the decline then occur, the losses on the stocks in the investor's portfolio will be offset, in part if not in whole, by the gains in either futures or options on stock-index averages.*

The Precious-Metals Options

There are only two metal contracts worth trading — gold and silver — and now there are options available on both. Options on gold futures were among the first of all options on futures to be introduced. Traded initially at the Commodity Exchange, Inc., in New York, the world's largest metals exchange, they are now also traded at the Mid-America Commodity Exchange in Chicago. Options on gold futures have proven to be among the most successful of all the new options on futures. More recently, the Comex introduced options on silver futures. And if the early performance results are any indication, the silver options will prove to be even more successful than the gold options.

Gold and silver have generally played the role of an inflation hedge. With the decline of inflation since 1980, gold and silver prices have fallen rather drastically — from more than $800 an ounce for gold to less than $300, and from more than $50 an ounce for silver to less than $6. But despite the bear market, the interest in metals remains undiminished. One can only expect that a resurgence in inflation will cause a wholesale march into gold and silver options as investors again seek an inflation hedge.

The leading precious-metals options are:

The gold option. Based on the Comex's 100-ounce contract, the gold option has the same delivery month as the underlying futures. The strikes are placed at $10 intervals, and each $1 move in the value of the option on a futures translates into a $100 gain or loss. Gold futures and options are widely traded and enjoy a popularity that is second only to the U.S. Treasury bond futures options at the Chicago Board of Trade. Options on so-called "mini-gold" contracts are available at the Mid-America Commodity Exchange in Chicago.

The silver option. Introduced two years after the gold options, silver

* For additional information on trading stock-index futures and options, I suggest you obtain a copy of my book *How to Triple Your Money Every Year with Stock-Index Futures*. It is available for $39.95 from Windsor Books, P.O. Box 280, Brightwaters, NY 11718.

options have quickly become one of the fastest-growing options. The strike prices are 50¢ apart, and the standardized contract calls for 5,000 ounces of silver. So-called "New York" silver futures—with delivery months and contract specifications identical to Comex silver futures—are also available at the MidAmerica Commodity Exchange in Chicago.

The easiest and most straightforward precious-metals strategy is to purchase call options in anticipation that renewed inflation will cause metal prices to rise. The metals have been in a bear market for so long that few expect higher prices. This is precisely the situation in which a lot of money can be made, since the majority of investors are rarely in the market when the major reversals occur.

The Interest-Rate Options

The U.S. Treasury bond futures option is the leading option on futures introduced to date. About 50,000 contracts change hands daily at the Chicago Board of Trade. Since they are based on the most popular futures contract in history, it probably isn't surprising that the options had a positive reception. They enable financial institutions to hedge their risk in the financial markets quite effectively.

One of the "first generation" options, options on U.S. Treasury bonds are quoted in terms slightly different from those of the underlying futures. Whereas the bond futures are quoted in intervals of $\frac{1}{32}$ (a quote such as 60-02 translating into $60\frac{2}{32}$ basis points), the options on the futures are quoted in $\frac{1}{64}$. Therefore, a quote of 5-19 for a June 60 call would mean $5\frac{19}{64}$, or approximately $5,297. First-time users of bond options will want to be aware of this feature.

A more recent entry into the interest-rate options market is the Eurodollar option, available at the Chicago Mercantile Exchange. The recent "internationalization" of the dollar and other factors have made the Eurodollar futures market one of the fastest-growing areas of the futures industry. The introduction of options on Eurodollar futures in early 1985 has likewise been met with wide acceptance in the international investor community.

The leading interest rate options are:

The U.S. Treasury bond option. The success of the U.S. Treasury bond futures contract at the Chicago Board of Trade is unparalleled in the history of futures trading. No other contract, including the once-booming soybean futures contract, has ever enjoyed the wide participation of bond futures. The futures contract, as we've mentioned, is quoted in basis points plus $\frac{1}{32}$ of a single basis point. To increase the depth and liquidity of the options, however, the quotations are in basis points plus $\frac{1}{64}$ of a basis point. Each basis point represents $1,000 in the value of the underlying instrument. Investors who are new to the interest-rate futures market must acquaint themselves with the reverse relationship that bond prices have to interest rates. Specifically, when interest rates *rise,* bond prices *fall;* and when interest rates *fall,* bond prices *rise.* So, if you were anticipating *declining* interest rates, you would be a bull on bond prices. You would, therefore, employ a bullish strategy to profit from the interest rise, such as buying call options on bond futures or buying the futures alone. An investor who anticipates *rising* interest rates would be a bear on bond prices and would sell futures or buy puts to profit from the move.

The Eurodollar option. Traded at the Chicago Mercantile Exchange, Eurodollar futures have enjoyed increasing popularity since their introduction in December 1981. The Eurodollar contract derives its popularity and liquidity from the trillion-dollar Eurodollar deposit market, which tracks short-term rates abroad. By contrast, bond futures track long-term interest rates. Like stock indexes, Eurodollar futures are settled for cash, as are the options. Futures and options stop trading on the same day. The futures and options have minimum fluctuations of .01 basis point, which is equal to $25. Strike prices for the options are set at .25-point intervals, and there are no daily price limits. Eurodollar futures prices are based on an index that is calculated by subtracting Eurodollar interest rates from 100. Thus, a Eurodollar interest rate of 9.07 percent would translate into a cash index price of 90.93. The individual months of the futures are based at progressively higher rates as you go out further in time. The option premiums, as with all options, reflect the futures prices, their relationship to the strike price, and time to expiration.

The Currency Options

Options on foreign-currency futures are one of the hottest areas of the investment business these days. The growth in the market has been spurred by rather dramatic gyrations of foreign-currency prices relative to the U.S. dollar. Moreover, the well-established interbank market in foreign exchange has created an interest in the futures market, which was once a relatively minor player on the foreign-exchange scene. No more. Today, the international interbank market follows the futures market in foreign exchange. One factor that helped was the new linkup between Chicago and Singapore, which created a system of *mutual off-set.* A trader can now initiate a trade in one market and close it out in another half way around the world.

Foreign-currency trading has spread from the original International Monetary Market in Chicago (a division of the Chicago Mercantile Exchange) to Philadelphia, where a new foreign-currency options market began last year. But for options on futures in foreign exchange, the Chicago Mercantile Exchange is likely to remain the leader.

Foreign-currency trading is vital to world trade. Moreover, it affects virtually every company or business that markets its product abroad or imports products from abroad. In recent years, companies involved in exporting have been especially hard hit by the strong U.S. dollar. Forced to pay wages and salaries here at home in a strong U.S. dollar, these companies were receiving relatively weak foreign currencies in payment abroad. By skillfully using the interbank or futures market for foreign exchange, however, these exporters were able to minimize their foreign-currency losses.

Farmers, of course, are among those hardest hit by the impact of a strong dollar abroad. This is because U.S. agricultural products can't compete on the international market against countries willing to be paid in softer currencies. As a result, foreign countries gladly accept payment in the strong U.S. currency but are quite unwilling to pay their creditors in the same currency. Another factor is disinflation, which causes currencies that retain some gold backing, such as the Swiss franc and the Deutschemark, to decline in terms of the dollar. This causes the trade imbalance to grow even more, as those who must rely on foreign-currency payments continue to suffer foreign-currency translation losses.

In response to the growth in international trade and the uncertainty in the foreign-exchange market, foreign-currency futures trading has soared in recent years. In just the past year, the first options on futures have been introduced in the foreign currencies, beginning with the successful options on Deutschemark futures. Since then, the Chicago Mercantile Exchange's Index and Options Market has introduced options trading on the Swiss franc and the British pound as well. More can be expected in the future.

If foreign-currency speculation isn't your specialty, you should know that foreign currencies allow you to profit from gyrations in the dollar. Essentially, when the dollar is strong, the foreign currencies are weak. Hence, if you were bullish on the U.S. dollar, you would sell foreign-currency futures; if you were bearish on the dollar, you would buy foreign-currency futures. In recent months, we've seen the U.S.

dollar soar to all-time highs; but in more recent weeks, a countertrend has begun, pushing the dollar lower and other currencies higher.

The options on the foreign-currency futures offer the same advantages as ag options. For a fixed, one-time premium payment, you can buy a put or a call and profit if your market judgment proves correct. Of course, you can also write foreign-currency puts and calls and receive the premium income.

The leading options on foreign-currency futures traded at the Chicago Mercantile Exchange are the following:

The Deutschemark option. Options on the popular Deutschemark futures, which are currently the most widely traded foreign-currency futures, are quoted in the same terms as the underlying futures. The option is for a futures contract consisting of 125,000 Deutschemarks. It is quoted in dollars per mark. This is the *reverse* of the way that foreign currencies are quoted in the interbank market, where the quote would be in marks per dollar. Hence, a quote of .3324 for September Deutschemark futures means $.3324 per mark, or 33.24¢ per mark. The options have strike prices placed at 1¢ intervals — 32¢, 33¢, 34¢, and so on. Each single point on the 125,000-Deutschemark contract is valued at $12.50. Thus, a September 34 put valued at 1.78 will cost precisely $2,225, or 178 times the value of one point, $12.50.

The Swiss franc option. A popular speculative currency, the Swiss franc tracks the Deutschemark pretty closely, although the latter currency enjoys a more prominent role in world trade. Because the Swiss franc options are much newer than the Deutschemark options, they haven't yet reached the same volume and open interest — they trade at only about one-tenth the rate of the Deutschemark. The futures contract for Swiss francs consists of 125,000 Swiss francs and is quoted in dollars per franc. The options on the futures are also quoted in 1¢ increments.

The British pound option. This newest entry on the options scene is based on the underlying British pound futures contract, which consists of 25,000 British pounds and is quoted in dollars per pound. So far, the trading in the options has been sluggish, but only time can tell if these options will eventually be successful. At present, several hundred option contracts on the British pound change hands daily, compared with almost 10,000 option transactions daily in the Deutschemark.

Trading Nonagricultural Options: Some Examples

The best way to acquaint yourself with some of the uses of nonagricultural options is to look at a few trading examples. As you must know by now, there are many, many ways to use options to capitalize on different market conditions. The only difference between agricultural and nonagricultural options is the underlying security.

For many first-time investors in the new options market, the first step will be to identify a situation in which you can use an option position to earn profits. Let's consider a few examples.

Example 1: Buy puts on Treasury bond futures to profit from a rise in long-term interest rates. Let's assume you envision higher interest rates in the future. As a borrower, you are concerned about the potential rise in interest rates, but you don't know what to do. One strategy is to purchase puts on Treasury bond futures. It works like this: With December Treasury bond futures trading at 68-00, you purchase a December 68 put for $1,000. In time, bond prices begin to fall as interest rates rise (remember, they move inversely). When December Treasury bond futures fall to 67-00, the December 68 puts are valued at $1,600. Let's say there are several months left to expiration. Because you now fear a decline in interest rates and a consequent rise in bond futures, you decide to take your profit. You sell the December 68 put for $1,600 and earn a profit of $600.

Example 2: Buy puts on the S&P 500 Index to hedge a stock portfolio against a temporary decline in prices. You may have purchased stock over the years, and you are reluctant to sell stock, because you are a long-term bull. Unfortunately, you interpret the market's hesitation to signal a temporary pullback that may take the Dow Jones Industrial Averages down 50 or 60 points, or even more. What can you do, short of selling stock? The answer is, buy puts on the S&P 500 Index futures. Assuming your stock holdings are representative of the market as a whole, chances are your stocks' performance will mirror that of the market as a whole. Let's say that June S&P 500 futures are trading at 180 and you purchase the June 180 put for $1,000. Four weeks later, June S&P 500 futures are at 170 and the June 180 put is now valued at $6,500 (10 points of intrinsic value at $500 per point, plus 3 points of remaining time value at $500 per point). The paper loss on the portfolio might have been $5,000. The net result is that you have made $5,500 on the put after expenses and have lost $5,000 on paper in your stock portfolio. Hence, the net profit is $500. This is not bad, considering that if you had *not* hedged by purchasing the put, you would have had just a $5,000 paper loss in your stock portfolio.

Example 3: Write puts on the S&P 500 Index to generate cash income during a stock-market rally. Many farmers and commercials engaged in agriculture own securities, though few think of aggressively writing options to enhance their overall portfolio income. With the introduction of stock-index futures several years ago and, more recently, options on stock-index futures, stock investors can increase their yield by writing options. Let's say you are bullish on the stock market, yet you are fully invested. One method of generating some income is to sell puts on the S&P 500 Index. In return for writing the puts, you will receive the premium income. Your risk, of course, is that the stock market declines rather than rises. At recent price levels, with the June S&P futures near the 182 level, the out-of-money June 180 puts were trading for about 2.50 points, or $1,250. Assuming the market stays *above* 180 at expiration, the June puts will expire worthless. So you might write ten June 180 puts and receive a total of $12,500 in premium income. Assuming the market is indeed bullish and prices rise, the puts will expire worthless and you will earn the full $12,500 premium income on the ten puts.

Example 4: Buy Deutschemark calls as insurance against a short sale in Deutschemark futures. Anticipating continued strength in the U.S. dollar, a futures speculator might sell Deutschemark futures in the hope of buying them back at a lower price. Yet he is reluctant to take the position unhedged, for fear that the dollar might slide and that the Deutschemark might soar in price. To provide a little protection, therefore, the speculator purchases call options. This limits his risk to the cost of the options. With September Deutschemark futures trading at 34¢, for example, a speculator might sell September futures while purchasing 34-strike calls. Let's say the calls are trading at 1.50 points, or $1,875, for the 125,000-Deutschemark contract. If prices slide as anticipated to 31¢ per Deutschemark, the speculator will earn a total of 3¢ per contract, or $3,750. At the same time, the 34-strike calls will lose value, since they remain out of the money. Hence, his profit will be offset by the amount he paid for the call, minus whatever he can earn on it by selling it later on. But let's assume he holds the call until expiration, when it has no value. The profit of $3,750 on the futures minus the cost of $1,875 on the call will result in a net profit of $1,875. Of course, had Deutschemark prices risen, the calls would have protected the speculator from losses on the short futures. His total risk: the cost of the calls.

Example 5: Write Deutschemark calls and purchase Deutschemark futures to profit from the writing income. One risk of writing "naked" options is the possibility of having the options exercised against you. What are you going to do if you receive a short futures position when writing a call? Since an option buyer will exercise only when he has a profit, you are going to have a built-in paper loss on any short position you receive. One strategy to avoid the losses associated with unwelcome exercise is to write only covered options. This means you already own the underlying security — in this instance, a long futures contract — at the strike price. Should the option be exercised against you, you still gain the writing income, although you will no longer own the futures.

For example, with September Deutschemark futures at 34¢ per mark, you decide to write an at-the-money September 34 call for a premium of 1.50, or $1,875. Assuming the market stays stationary or moves higher, your profit is $1,875 in writing income. Why? Because you are protected against exercise by holding a long position in the underlying futures. If the market rises, the call will be exercised and you will be given a *short* position at the strike of 34¢. But you are already long at 34¢. The net result is a wash on the futures. That is, you bought at 34 and sold at 34. That's the futures. In the options market, however, you have gained the premium income, which is yours to keep no matter what the futures do. However, there is some risk here on the down side. Should Deutschemark futures move lower, you will lose on the long futures. In part, this loss can be offset by the writing income. So you have 1½¢ in down-side protection. Below that price you will sustain a loss. The breakeven point is at the premium received minus the strike (when you write an at-the-money call). In this example, where you initially took in 1.50 points in writing income, the breakeven point will be at 32.50 in the underlying September futures.

Example 6: Write calls on the NYSE Composite Index to generate income in a declining stock market. You may see a declining stock market as an opportunity to pick up some money writing calls — *if* you see the decline as temporary. Perhaps you are unwilling to sell stock. Capital-gains tax and other factors might militate against a sale of the securities, yet you don't want to feel helpless either. One solution is to write calls. As long as the calls remain out of the money, they won't be exercised, and the steady decline in time value will be yours to keep. Let's say the NYSE Composite Index June futures are trading at 105, and you decide to write a June 106 call for a premium of $1,000. As long as NYSE Composite futures remain below the 106 strike, the call will remain unexercised and you will earn the entire $1,000 writing income. After all, for you to profit, the market doesn't even have to decline; in fact, it can rise 100 points, and you will still keep the entire premium at expiration. However, the margining process may present some problems. So you write seven or eight calls for $7,000 or $8,000. While you may sustain a paper loss in your stock portfolio, the gain in the call-writing income should offset any losses.

Example 7: Write a naked straddle in Swiss franc options to capitalize on stationary foreign-currency prices. Many investors claim that they can't make money in stationary markets. The market goes up a little and down a little and ends up pretty much the same. All markets enter occasional periods of stagnation. Rather than yawn and complain that you can't make money during such market periods, why not go with the trend and write straddles, capitalizing on the inevitable decline in time premiums? One method is to write a naked straddle. With the naked straddle, you don't have a long or short position, so you cannot afford to let the market run on you. The strategy is to write a put and a call at the same strike, preferably near the market price of the underlying futures. Let's look at our example. Swiss franc futures are dead in the water and trading about 41¢ per franc. The June 41 call and the June 41 put are each trading at 1 point, or $2,500 for both. So you write one of each and collect the $2,500 as writing income. Now, as long as June Swiss franc futures remain stationary, the writing income — or at least *most* of it — is yours to keep. Let's say that at expiration, June Swiss franc futures are at 41.50. You have lost .50 points, or $625, on the call, but you have picked up 2.00 points, or $2,500 in writing income. You still come out ahead by the difference between your writing income and what you paid out, or $1,875. Typically, you can earn such writing income in 35 to 40 calendar days. So, on an annual basis, the percentage profit on the invested margin can be quite high.

Example 8: Buy deeply out-of-the-money calls on S&P Index futures to gain tremendous leverage in a bull market. Calls are relatively cheap when they are trading deeply out of the money. And for good reason. Their chances of ever proving profitable are slim. As a result, the writers of such calls consider it a good risk to capture whatever time value exists in return for writing the call. They write them by the hundreds and generally forget about them. That is, until a genuine bull market gets under way and the calls suddenly come to life overnight. Granted, the chances of making money in a call that is far out of the money are not good. But the leverage can't be beat. And when the market runs, that leverage can turn into a quick fortune. For instance, you can currently buy a call on the June S&P futures contract for just $175. That's just $175 to control an asset worth over $90,000! But there's a catch. The underlying June futures are trading at about 182, and the strike on the cheap call is 195, so you are looking at 13 points in appreciation needed to just get to the strike! The option won't have any cash value until it goes *above* the strike. What's more, time on the option is running out. We are looking at just eight weeks left to expiration (S&P options, because of the cash settlement provision, expire at the same time as the underlying futures, namely, in the latter half of the expiration month). In five more trading days, the option will have just seven weeks left to expiration, and the chance that it will still be out of the money is almost 100 percent.

Still, buying these deeply out-of-the-money calls might make sense.

The reason? The option doesn't have to go into the money for you to make money. On the contrary, almost any bull move will push the calls higher in price. If the calls were to rise $500 each, you would have a profit of 175 percent! Thus, even a temporary surge in volatility would make these out-of-the-money call options more valuable. But you better be right when you purchase options that are deeply out of the money. Two weeks ago, these same June 195 calls were valued $100 higher (that's right, they have *lost* 36 percent since then) — and, significantly, the market has moved *up* almost a point since then. As time passes (unless a real runaway bull market comes along), these out-of-the-moneys are going to remain just that — out, a total loss for their buyers.

Example 9: Write puts on Deutschemark futures to bet against a weakening dollar. As the era of the strong U.S. dollar comes to an end and our exports become more attractive abroad, foreign currencies will surely rise. One way to profit from this appreciation of the Deutschemark is to write put options. A rising currency market will cause the puts to lose value and let the put writer capture the premium income. An example: With September Deutschemark futures trading at 34¢ per mark, you can write a September 34 put for a premium of 1.50 points, or $1,875. If you hold the short position until the expiration of the put — and, of course, assuming the put remains unexercised — you will receive the entire premium if September Deutschemark futures are above 34¢ per mark at expiration of the September options. Your profit: $1,875.

Example 10: Place a vertical bear call spread in Swiss franc options to capture the initial net credit on a declining currency market. You may be bearish on Swiss franc prices and wish to capitalize on the situation by placing the bear spread. Let's assume June Swiss franc futures are trading at 41¢ per franc and that you buy the higher-strike June 41 call for a premium of 1.00, or $1,250, and write the lower-strike June 39 call for a premium of 2.00, or $2,500. Since you received twice as much as you paid, the initial net credit is $1,250. This is the maximum profit on the spread. At expiration, if the June futures are at 39¢ or lower, you will earn the full $1,250 net credit. At the price of 39¢, the short call will expire worthless, earning you $2,500 in writing income; at the same time, the higher-strike 41 call, for which you paid $1,250, will also expire worthless. Your profit: $1,250.

A Final Word of Caution

Whether you decide to buy or write agricultural or nonagricultural options — or, for that matter, engage in a more sophisticated strategy

— be forewarned that there are no guarantees. Even the most carefully thought-out trading plan is apt to go awry when the markets change, as they so often do. Anyone who claims that a particular options trading strategy is certain to return a profit is either misinformed or unethical. There are no certainties in options trading.

The examples provided here were intended to show you how a given strategy might work under actual market conditions. This book is intended as a guide, nothing more. The new agricultural options market will continue to offer an abundance of opportunities to those with the patience and understanding to find them. I hope that, armed with the information in this book, you can go out and find those opportunities.

Appendix I:

The Leading Speculative Strategies

This Appendix is designed as a ready reference for the rest of the book. If, for instance, in reading the chapter on option spreads, you want a thumbnail refresher on the vertical bear call spread, you can simply turn to the section in this Appendix and go over the details of the strategy.

We've dealt in Chapter 2 with the four basic option strategies: buying calls, buying puts, writing calls, and writing puts. Every advanced option strategy relies on these four basic strategies. So if you have understood what we've been talking about so far, you are in a good position to understand the slightly more advanced strategies covered here.

Every strategy can be broken down into its component buy or write, put or call strategies. So when you are uncertain about a particular strategy, try to isolate its component parts in order to understand the dynamics at work. Also, in some of the more advanced strategies, you will be using both options and futures contracts. In some strategies, the options serve as the "insurance" for the risk of holding the futures contract; in others, the options are just another leverage-enhancement tool. In virtually every strategy, however, there will be a trade-off between higher risk and higher reward.

The important thing to remember is that there is an option strategy for virtually every market condition. Indeed, your problem won't be finding a strategy to cope with a particular market condition but deciding which of five or more strategies best accommodates your circumstances. Finally, in sizing up a strategy, you have to place yourself in the camp of a commercial hedger or a speculator. Commercials will find options useful for such purposes as controlling their business expenses and timing the marketing of their product. To the speculator, whose only real concern is a profitable trade, the new farm options will offer an unprecedented opportunity to hone his trading skills and specialize in one aspect of options trading. Not every strategy will be applicable to every trader. But rest assured there's something here for everyone, commercial and speculator alike.

Coping with a Stationary Market

In recent years, the agricultural sector of the futures industry has suffered from markets that have been in the doldrums. With the breaking of the inflationary cycle of the late 1970s, the markets of the 1980s have moved primarily down or sideways. For the farmer, the low prices have been a disaster. Unable to meet the cost of production, the farmers have had little opportunity to profit from either the cash or the futures markets. Perhaps some of these new options strategies will enable them to generate a little income while remaining protected by virtue of owning the cash crops. Likewise, for the speculators, who have abandoned the agricultural futures markets in droves in recent years for more lucrative pastures, the new agricultural options market might represent a new frontier of opportunity. Quite simply, with the new ag options, you don't need a market that goes up or down. That's right, by using specific strategies, you can capitalize on selling time premium to create a profit stream. Let's look at the most widespread techniques for profiting from a stationary market.

Selling the Naked Straddle

We've discussed the pros and cons of selling naked puts and calls. The naked writer grants a put or call to the buyer in return for a premium payment. The premium payment is the most that the writer can gain from a transaction. In return for granting the option, the writer must be willing to pay the buyer for any profit that accrues on the open option position. Thus, his return is strictly limited to the premium he receives, but his potential liability is unlimited.

Generally, the option writer has a point of view on the market. The put writer expects prices to remain stationary or rise; the call writer expects prices to remain stationary or decline. Both want the options to be out of the money at expiration.

Now we turn to a slightly more sophisticated strategy that involves writing both put *and* call options on the same futures. Known as *selling the naked straddle*, the strategy involves the simultaneous writing of both a put and a call with identical exercise prices and expiration dates. Moreover, the strategy is accomplished without an accompanying futures position. Thus the term "naked," which refers to an uncovered short position in the futures.

Because the options are sold without a futures position, the likelihood of assignment on one option or another is great. This possibility must be taken into account in planning the naked option straddle strategy.

Let's look at an example. Assume you are indifferent concerning live-cattle prices. The market has been trading around $68 a hundredweight, and you fully expect the price two months from now also to be around $68. Supply and demand are in balance, the Cattle on Feed reports are all neutral, you don't expect a sharp hike or decline in interest rates, and there is just nothing on the horizon to suggest substantially higher or lower cattle prices. One method of capitalizing on this situation is to write a naked straddle.

You might, therefore, sell an at-the-money 68 put for a premium of, let's say, 1.00 and simultaneously sell an at-the-money 68 call for the same premium. Your total income per straddle is therefore $800, or $400 on each side. Your obligation is to provide the call buyer with a long live-cattle futures position at the strike of 68 and to provide the put buyer with a short live-cattle futures position at the strike of 68. Naturally, the call will be exercised only when futures are above 68, and the put will be exercised only when futures are below 68. In the two months prior to expiration, you will be expected to provide sufficient margin for both positions. And if prices begin to move substantially away from the strike price, you may very well want to take a defensive position by buying back one of the options. But in the meanwhile, you are content to earn the premium income as time passes and the time value steadily erodes.

We know that the maximum potential return on the position is at the strike of 68. At that price, neither call nor put will have any value, and you will collect 100 percent of the premium income. But more likely, even if prices are stationary, prices will move away from the strike to some degree. Let's say the movement is down—to 67.50 at expiration. Now the call will have expired worthless, while the put will have a .50 value. The put option will be exercised against you (requiring you to provide the put buyer with a short position at the strike of 68.00), and you will be able to offset the futures position in the market for a .50 point loss, or $200. Your net profit, commission costs aside, will be the difference between what you took in originally on the straddle sale and the amount you paid out. In this instance, the $800 constituted the income, and the $200 loss on the exercised put constituted the loss. The net gain will be the difference of $600—again, before commission costs are factored in.

The breakeven points on such a straddle sale can also be calculated easily. Since you took in 2 points, or $800, in premium income, you can afford to lose a comparable amount and still break even. Thus the strike plus-or-minus the writing income will be the breakeven points. In this instance, with a strike of 68, the breakeven points on the straddle will be 70 and 66.

In summary, selling a straddle involves writing both a put and a call for the same expiration at the same strike price. Most profitable in a stationary market, the strategy provides a fixed premium return coupled with an unlimited risk should prices move sharply higher or lower. The maximum gain will exist at the strike price. The profit will become decreasingly smaller as the underlying futures move away from the strike price in either direction.

Typical results if the straddle is written at 68 on April live-cattle futures are as follows (see also Figure 13):

Example:

Sell 1 April live-cattle 68 call at $1.00 = $400
Sell 1 April live-cattle 68 put at $1.00 =   400
                                 Net inflow = $800

Hypothetical Results:

	Change In Value Points	Dollar Value
If futures price = $68.50		
1 April 68 call at .50 =	.50	$200
1 April 68 put at 0 =	1.00	400
Net =	1.50	$600
If futures price = $68.00		
1 April 68 call at 0 =	1.00	$400
1 April 68 put at 0 =	1.00	400
Net =	2.00	$800

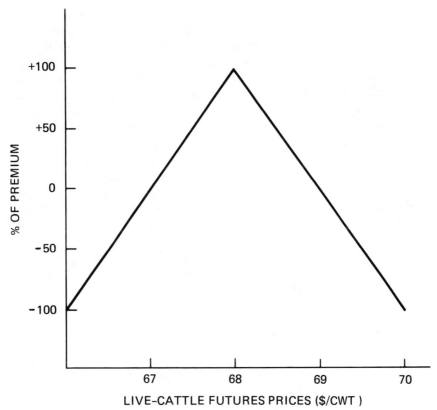

Figure 13. Selling the naked straddle.

If futures price = $67.50

I April 68 call at 0 =	1.00	$400
I April 68 put at .50 =	.50	200
Net =	1.50	$600

Maximum profit: $800
Maximum loss: unlimited
Breakeven point: $70.00 and $66.00 — a 4.00-point range

Selling the Naked Strangle

The strangle, which is also known as the *combination*, involves a put and a call with *different* strike prices. The naked-strangle writer sells a call at one strike price and a put at another strike. Typically, both options are out of the money. Like the straddle writer, the writer of a strangle hopes to capture declining time value by selling the out-of-the-moneys and waiting for time value to erode. Because both options in the strangle write are out of the money, the premium received is apt to be less than for the straddle write. This decreased income, however, is offset by a greater likelihood of keeping the entire premium, since the market must move in order for either the put or the call to prove profitable to the buyer.

With April live-cattle futures trading at $68 per hundredweight, the naked-strangle writer might sell an out-of-the money 66 put for .15 points, or $60, and an out-of-the-money 70 call for .40 points, or $160. His total income, therefore, will be $220 on the strangle. As long as the price of April live-cattle futures remains between $66 and $70 per hundredweight at the time of expiration of the options (in late March), the strangle writer will keep the entire premium received. His risk is that April live-cattle futures will rise above the higher strike of 70 or fall below the lower strike of 66 prior to expiration. Breakeven will exist at expiration at 70.55 or 65.45 — the difference between the strike, where the put or call goes into the money, and the premium received. See the example that follows:

Example:

```
Sell 1 April live-cattle 70 call at $.40 = $160
Sell 1 April live-cattle 66 put for $.15 =    60
                            Net inflow = $220
```

Hypothetical Results:

	Change In Value Points	Dollar Value
If futures price = $68.50		
1 April 70 call at 0 =	.40	$160
1 April 66 put at 0 =	.15	60
Net =	.55	$220
If futures price = $68.00		
1 April 70 call at 0 =	.40	$160
1 April 66 put at 0 =	.15	60
Net =	.55	$220
If futures price = $67.50		
1 April 70 call at 0 =	.40	$160
1 April 66 put at 0 =	.15	60
Net =	.55	$220

Maximum profit: $220
Maximum loss: unlimited
Breakeven point: $70.55 and $65.45 — a 5.10-point range

A word of caution. When selling the naked strangle, you must remember that you are taking in a comparatively small premium while risking an unlimited amount. Therefore, you must be careful not to let the market get away from you. The first sign of trouble in this strategy is an increase in volatility. Increased volatility will translate into higher premiums. Moreover, when the volatility increases, *both* puts and calls tend to increase in value, *even if* the market heads in one direction.

For instance, let's say you have sold an out-of-the-money put and an out-of-the-money call and the market takes a tumble. Naturally, the puts will increase in value, since the market is heading down. However, the calls may very well also increase in value, because the market has suddenly become more volatile and option buyers might reason if it can go down rapidly, it can also rise rapidly. This is especially true following a period of relatively quiet prices. For the hapless sellers of options, the situation calls for immediate withdrawal from the market. Not to do so can result in large losses — a strangle writer in pursuit of a $600 profit in writing income may soon find himself owing many times as much to lucky option buyers.

Be forewarned of the risk involved here. While writing strategies in stationary markets often result in steady writing income, the one exception — when the market suddenly comes alive — will ruin even the best-financed trader if he is not quick to take a loss and run.

Now take a look at Figure 14, which shows how you will retain 100 percent of the premium when live-cattle futures prices are between the strike prices and how you will quickly go into a low position as prices move either above the call's strike price or below the put's strike price.

Selling the Naked Safety Straddle

If you are neutral on the market but would prefer to hedge your bets in case a rally or decline takes place, you'll want to consider the safety straddle. The naked safety straddle involves no futures positions, just options. As the name suggests, the safety straddle is a straddle (short one put, short one call at the same strike) with a higher-strike long call and a lower-strike long put, or four options in all. Assuming the straddle portion is written at-the-money, the call will be out of the money, as will be the put. Thus, the "safety" portion of the safety straddle is a little extra insurance to help you out in case you get in trouble and the market takes off.

In the short straddle and short strangle, which we previously dis-

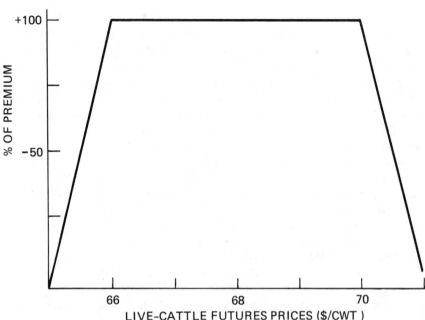

Figure 14.   Selling the naked strangle.

cussed, the risk was that the market stopped what it was doing—namely, moving sideways—and turned into a roaring bull or bear. In either instance, the seller of a straddle or strangle would find himself in trouble. In the case of the safety straddle, however, for a payment of two extra premiums, the straddle writer provides himself with a little extra insurance. In the event of a rise in prices, the long call will partly offset the losses on the short call that he sold at the lower strike. Depending on the premiums he received and paid, the straddle writer will have either a small profit or a small loss on the position. Likewise, in the event of a sharp decline in prices, the long put at the lower strike will partly offset the loss on the short put that he sold as part of the straddle.

In summary, selling a naked safety straddle involves four option transactions: selling a put and a call at the same strike price, and purchasing one call at a higher strike and one put at a lower strike. Both potential gains and losses are, therefore, limited. This is in contrast to the short straddle or strangle, which has unlimited risk. Because you must pay out money to purchase the long call and the long put (the ''insurance'' options), the range of profitability will be narrower than it would be in a simple short straddle. But this is the price you pay for safety. You sell a safety straddle when you are anticipating stationary prices but fear that a sharp rally or decline might prove ruinous to the straddle position.

Consider the following example. See also Figure 15, which shows how the naked straddle is profitable over a narrow range of prices. The "safety" is provided by the out-of-the-money long put or call.

Example:

Sell 1 live-hogs July 54 call at $1.00 = $300
Sell 1 live-hogs July 54 put at $1.00 =   300
Buy 1 live-hogs July 56 call at $.50   = (150)
Buy 1 live-hogs July 52 put at $.50   = (150)
Net inflow = $300

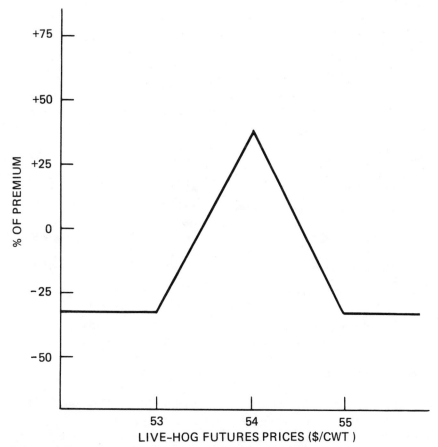

Figure 15.   Selling the naked safety straddle.

Hypothetical Results:

	Change In Value Points	Dollar Value
If futures price = $58.00		
July 54 call at 4.00 =	(3.00)	($900)
July 54 put at 0 =	1.00	300
July 56 call at 2.00 =	1.50	450
July 52 put at 0 =	(.50)	(150)
Net =	(1.00)	($300)
If futures price = $56.00		
July 54 call at 2.00 =	(1.00)	($300)
July 54 put at 0 =	1.00	300
July 56 put at 0 =	(.50)	(150)
July 52 put at 0 =	(.50)	(150)
Net =	(1.00)	($300)
If futures price = $54.00		
July 54 call at 0 =	1.00	$300
July 54 put at 0 =	1.00	300
July 56 call at 0 =	(.50)	(150)
July 52 put at 0 =	(.50)	(150)
Net =	1.00	$300
If futures price = $52.00		
July 54 call at 0 =	1.00	$300
July 54 put at 2.00 =	(1.00)	(300)
July 56 call at 0 =	(.50)	(150)
July 52 put at 0 =	(.50)	(150)
Net =	(1.00)	($300)
If futures price = $51.00		
July 54 call at 0 =	1.00	$300
July 54 put at 3.00 =	(2.00)	(600)
July 56 call at 0 =	(.50)	(150)
July 52 put at 1.00 =	.50	150
Net =	(1.00)	($300)

Maximum profit: $300
Maximum loss: $300
Breakeven point: $55.00 and $53.00 — a 2.00-point range

The Butterfly Spread

The butterfly spread is among the most popular strategies for coping with a stationary market, especially among members of the floor who don't have to take the cost of commissions into account. For if there is any drawback to this strategy, it is commission costs. The butterfly involves four options and three strikes—using just calls, although advanced students could well construct the spread using puts. These options are arranged in two different spreads. A spread transaction is composed of a long (buying) position and a short (selling) position. The call you purchase will cost you money, whereas the call you sell will generate premium income. The difference between the spread of the two legs of the position when you initiate it and when you subsequently ''unwind'' it will constitute your profit.

Specifically, the butterfly consists of two shorts calls at a middle strike, a long call at a higher strike, and a long call at a lower strike. Assuming the two calls you write are initiated at the money, the higher-strike long call will be out of the money (hence cheaper) than the lower-strike call, which will be in the money. Added together, you have two short (selling) calls and two long (buying) calls, for a total of four.

Let's take an example. Let's say April live hogs are trading at $48 per hundredweight and you decide to put on the butterfly. You instruct your broker to sell two at-the-money April 48 calls and simultaneously purchase one in-the-money April 46 call and one out-of-the-money April 50 call. You are now long two and short two. Since this is a stationary market strategy, you greatest point of profit will exist right at the middle strike, $48. At that price, both 48-strike calls will expire worthless and you will gain the entire writing income on the two calls you sold. At the same time, the in-the-money April 46 call will still be in the money, although you probably won't recover what you paid for it, because the time premium has now disappeared and it will retain cash value alone. The higher-strike April 50 will be worthless, and you will have to offset the loss with the profits you earned on writing the two April 48s.

As prices move away from the middle strike price, the profits will tend to lessen, until you get to a point where no matter how high or low futures trade, the loss will be the same. The strategy is best illustrated by the example that follows. Look also at Figure 16, which shows that the maximum profit results at the middle strike.

Example:

```
Buy 1 live-hogs April 46 call for $2.00  = ($600)
Sell 2 live-hogs April 48 calls for $1.00 =   600
Buy 1 live-hogs April 50 call for $.30    =   (90)
                 Initial investment cost = $  90
```

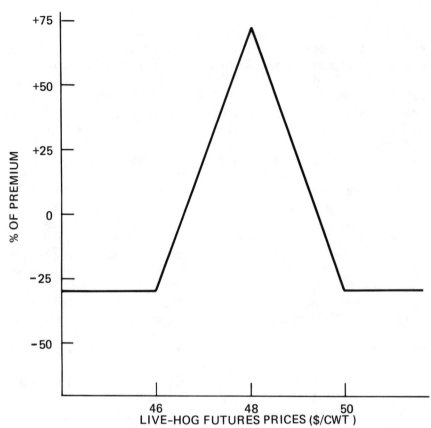

Figure 16.   The butterfly spread.

Hypothetical Results:

	Change In *Value Points*	*Dollar Value*
If futures price = $50.00		
1 April 46 call at 4.00 =	2.00	$600
2 April 48 calls at 2.00 =	(2.00)	(600)
1 April 50 call at 0 =	(.30)	(90)
Net =	(.30)	($ 90)
If futures price = $48.00		
1 April 46 call at 2.00 =	0	$ 0
2 April 48 calls at 0 =	2.00	600
1 April 50 call at 0 =	(.30)	(90)
Net =	1.70	$510

If futures price = $46.00

1 April 46 call at 0	=	(2.00)	($600)
2 April 48 calls at 0	=	2.00	600
1 April 50 call at 0	=	(.30)	(90)
	Net =	(.30)	($ 90)

Maximum profit: $510
Maximum loss: $ 90
Breakeven point: $ 49.70 and $46.30 — a 3.40-point range

Option Strategies for Rising Markets

Since flexibility is the key to market success, you'll want to know how to switch into different option strategies to cope with changing market conditions. We've discussed some of the important strategies for dealing with sideways markets. Now, what about rising markets? Are you limited to simply buying a call and hoping for the best? Absolutely not. Call buying has its place in the option strategist's portfolio. We've covered some of the advantages: fixed premium, limited risk, and so on. But more complicated strategies, some of them using call buying, have added advantages such as reduced overall option investment cost and wider profit zones. Some of them, such as the bull spread using calls, enhance profitability within a given range of prices. So, if you expect a modest rise in prices rather then a runaway bull market, you might want to consider this particular stategy.

Most significant, the introduction of options on futures enables you to tailor your strategy to a particular market condition. It is this increased choice of strategies that makes options trading so interesting and rewarding to the knowledgeable options trader. Let's look now at some of the alternatives for dealing with a rising market.

The Bull Call Spread

As the name suggests, the bull call spread involves the spreading of calls — buying one call and selling another — to cope with a bull market. Specifically, it consists of buying one call and writing another at a higher strike price. For example, you might buy a June 68 live-cattle call and simultaneously write a June 70 live-cattle call.

Since lower-strike calls, by definition, are more expensive than higher-strike calls of the same commodity and expiration date, the bull call spread will involve an outlay of cash. This is because you will be purchasing a more expensive call and writing a less expensive call.

Whether or not you will ultimately profit from the spread will depend on the action of the underlying futures contract. If futures prices rise, there is a good chance you will profit. If they remain stationary or decline, however, chances are you will lose money.

In general, the bull spread will be less expensive than an outright purchase of a call option. This is because you will generate writing income by selling the higher-strike call. However, the trade-off will be a limitation of your maximum profit. Hence, this strategy is generally best when you anticipate slightly higher prices. The maximum profit is at the higher strike. As for the cost of the spread, the down-side risk is limited to the initial debit when you put on the spread. See the next example. Also look at Figure 17, which shows that you obtain the maximum profit at the higher strike or above and the maximum loss at the lower strike or below.

Example:

Buy 1 May 575 soybean call for $13\frac{1}{2}¢$ = ($675)
Sell 1 May 600 soybean call for $5\frac{1}{2}¢$ = <u>275</u>
Initial investment cost = ($400)

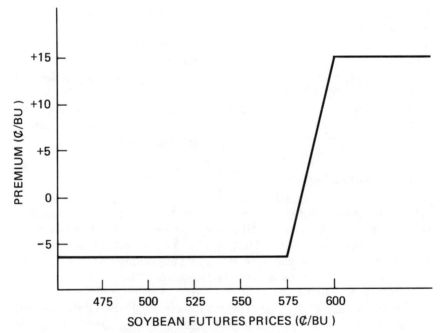

Figure 17. The bull call spread.

Hypothetical Results:

	Change In Value Points	Dollar Value
If futures price = $6.00		
1 May 575 call at 25¢ =	11½¢	$575
1 May 600 call at 0 =	5½¢	275
Net =	17¢	$850
If futures price = $5.85		
1 May 575 call at 10¢ =	(3½¢)	($175)
1 May 600 call at 0 =	5½¢	275
Net =	2¢	$100
If futures price = $5.75		
1 May 575 call at 0 =	(13½¢)	($675)
1 May 600 call at 0 =	5½¢	275
Net =	(8¢)	($400)

Maximum profit: $850
Maximum loss: $400 (initial net debit)
Breakeven point: $ 5.83 (value of initial net debit plus lower strike)

The Bull Put Spread

The bull put spread consists of one long put and one short put that is written at a higher strike. The spread will result in a net credit at the outset, since higher-strike puts have greater value than lower-strike puts. Like the bull call spread, the bull put spread will prove profitable if prices rise. Maximum profitability is at the higher strike, where the short put will expire worthless. At that price, the spread will return the entire initial net credit. Because the lower-strike put is purchased in this strategy, any movement below the lower strike will result in a fixed loss, which is the loss incurred at the lower strike. Consider the example below as well as Figure 18, which shows that the maximum profit is realized at the higher strike or above and that the maximum loss is incurred at the lower strike or below.

Example:

Sell 1 May 575 soybean put for $.13 = $650
Buy 1 May 550 soybean put for $.04 = (200)
               Net credit = $450

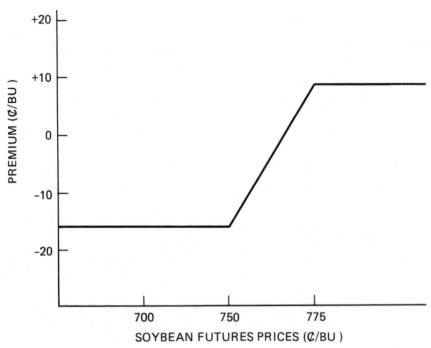

Figure 18. The bull put spread.

Hypothetical Results:

	Change In Value Points	Dollar Value
If futures price = $5.75		
1 May 575 put at 0 =	.13	$650
1 May 550 put at 0 =	(.04)	(200)
Net =	.09	$450
If futures price = $5.50		
1 May 575 put at 25¢ =	(.12)	($600)
1 May 550 put at 0 =	(.04)	(200)
Net =	(.16)	($800)
If futures price = $5.25		
1 May 575 put at 50¢ =	(.37)	($1,850)
1 May 550 put at 25¢ =	.21	1,050
Net =	(.16)	($ 800)

Maximum profit: $450
Maximum loss: $800
Breakeven point: $ 5.66 (higher strike minus net initial credit)

The Buy – Write

Another bullish to slightly bullish strategy is the buy–write, which involves buying a long futures contract and simultaneously writing a call. The purpose of the strategy is to lock in the call's premium in the event that prices stabilize or move higher. The futures contract serves as the underlying instrument that will be called away in the event of higher prices—which is precisely what the buy–write strategist anticipates. The call's premium, which is received as income at the outset of the transaction, serves to provide a relatively small profit cushion in the event of slightly lower prices. But this protection is marginal and limited to the income received. As a result, any downward movement in price will require defensive action, since the potential loss is unlimited. Refer to the example. Also look at Figure 19, in which you can see that the maximum profit exists at the strike price of the short call and above.

Example:

Sell 1 May 575 soybean call at $12\frac{1}{2}$¢ = $625
Buy 1 May soybean futures at $5.75 = ___0
Net inflow = $625

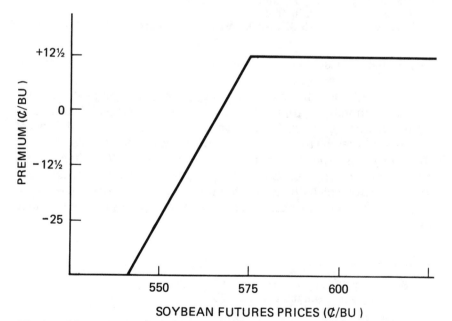

Figure 19.   The buy-write strategy.

Hypothetical Results:

	Change In Value Points	Dollar Value
If May futures price = $6.00		
1 May 575 soybean call at 25¢ =	(12½¢)	($625)
1 May soybean futures at $6.00 =	25 ¢	1,250
Net =	12½¢	$625
If May futures price = $5.75		
1 May 575 soybean call at 0 =	12½¢	$625
1 May soybean futures at $5.75 =	0	0
Net =	12½¢	$625
If May futures price = $5.50		
1 May 575 soybean call at 0 =	12½¢	$625
1 May soybean futures at $5.50 =	(25 ¢)	(1,250)
Net =	(12½¢)	($625)
If May futures price = $5.25		
1 May 575 soybean call at 0 =	12½¢	$ 625
1 May soybean futures at $5.25 =	(50 ¢)	(2,500)
Net =	(37½¢)	($1,875)

Maximum profit: $625 (initial net inflow)
Maximum loss: unlimited
Breakeven point: $5.62½ (strike price minus net inflow)

The Synthetic Call

The synthetic call consists of a long futures position protected by a long put option. The profitability/loss on the synthetic call is comparable to that on buying a call option. The risk is limited to the initial cost of the option, whereas the upward potential is unlimited. Because puts are frequently less expensive than calls, the synthetic call is often a good proxy for the outright purchase of a call option. Read the example and see Figure 20, which illustrates that with a synthetic call the cost of the put is the maximum loss and, on the other hand, that profit potential is unlimited.

Example:

Buy 1 May 575 soybean put for $.13 = ($650)
Buy 1 May soybean futures at $5.75 =   0
                Net initial investment = $650

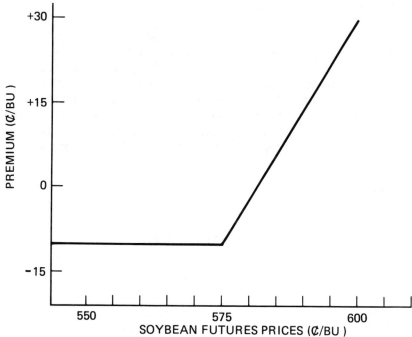

Figure 20. The synthetic call.

Hypothetical Results:

	Change In Value Points	Dollar Value
If futures price = $6.00		
1 May 575 soybean put at 0 =	(.13)	($650)
1 May futures at $6.00 =	.25	1,250
Net =	.12	$600
If futures price = $5.87		
1 May 575 soybean put at 0 =	(.13)	($650)
1 May futures at $5.87 =	.12	600
Net =	(.01)	($ 50)
If futures price = $5.75		
1 May 575 soybean put at 0 =	(.13)	($650)
1 May futures at $5.75 =	0	0
Net =	(.13)	($650)

Maximum profit: unlimited
Maximum loss: $650 (cost of put)
Breakeven point: $ 5.88 (entry price of long futures plus cost of put)

The Synthetic Long Futures

The synthetic long futures position consists of buying a call and selling a put at the same strike. The potential profit and loss on the synthetic long futures are comparable to those on an outright long futures position when the market price is close to the strike price of the call and the put. Since the prices of an at-the-money put and a call are often close, the position can often be taken for very little cost. See the example that follows. Figure 21 indicates that the synthetic long futures position has the same risk and the same reward as the long futures position.

Example:

Buy 1 May 575 soybean call for $13\frac{1}{2}¢$ = ($675)
Sell 1 May 575 put for 13¢   =   650
Net initial investment = $ 25

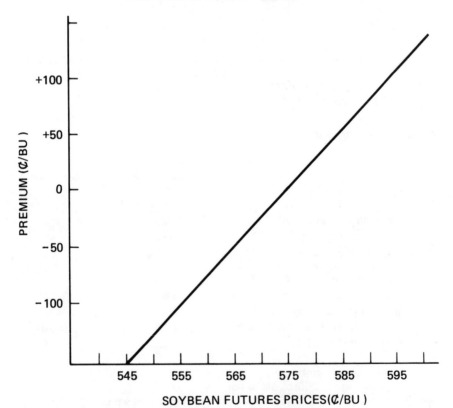

Figure 21. **The synthetic long futures position.**

Hypothetical Results:

	Change In Value Points	Dollar Value
If futures price = $6.08		
1 May 575 soybean call at 33¢ =	19¼¢	$ 975
1 May 575 soybean put at 0 =	13 ¢	650
Net =	32¼¢	$1,625
If futures price = $6.00		
1 May 575 soybean call at 25¢ =	11½¢	$ 575
1 May 575 soybean put at 0 =	13 ¢	650
Net =	24½¢	$1,225
If futures price = $5.75		
1 May 575 soybean call at 0 =	(13¼¢)	($675)
1 May 575 soybean put at 0 =	13 ¢	(650)
Net =	(¼¢)	($ 25)

Maximum profit: unlimited
Maximum loss: unlimited
Breakeven point: $5.75½ (strike price plus cost of position)

Buying the Straddle

For truly volatile markets, the buy straddle can prove an effective strategy. This is especially true when the market has recently put in a lackluster performance and premiums are low because of low volatility. At such times, the buy straddle can prove a moneymaker, because the subsequent volatility will make both put and call premiums rise, perhaps resulting in profits on both legs of the straddle.

Here's how it works. You purchase a put and a call at the same strike. Sometimes called a "double option," the resultant straddle is nothing more than a put and a call. As long as the market moves sufficiently up or down from the strike to win back the premium cost, the buyer of the straddle will have a profit. The cost of the straddle, of course, is fixed at the initial cost of the two premiums. Chances are, even if the market doesn't move sufficiently to win back the entire premium cost, it will move sufficiently to return at least a portion of the premium cost. Read the following example. Examine Figure 22, which shows the straddle provides a return as soon as prices move away from the strike price in either direction.

Example:

Buy 1 July 330 wheat call at $.06 = ($300)
Buy 1 July 330 wheat put at $.06 = (300)
Net initial investment = $600

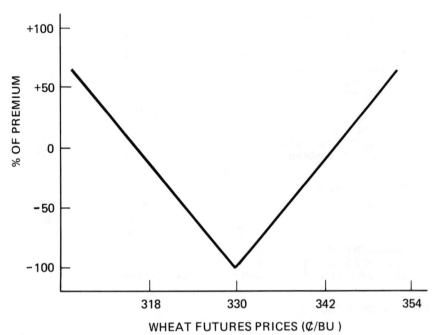

Figure 22.   Buying the straddle.

Hypothetical Results:

	Change In Value Points	Dollar Value
If futures price = $3.80		
1 July 330 wheat call at 50¢ =	.44	$2,200
1 July 330 wheat put at 0 =	(.06)	(300)
Net =	.38	$1,900
If futures price = $3.30		
1 July 330 wheat call at 0 =	(.06)	($300)
1 July 330 wheat put at 0 =	(.06)	(300)
Net =	(.12)	($600)
If futures price = $2.70		
1 July 330 wheat call at 0 =	(.06)	($ 300)
1 July 330 wheat put at 60¢ =	.54	2,700
Net =	.48	$2,400

Maximum profit: unlimited
Maximum loss: $600
Breakeven point: $ 3.42 on up side and $3.18 on down side (strike price
                         plus or minus cost of straddle)

The Buy Combination, Or Buying the Strangle

Like the straddle, the buy combination, or long strangle, returns a profit in a highly volatile market. Typically, the buy combination consists of buying a put and a call at different strikes, both out of the money. For example, with live-cattle futures trading at $67, the combination buyer would purchase an out-of-the-money 68 call and an out-of-the-money 66 put. The advantage of the combination over the straddle is that it costs less to initiate, since both options are out of the money. As a result, the position must overcome less premium expense in order to recover the initial investment and become profitable.

The drawback of the long strangle or combination is this: should prices stabilize, the investor will lose his entire premium cost if the futures trade between the two strikes at expiration. Given the lower cost of the combination, however, the strategy should return a higher percentage than the straddle in the event of volatile prices in either direction. See the following example. Figure 23 shows that the buy combination results in a 100 percent loss within the range between the two

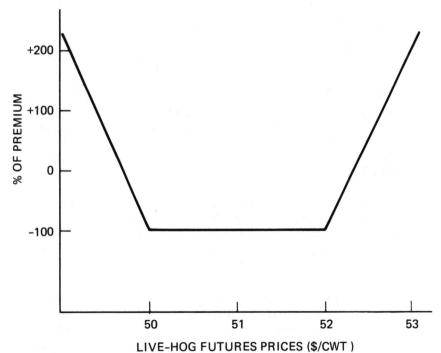

Figure 23. The buy combination, or buying the strangle.

strike prices but provides a return as prices move above the higher strike or below the lower strike.

Example:

When June live hogs trade at 51.00
Buy 1 June 52 call at $1.90 = ($570)
Buy 1 June 50 put at $1.00 =   (300)
Net initial investment = $870

Hypothetical Results:

	Change In Value Points	Dollar Value
If futures price = $63.00		
1 June 52 live-hogs call at 11 =	9.10	$2,730
1 June 50 live-hogs put at 0 =	(1.00)	(300)
Net =	8.10	$2,430
If futures price = $51.00		
1 June 52 live-hogs call at 0 =	(1.90)	($570)
1 June 50 live-hogs put at 0 =	(1.00)	(300)
Net =	(2.90)	($870)
If futures price = $39.00		
1 June 52 live-hogs call at 0 =	(1.90)	($ 570)
1 June 50 live-hogs put at 11 =	10.00	3,000
Net =	8.10	$2,430

Maximum profit: unlimited
Maximum loss: $870 (sum of two initial premiums)
Breakeven point: $ 54.90 on up side and $47.10 on down side (call strike
                 plus premium cost or put strike minus premium cost)

Option Strategies for Declining Markets

Over the past several years, the predominent trend in the futures markets has been downward. Disinflation, such as we've experienced in recent years, tends to affect commodity prices severely. Indeed, had options on futures been available two or three years ago, chances are agricultural producers and speculators alike could have profited handsomely from the slowdown in agriculture and avoided much of the financial difficulties of the past few years.

Although it is true that only a small percentage of farmers use the futures markets, chances are that more and more farmers will hedge using the new options. For one, if recent experience has taught the farmers anything, it is that some type of hedge could help them maintain a healthy bottom line. For another, the new options on farm commodities enable the farmer for the first time to place a hedge with limited risk — an opportunity that simply didn't exist prior to the introduction of options on farm futures. In the following pages, I have listed some of the more sophisticated strategies for coping with a declining market.

The Bear Call Spread

The bear call spread is simply the opposite of the bull call spread. Using calls, you buy the higher-strike option and sell the lower-strike option. Since calls with lower strikes are more valuable, the bear call spread results in an initial net credit — a position that must be margined until expiration. Among its features are a known maximum profit and maximum loss. The maximum profit will be the initial cash inflow, or the income generated by the lower-strike call minus the cost of the higher-strike call. Maximum profitability will exist at the lower strike and maximum potential loss at the higher strike. Below the lower strike, the bear call spread will not provide greater profits; conversely, above the higher strike, losses won't increase either. In general, the bear call spread is best employed when you anticipate a modest decline in prices. If you expect a precipitous decline in prices, other strategies, including simple put buying, are recommended. An example of the bear call spread follows. Figure 24 shows how this strategy proves profitable in a declining market.

Example:

Buy 1 August 52 live-hogs call at $1.35 = ($405)
Sell 1 August 50 live-hogs call at $2.25 = <u>675</u>
Net cash credit = $270

Hypothetical Results:

	Change In Value Points	Dollar Value
If futures price = $54.00		
1 August 52 live-hogs call at 2 =	.65	$195
1 August 50 live-hogs call at 4 =	(1.75)	(525)
Net =	(1.10)	($330)
If futures price = $52.00		
1 August 52 live-hogs call at 0 =	(1.35)	($405)
1 August 50 live-hogs call at 2 =	.25	75
Net =	(1.10)	($330)

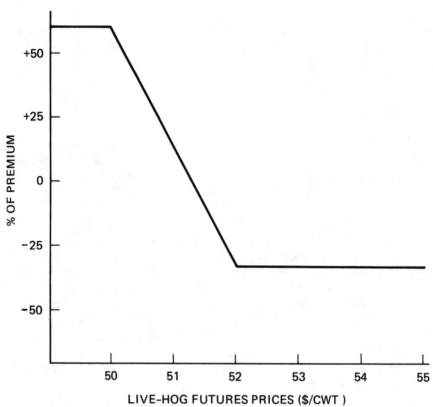

Figure 24.   The bear call spread.

If futures price = $51.00
   1 August 52 live-hogs call at 0 =   (1.35)   ($405)
   1 August 50 live-hogs call at 1 =   <u>1.25</u>   <u>375</u>
                    Net =   (.10)   ($ 30)

If futures price = $50.00
   1 August 52 live-hogs call at 0 =   (1.35)   ($405)
   1 August 50 live-hogs call at 0 =   <u>2.25</u>   <u>675</u>
                    Net =   .90 $270

If futures price = $47.00
   1 August 52 live-hogs call at 0 =   (1.35)   ($405)
   1 August 50 live-hogs call at 0 =   <u>2.25</u>   <u>675</u>
                    Net =   .90 $270

Maximum profit: $270
Maximum loss: $330
Breakeven point: $ 50.90 (lower price plus net credit)

The Bear Put Spread

The bear put spread involves buying a higher-strike put and selling a lower-strike put with the same expiration month. The spread is placed at an initial debit, which constitutes the maximum total risk on the position. The spread's maximum profit will exist at the lower strike; the maximum loss at the higher strike. Above the higher strike, losses cannot grow larger, since the long put will just be abandoned and the lower-strike put will be worthless. Below the lower strike, the losses on the short put will be offset by the gains in the long put, resulting in no additional profit. An example follows. In Figure 25 you can see that in a bear put spread the maximum profit is realized at the lower strike and below and the maximum loss is realized at the higher strike and above.

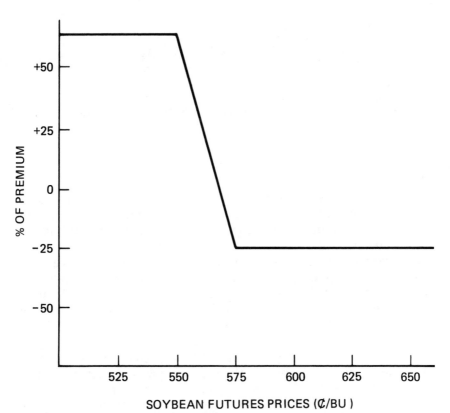

Figure 25. The bear put spread.

Example:

Buy 1 May 575 soybean put at 12¢ = ($600)
Sell 1 May 550 soybean put for 3½¢ =   175
                      Net initial cost = $425

Hypothetical Results:

	Change In Value Points	Dollar Value
If futures prices = $5.75		
1 May 575 soybean put at 0 =	(12 ¢)	($600)
1 May 550 soybean put at 0 =	3½¢	175
Net =	(8½¢)	($425)
If futures price = $5.55		
1 May 575 soybean put at 20¢ =	8 ¢	$400
1 May 550 soybean put at 0 =	3½¢	175
Net =	11½¢	$575
If futures price = $5.50		
1 May 575 soybean put at 25¢ =	13 ¢	$650
1 May 550 soybean put at 0 =	3½¢	175
Net =	16½¢	$825

Maximum profit: $825
Maximum loss: $425
Breakeven point: $ 5.66½ (higher strike minus cost of spread)

The Sell–Write

The sell–write strategy provides a means of capitalizing on a slightly bearish market by writing a put and simultaneously selling short a futures contract. The drawback of the strategy is that it leaves little protection in the event of a rising market, but the trader can always take defensive action to run from potential losses should prices rise. Moreover, by writing a put, the sell–write investor creates a cushion of safety that the outright short seller does not have. That is, the sell–write strategy provides its user with the writing income from the put; the outright short seller, of course, doesn't enjoy this protection. Like simply writing options, the sell–write strategy attempts to capture the writing income. Thus, the potential profit is limited to the initial income generated, whereas the potential losses are unlimited. An example is shown. Also see Figure 26, which shows that with this strategy the maximum profit will be realized in a declining market; however, losses will mount dramatically if prices rise.

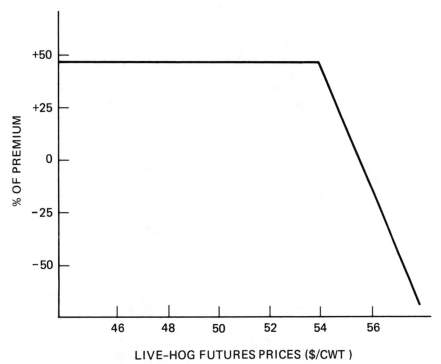

Figure 26.   The sell-write.

Example:

Sell 1 July 52 live-hogs put for $1.70   = $510
Sell 1 July 52 live-hogs futures at $.52 =   0
                       Net inflow = $510

Hypothetical Results:

	Change In Value Points	Dollar Value
If futures price = $54.00		
1 July 52 live-hogs put at 0 =	1.70	$510
1 July futures at 54.00 =	(2.00)	(600)
Net =	(.30)	($ 90)
If futures price = $52.00		
1 July 52 live-hogs put at 0 =	1.70	$510
1 July futures at 52.00 =	0	0
Net =	1.70	$510

If futures price = $50.00

1 July 52 live-hogs put at 2 =	(.30)	($ 90)
1 July futures at 50.00 =	2.00	600
Net =	1.70	$510

Maximum profit: $510
Maximum loss: unlimited
Breakeven point: $53.70 (strike price plus initial credit)

The Synthetic Put

The synthetic put, the mirror image of the synthetic call, consists of a short futures contract and a long call option. As the name suggests, the synthetic put has a risk/reward ratio similar to that of an outright purchase of a put option. That is, in the event of higher subsequent prices, the risk is strictly limited to the initial cost of the synthetic put; on the other hand, the down-side profit opportunity is unlimited — at least to zero.

The long call, which is purchased at the time the transaction is initiated, serves as the insurance in the strategy. An unprotected short futures position would result in unlimited liability should futures prices soar. With the call, the short seller can rest assured that above the strike price, the losses on the short position are offset by the gain on the call. The cost for this protection, of course, will be the premium on the call — the maximum one can lose on the strategy.

The one drawback of the strategy is that the market move downward must be sufficient to offset the cost of the long call. Hence, if you pay 10¢ per bushel for the call, the market must decline at least by this amount for the cost of the premium to be offset by the profits on the short futures position. Note the example and see Figure 27, which depicts how the synthetic-put strategy results in profits as prices fall with a fixed, predetermined risk.

Example:

Buy 1 August 52 live-hogs call for $1.90 =	($570)	
Sell 1 August futures at $52.00 =	0	
Initial cost =	$570	

Hypothetical Results:

	Change In Value Points	Dollar Value
If August futures price = $56.00		
1 August 52 call at 4.00 =	2.10	$630
1 August futures at 56.00 =	(4.00)	(1,200)
Net =	(1.90)	($570)

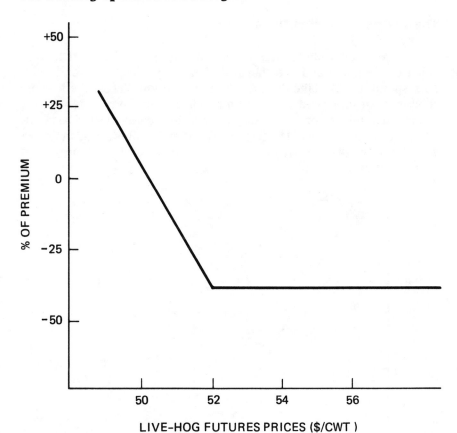

Figure 27.   The synthetic put.

If August futures price = $52.00
    I August 52 call at 0   =   (1.90)   ($570)
    I August futures at 52.00 =   0   0
                        Net =   (1.90)   ($570)

If August futures price = $51.00
    I August 52 call at 0   =   (1.90)   ($570)
    I August futures at 51.00 =   1.00   300
                        Net =   (.90)   ($270)

If August futures price = $44.00
    I August 52 call at 0   =   (1.90)   ($ 570)
    I August futures at 44.00 =   8.00   2,400
                        Net =   6.10 $1,830

Maximum profit: unlimited
Maximum loss: $570
Breakeven point: $ 50.10 (strike price minus cost of call)

The Synthetic Short Futures

A proxy for a short futures position, the synthetic short futures consists of a long put and a short call. That is, you buy a put and sell a corresponding call. Like the short futures position, the synthetic short combines an unlimited potential for gain on the down side with an unlimited potential for loss on the up side. This position would be taken when futures are expected to decline. An example follows, and in Figure 28 you can see that this strategy has the same risk and the same reward as a short futures position.

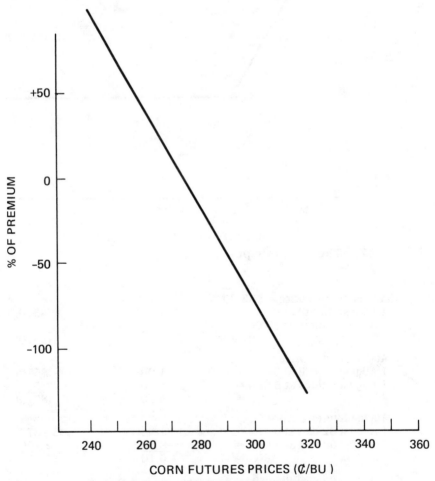

Figure 28.   The synthetic short futures position.

Example:

Sell 1 May 270 corn call at 4¢ = $200
Buy 1 May 270 put at 2½¢   = (125)
Net inflow = $ 75

Hypothetical Results:

	Change In Value Points	Dollar Value
If corn futures price = $3.08		
1 May 270 corn call at 38¢ =	(34 ¢)	($1,700)
1 May 270 corn put at 0 =	(2½¢)	(125)
Net =	(36½¢)	($1,825)
If corn futures price = $2.70		
1 May 270 corn call at 0 =	4 ¢	$200
1 May 270 corn put at 0 =	(2½¢)	(125)
Net =	1½¢	$ 75
If corn futures price = $2.50		
1 May 270 corn call at 0 =	4¢	$ 200
1 May 270 corn put at 20¢ =	17½¢	875
Net =	21½¢	$1,075

Maximum profit: unlimited
Maximum loss: unlimited
Breakeven point: $2.71½

APPENDIX II

Contract Specifications

Commodity	Strike Price Intervals	Minimum Price Fluctuations	Daily Limits	Exchange
Corn (5,000 bushels)	10¢/bu	$\frac{1}{8}$¢/bu	10¢/bu	CBOT
Soybeans (5,000 bushels)	25¢/bu	$\frac{1}{8}$¢/bu	30¢/bu	CBOT
Soybeans (1,000 bushels)	25¢/bu	$\frac{1}{8}$¢/bu	30¢/bu	MidAm
Wheat (5,000 bushels)	10¢/bu	$\frac{1}{8}$¢/bu	20¢/bu	MidAm
Wheat (5,000 bushels)	10¢/bu	$\frac{1}{4}$¢/bu	25¢/bu	KCBT
Wheat (5,000 bushels)	10¢/bu	$\frac{1}{8}$¢/bu	20¢/bu	MGE
Live cattle (40,000 lbs)	2¢/lb	$2\frac{1}{2}$¢/lb	None	CME
Live hogs (30,000 lbs)	2¢/lb	$2\frac{1}{2}$¢/lb	None	CME
Cotton (50,000 lbs)	1¢/lb	$\frac{1}{100}$¢/lb	None	NYCE

Glossary of Terms

Arbitrage: Purchase of a commodity or option in one market for immediate sale in another market.

At the money: An option is at the money if its strike price is the same as the current price of the underlying futures.

Back month: Same as *distant month*.

Basis: The difference between a cash price for a specific location and a particular futures price.

Bear: One who anticipates a downtrend.

Bear spread: A spread that makes money when prices go down.

Breakeven point: The futures price (or prices) at which a particular strategy neither makes nor loses money. A "dynamic" breakeven point is one that changes as time passes.

Bull: One who anticipates an uptrend.

Bull spread: A spread that makes money when prices go up.

Butterfly spread: Using either puts or calls with three different strike prices and the same expiration.

Buyer: The purchaser of an option, either a call option or a put option. The buyer may also be referred to as the *option holder*. Option buyers receive the right, but not the obligation, to enter a futures market position.

Calendar spread: Consists of the sale of an option and the purchase of a more distant option with the same strike price.

Call option or call: The right to purchase some asset at the stated strike price on or before the expiration date.

Carrying charges: The costs associated with storing and transporting a commodity.

Cash value: The value an option has if it were to be exercised now.

CBOT: Chicago Board of Trade.

CFTC: Commodity Futures Trading Commission.

Class of options: All call options — or all put options — on the same underlying futures.

Clearing corporation: A nonprofit corporation whose function it is to clear all purchases and sales and to ensure the financial integrity of all futures and options transactions on a futures exchange.

Closing transaction: The sale of an option or futures by someone who owns the option or has a long position on the futures, or the purchase of an option or futures position by a person who previously sold it short. These transactions terminate the investor's position.

CME: Chicago Mercantile Exchange.

217

Combination: A position created either by purchasing both a put and a call or by writing both a put and a call on the same underlying futures contract.

Commission: Fees paid to the broker for execution of an order.

Covered writing: Writing an option when one holds a corresponding position in the underlying futures.

Cross hedge: A hedge in which the hedged commodity does not respond to a change in economic factors in the same way the cash item underlying the futures contract does.

Delivery: The tender and receipt of the cash commodity in settlement of a futures contract.

Delta: The expected percentage change in the option premium, given a fluctuation in the price of the underlying futures. Delta factors are frequently considered in a "ratio hedge"—hedging a commodity position with options.

Delta spread: A ratio spread that is established as a neutral position by using the deltas of the options involved. The neutral ratio is determined by dividing the delta of the purchased option by the delta of the written option.

Diagonal spread: A spread in which a long-term option of one strike price is purchased and a shorter-term option of another strike is sold.

Dip: A period of falling market prices.

Distant month: Any contract month other than the nearby month or most recent month.

Erosion: The dissipation of time value of a given option contract.

Exercise: The process whereby the option buyer uses the right to enter the underlying futures contract.

Exercise price: The price at which the option holder may buy or sell the underlying future, as defined in the terms of his option contract. Same as *strike price.*

Expiration: The day when the owner of the option loses the right to exercise an option.

Front month: Same as *nearby month.*

Futures contract: A current contract for future delivery of a specific commodity.

Future time value: That part of the option price which does not represent cash value.

Gap down: A day whose highest price is lower than the previous day's lowest price.

Gap up: A day whose lowest price is higher than the previous day's highest price.

Hedge: The sale or purchase of offsetting positions in options, futures, or commodities; designed to reduce potential loss in the event of price fluctuation.

Hedge ratio: The mathematical quantity that is equal to the delta of an option.

Holder: Same as *buyer.*

Horizontal spread: Long or short in a nearby month with the opposite position in a more distant month in the same commodity option or futures.

Implied volatility: A measure of the volatility of the underlying futures. It is determined by using current prices in the market, not historical data on the price changes of the underlying futures.

In the money: A *call* is in the money if its strike price is *below* the current price of the underlying futures contract. A *put* is in the money if its strike price is *above* the current price of the underlying futures contract.

Intrinsic value: For call options, the amount by which the futures price exceeds the strike price. For put options, the amount by which the futures price is lower than the strike price.

KCBT: Kansas City Board of Trade.

Liquidation: A purchase or sale that offsets an existing position.

Liquid market: A market in which selling and buying can easily be accomplished because of a large number of buyers and sellers.

Long: The position established by the purchase of a futures contract or an option (either a call or a put) if there is no offsetting position.

Margin: In commodities, an amount of money deposited to insure performance of an obligation at a future date. Buyers of options do not post margin, only sellers do.

Naked writing: Writing a call or a put on a futures contract in which the writer has no opposite cash or futures market position.

Nearby month: The closest contract month in time; often the most active month.

Off-floor trader: One who trades through a broker, usually by phoning in an order.

Opening transaction: A purchase or sale that establishes a new position.

Open order: An order good until canceled.

Option: A right that can be exercised at any time until expiration.

Option pricing curve: A graphical representation of the projected price of an option at a fixed point in time.

Out of the money: A put or call option that currently has no intrinsic value.

Point: The minimum unit by which an option or a futures position changes.

Position: To be either long or short in the market.

Premium: The price of an option—the money the option buyer *pays* and the option seller *receives* for the rights conveyed by the option.

Put option or put: An option granting the holder the right to sell the underlying futures at a certain price for a specified period of time.

Ratio write: Buying a futures contract and selling a greater number of calls. Also refers to selling futures and selling a greater number of puts. Ratio write also refers to writing options and buying a lesser number of options at another strike.

Reverse conversion: A trade in which an options investor buys a call, sells the underlying futures, and sells a put; a call disappears and a put is created, offsetting the put that was sold.

Rolling down: Switching into lower-strike options.

Rolling up: Switching into higher-strike options.

Settlement price: A price based on the day's closing range. Used to determine daily gains and losses.

Seller: One who sells an option. Also referred to as the *writer* or grantor of an option.

Short hedger: One who owns the underlying futures commodity and seeks to forward-price that product.

Short: The position of a net seller of a specific option or futures contract.

Spread: Any combination of positions that involves more than one strike price or expiration month.

Straddle: A combination in which the put and the call have the same strike price and the same expiration.

Strike price: See *exercise price.*

Time value: Premium minus the intrinsic value.

Underlying futures contract: The futures contract designated for purchase or sale on exercise of a particular option.

Vertical spread: Long or short at one strike price with the opposite position at a higher or lower strike price on the same commodity and the same contract month.

Writing: The sale of an option in an opening transaction.

Index